Tales from the Gamecock Roost

By Tom Price

Sports Publishing, LLC
www.SportsPublishingLLC.com

Director of production: Susan M. Moyer
Senior project manager, book design: Jennifer L. Polson
Dust jacket design: Kenneth J. Higgerson
Editor: David Hamburg

ISBN: 1-58261-342-7

Printed in the United States.

SPORTS PUBLISHING, LLC
www.SportsPublishingLLC.com

This book is dedicated to the memory of Jim Price,
an outstanding athletics trainer and, for more than
30 years, a dedicated member of the Gamecock family.
Although we shared a surname, we were not biologically related.
Nevertheless, he was my brother.

Tom Price

Acknowledgments

The author extends heartfelt thanks to all the athletes, coaches, fans, and others who shared memories and otherwise contributed to the contents of *Tales from the Gamecock Roost.*

Special thanks to Sarge Frye, Sid Kenyon, Sue "Mrs. K" Kurpiewski, Jack Wilson, Randy Herald, Ed Pitts, Dennis Powell, Bobby Cremins, Skip Harlicka, Dom Fusci, Bob Fulton, Van Newman, Tony Ciuffo, and the Legends in Their own Minds, who dipped deep into their memory banks for many of the anecdotes cited within these pages.

Also, thanks to Coach Lou Holtz for brightening this volume with his wit and for directing the second-greatest turnaround in NCAA football history, from 0-21 to a New Year's Day bowl victory over Ohio State in his second season at South Carolina.

Thanks to Russell "Chip" McKinney, University of South Carolina director of public affairs, for granting permission to use the Gamecock logo. Extra-special thanks to Kerry Tharp, assistant athletics director for media relations, and his staff for their cooperation and permission to use photographs from the sports information files. Particular thanks for assistant SID Brian Binette for all his help.

Also, thanks to Steven "Dry Rock" Whetstone, a talented artist and baseball pitcher, for permission to use his drawings.

Thanks to a great university, which celebrated its 200th birthday in 2001.

Last, but not least, thanks to Margaret, my wife since June 10, 1950, in most respects, not a sports fan, but nevertheless an adept proofreader. We've been happily married more than 45 years, and 45 out of 51 is batting nearly .900.

—TP

Contents

1
What's a Gamecock?

The University of South Carolina is one of only two institutions of higher learning in the United States that uses a gamecock as its athletic mascot. The other is Jacksonville State University in Alabama.

There are three, if the University of Puerto Rico is included. The mascot of Coastal Carolina University, which began as a regional campus of the University of South Carolina, is a chanticleer, the name of a rooster in the *Nun's Priest Tale*, one of the *Canterbury Tales* by Geoffrey Chaucer (1342–1400). The chanticleer also appears in the medieval epic *Reynard the Fox.*

Webster's New World Dictionary of American English defines a gamecock as "a specially bred rooster trained for cock-fighting." Gamecocks are known for their courage in battle and willingness to fight to the death.

The *St. Petersburg Times* published a piece on cock-fighting December 31, 2000, the day before the South Carolina Gamecocks met the Ohio State Buckeyes in the Outback Bowl across the bay in nearby Tampa, Fla.

The piece was written by Jim Soliski, a freelance writer from Canada, and described a cock-fight Soliski had witnessed in Manila. Soliski wrote that Filipinos combine their two religions on Sundays; they attend Mass in the morning, and "then [they] prepare for the afternoon service—cockfights."

"The roosters are beautiful birds," Soliski wrote. "Some are snow white. Others have black tails and wings with a cream-colored chest, complete with matching head feathers cascading over their shoulders and back like a lion's mane. Others are brilliantly colored with teal, green, harvest gold, burnt orange, burgundy and liver red."

Soliski said the winner of the fight was the rooster that remained alive.

Cock-fighting was a popular sport throughout the American colonies, and many prominent South Carolinians raised and trained gamecocks. One of them was Gen. Thomas Sumter, one of two famous guerilla fighters who harassed British forces during the revolution that resulted in the creation of the United States of America.

Sumter's nickname was "The Gamecock," while the other South Carolina guerilla general, Francis Marion, was called "The Swamp Fox."

One president of the United States kept gamecocks at the White House. Some Southerners might be surprised to learn that the president was Ulysses S. Grant.

Cock-fighting has long been outlawed for humanitarian reasons throughout most of the United States but is still practiced legally in many other parts of the world.

South Carolina athletic teams were referred to by several nicknames in the early days before becoming Gamecocks in 1902. A newspaper story following a particularly hard-fought game said the South Carolina players "fought like gamecocks."

It's quite possible that this reference resulted in the nickname, because newspaper writers frequently coined nicknames for teams early in the 20th century. For example, the Brooklyn National League baseball team was called the Bridegrooms and the Superbas before a newspaper referred to fans walking along the trolley tracks to games as "Trolley Dodgers," which soon was shortened to "Dodgers."

The 1902 season, South Carolina's first under the Gamecock banner, included a post-game confrontation that resulted in a six-year break in the series with archrival Clemson.

Clemson was a military school, and after losing its first game against South Carolina in 1896, it reeled off four consecutive wins. No game was played in 1901 due to scheduling conflicts. Clemson's cadet corps traditionally remained overnight in Columbia after the game to enjoy the state fair and at one time celebrated victories by parading Columbia streets with shoes draped in garnet-and-black cloth—South Carolina's school colors.

It was South Carolina's turn to celebrate after the 12-6 Gamecock victory in 1902, and students paraded a transparency of a gamecock crowing over a fallen tiger through the streets. They defied a law-enforcement recommendation and included the transparency in the Elks parade the following day.

Enraged Clemson cadets formed and marched on the South Carolina campus with swords and fixed bayonets. A small band of South Carolina's "civilian" students, armed with pistols and clubs, rallied to the defense. Christie Benet, a Columbia attorney and South Carolina assistant coach, acted as mediator and offered to fight any selected Clemson supporter to settle the dispute. Some accounts said the offer was to take on any two from the Clemson side.

Police and faculty members arrived in time to prevent bloodshed, and finally the transparency was burned as both sides cheered. Because of the near riot, however, the Gamecocks and Tigers did not meet again until 1909. The rivalry has continued ever since.

Modern Definition

A bumper sticker that appeared on automobiles throughout South Carolina around 1984 defined a Gamecock as an "Ass Kickin' Chicken."

One-Year Hiatus

South Carolina took a one-year break from football in 1906. President Theodore Roosevelt threatened to ban the sport on grounds of brutality when several deaths and severe injuries were reported. South Carolina trustees, acting on the threat by Roosevelt, banned the sport but relented after one season. Football was reinstated in 1907 with a three-game schedule, and the Gamecocks went undefeated against College of Charleston, Georgia College, and The Citadel. Columbia attorney Douglas McKay coached the team.

Snuffy

After World War II ended, Rear Admiral Norman M. Smith, commander of the Construction Battalions (Seabees) retired from the U.S. Navy and became president of the University of South Carolina. Irreverent students immediately nicknamed him "Snuffy," after Snuffy Smith, the comic-strip character.

It naturally followed that a live gamecock presented to the university, should also be named Snuffy. Snuffy—the bird, not the admiral—strutted along the sidelines on a leash fastened to one leg and crowed the football team on to victory, or at least to a superb effort.

There have been a number of live gamecock mascots since, including a magnificent bird whose owner brought it to home baseball games during the 2000 season when the team led the nation with a school-record 56 victories. This bird paraded atop the first-base dugout, pausing every few minutes to throw his head back and crow loudly.

Gamecocks mounted by a taxidermist were presented in 2000 to football coach Lou Holtz and baseball coach Ray Tanner by an admiring fan.

Cocky

"Big Spur," a seven-foot-tall bird suit with a student named Chuck Eaton inside, paraded the sidelines for a few years in the late 1970s, but Big Spur was too big and cumbersome to be adopted as the permanent official mascot.

A student named John Routh came up with "Cocky," a nimble bird with skinny legs that initially performed only at women's basketball games until the powers that be realized that this was the real thing.

Cocky accompanied the Gamecock baseball team to Omaha for the 1981 College World Series but was initially barred from performing on the field. University of Miami coach Ron Fraser, a genius at promoting college baseball, interceded on Cocky's behalf,

Cocky and friend. (USC Sports Information)

and a compromise was reached. Cocky removed his garnet-and-black vest and other trappings identifying him with South Carolina and became the mascot for all eight teams in the World Series.

Cocky returned to the World Series with the South Carolina team in 1982 and in 1985. For several years, although the Gamecock team didn't make it, Cocky was there performing at Rosenblatt Stadium.

When John Routh graduated, assistant athletics director Ron Dickerson recommended in a staff meeting that he be hired as a full-time mascot, an idea that was turned down by Athletics Director Bob Marcum, who thought the mascot should remain a student.

Ron Fraser immediately hired Routh to become the "Miami Maniac," and he served in that role a number of years, until major league baseball came to Miami, and Routh became "Billy the Marlin."

Since Routh's departure, quite a few students—both male and female—have donned the Cocky suit. Cocky has won several national mascot titles.

The Other Gamecocks

Except for having the same mascot, the athletic teams of the University of South Carolina and Jacksonville State University have had little contact over the years.

The women's basketball team from Jacksonville State came to Columbia to play in a tournament during the 1999–2000 season. Jacksonville State lost in the opening round, while South Carolina won, so the two teams of Lady Gamecocks missed playing against each other, even though they performed in the same arena for two nights.

During the 1988 soccer season, the South Carolina men's team played at the College of Charleston in the first game of a double-header, while the Jacksonville State women's team played the College of Charleston in the nightcap. Two sets of Gamecocks played on the same field on the same day, but not against each other.

There was an occasion in the early 1970s, however, when I — as sports information director—was invited to address the Anniston,

Ala., Touchdown Club. Anniston is near Jacksonville, and the Jacksonville State Gamecocks are the Anniston Touchdown Club's home team.

Anniston isn't the easiest place to get to from Columbia, so rather than miss two days from the office, pilot Roger Booco took me to Anniston in the school plane. I shared part of the honorarium for the speaking engagement with him.

"I've been flying coaches to speaking engagements for a long time," Roger said. "This is the first time I've received any of the money."

That was one of the very few times that I received an honorarium for speaking. The sports information director usually is assigned to the freebies, and I have quite a few framed copies of the Optimist Creed and Sertoma and Kiwanis certificates.

Clemson Sports information Director Bob Bradley and I shared the speaker's podium before the touchdown club at Charleston one season during the week of the Carolina-Clemson game. Both of us thought it was a freebie, but after the meeting, the club president asked if it was okay by us if we split $500.

We didn't turn him down.

On another occasion, I spoke at the Flat Creek High School football banquet. The Flat Creek football coach was my first cousin, Jim Hart. He presented me with a check for $20.50 to cover my mileage.

Lady Gamecocks

When women's sports teams were first organized at the University of South Carolina, they were under the jurisdiction of the Office of Student Affairs. In 1974, the women's program was transferred to and funded by the Department of Athletics.

The highest-profile women's sport from the outset was basketball, and the players themselves had adopted the nickname "Chicks." Helen Timmermans, the senior women's administrator and a professor of physical education, had a vanity license plate on her automobile that read, "Chicks."

After a short time, members of the women's teams felt the name "Chicks" was degrading, so all the teams in the women's intercollegiate program became "Lady Gamecocks," even though a gamecock is a male bird.

Chicken Curse

Whenever a University of South Carolina athletic team falls on hard times, media reports of the "Chicken Curse" appear in print and on TV and radio.

It has been said that Edgefield farmer "Pitchfork Ben" Tillman put a curse on the university late in the 19th century. Tillman was instrumental in the founding of Clemson College in 1890 and the downgrading of South Carolina from university to college status.

Tillman was a member of the state legislature from Edgefield County and later was elected governor. If old Pitchfork Ben did lay a curse on the institution of higher learning in Columbia, it wasn't a chicken curse, because the gamecock didn't become the school mascot until 1902, more than a decade later.

As a retired sports information director and unofficial South Carolina athletics historian, I am often asked about the origin of the chicken curse.

My best recollection is that during the 1963 football season, when the Gamecocks were struggling to a 1-8-1 record, newspaper writer Doug Nye made reference to the chicken curse in a column.

Nye, now the television editor of *The State* in Columbia, brought up the spectre of a chicken curse when he was sports editor of the *Sumter Item*. The reference prompted a protesting telephone call from Coach Marvin Bass. Nye mentioned the chicken curse again after he became sports editor of the *Columbia Record.*

Those who believe in the chicken curse can point to a number of times when South Carolina has lost when it was supposed to have won, or has missed an opportunity for victory in the closing moments.

A few examples in support of the chicken curse theory:

- In 1956, fullback Don Johnson fumbled just before crossing the goal line, and Clemson recovered for a touchback to preserve a 7-0 win.

- South Carolina led Maryland 6-3 in the closing moments in 1958, when a bad snap from center on a punt attempt gave the Terps the football at Carolina's one-yard line. Maryland scored to win 10-6. South Carolina led Wake Forest 19-7 at halftime in 1963, but gained only one yard in the second half to lose 20-19 and break Wake's nation's-longest losing streak.

- South Carolina was 9-0 and ranked second in the national polls in 1984, before being upset by Navy to be denied an unbeaten season.

- In 1991, the Gamecocks led Duke by 14 points with two minutes left in the game. Duke scored, missed a two-point conversion, recovered an onside kick, and was aided by an official who erroneously stopped the clock after a play. Duke scored on the last play of the game and converted a two-point try to forge a 14-14 tie.

- During the same season, a late score resulted in a 12-7 lead over Louisiana Tech. The Gamecocks went for two points in hopes of expanding the lead to 14-7. Louisiana Tech intercepted the pass and returned it 100 yards for the only reverse two-pointer ever scored against South Carolina. Louisiana Tech kicked a last-second field goal to earn a 12-12 tie.

- South Carolina, leading N.C. State by five points in 1986, jumped offside on the last play of the game to give the Wolfpack one more play. A South Carolina defender was thrown to the ground by one N.C. State receiver, while another caught a "Hail Mary" pass for a touchdown. The official closest to the play threw a penalty flag, but stuffed it back in his pocket when Wolfpack students surged onto the field.

- In 2000, Clemson kicked a field goal with three seconds remaining in the half to take a 10-7 lead. South Carolina drove for a touchdown with less than three minutes remaining in the game to take a 14-13 lead. Clemson then completed a 50-yard pass to set up a field goal, again with three seconds remaining, to win 16-14.

- In basketball, heavily favored South Carolina played N.C. State for the championship of the 1969 Atlantic Coast Conference tournament after Gamecock All-America guard John Roche had suffered a serious ankle injury. N.C. State played a slow-down game and won 42-39 in double overtime. At that time, only one conference team went to the NCAA Tournament, and and South Carolina was prohibited from playing in the National Invitation Tournament because the school was hosting an NCAA regional. The Gamecocks stayed home with a 25-3 record.

- South Carolina led Louisville by 14 points with two minutes to play in 1988, when a fight broke out during a free-throw try. Multiple technical fouls were called. Louisville made its technical shots, South Carolina missed most of its, and the Cardinals sent the game into overtime. Louisville eventually won.

On the other hand, there are just as many examples of upset victories by underdog South Carolina teams and amazing comebacks to disprove the chicken curse theory:

- In the championship game of the 1971 Atlantic Coast Conference basketball tournament, North Carolina led South Carolina by one point with five seconds remaining, when a jump ball was called between 6-3 Kevin Joyce of South Carolina and 6-10 Lee Dedmon of North Carolina. Joyce outjumped Dedmon and tipped the ball to Tom Owens, who scored for a 52-51 South Carolina victory and the ACC tourney championship.

- Bobby Cremins, the team's worst free-throw shooter, made six in a row in the final minutes to preserve an 87-86 win over North Carolina at Chapel Hill in 1968.

- South Carolina trailed Indiana by 16 points in the second half in 1972, but came back to win 88-85 on a 41-point effort by Kevin Joyce.

- South Carolina's football team trailed Virginia 14-0 in the fourth quarter in 1952, but scored three touchdowns in less than two minutes to win 21-14.

- South Carolina rolled up 446 yards rushing against a heavily favored Army team in 1954 to win 34-20.
- The Gamecocks trailed North Carolina 27-3 after three quarters at Chapel Hill in 1968, before rallying to win 32-27.
- North Carolina was undefeated and the nation's third-ranked team in 1981, but Gamecock quarterback Gordon Beckham completed 16 of 17 passes to lead South Carolina to a 31-13 upset.
- One of the strongest outbursts of comeback power occurred on the baseball diamond. Trailing 5-0 after half an inning, the Gamecocks set numerous school records in a 38-16 win over Clemson in 1997.

Is there a chicken curse or isn't there a chicken curse? Take your pick. It's all in the mind.

Happy Birthday

The University of South Carolina kicked off its bicentennial celebration January 10, 2001, and it was inevitable that the university's athletics history and its gamecock mascot would be woven into the opening ceremony.

Dr. John M. Palms, the university's president, pointed out that the Greek translation of the word "gamecock" is "announcer of the sun," which seemed appropriate, since cocks (roosters) always crow at sunrise.

Dr. Jaroslav Pelikan, sterling professor emeritus of history at Yale University, was one of the ceremonial speakers. He said he was chosen "to speak before all these gamecocks" because he had the name of a bird (Pelican).

Secretary of Education Richard W. Riley, an alumnus of the University of South Carolina Law School, was the ceremony's principal speaker.

Riley said if he were stocking a time capsule of the university's first 200 years to be opened two centuries later, he would include, in addition to many artifacts of academic achievements, two mementos from early 2001 athletics triumphs.

They would be "the basketball that Travis Kraft shot last Sunday [a three-point goal as time expired to defeat fifth-ranked Florida 69-68] and the football Ryan Brewer used to score three touchdowns against Ohio State." Brewer was the MVP of South Carolina's 24-7 Outback Bowl win on January 1, 2001.

The South Carolina Legislature passed a founding resolution that chartered South Carolina College on December 19, 1801. However, the first students did not enroll until January 10, 1805, when a student body of nine began studying under a faculty of two.

The bicentennial celebration began on the 195th anniversary of the first matriculation and was scheduled to end on December 19, the 200th anniversary of the charter.

When Joe Morrison became South Carolina's head football coach in 1983, he began a tradition of having the team enter the field just before kickoff each home game through a cloud of manufactured white smoke to the music from *2001: A Space Odyssey*. It naturally followed that this theme would be incorporated into the bicentennial celebration in 2001.

As the university symphony orchestra played the theme from *2001* as a finale to the bicentennial kickoff ceremony and the procession of deans and dignitaries exited the huge outdoor stage on the Horseshoe, at least one spectator in the crowd of more than 3,000 asked, "Where's the smoke?"

Alma Mater

The words to the University of South Carolina Alma Mater were written by Dr. George Armstrong Wauchope in 1911. He taught English and literature at the university from 1898 to the first few years of the 20th century. The lyrics were set to the tune of the poem *Flow Gently Sweet Afton*, penned by the Scottish poet Robert Burns (1759–96). When Gamecock fans sing the refrain—"Here's a health Carolina forever to thee!"—they raise their right arms as if holding a glass of cheer.

The Alma Mater:

We hail thee, Carolina, and sing thy high praise;
With loyal devotion, rememb'ring the days.
When proudly we sought thee, thy children to be;
Here's a health, Carolina, forever to thee!

Since pilgrims of learning, we entered thy walls
And found dearest comrades in thy classic halls;
We've honored and loved thee, as sons faithfully;
Here's a health, Carolina, forever to thee!

Generations of sons have rejoiced to proclaim
Thy watchword of service, thy beauty and fame;
For ages to come shall their rallying cry be;
Here's a health, Carolina, forever to thee.

Fair shrine of high honor and truth, thou shalt still
Blaze forth as a beacon thy mission fulfill;
And be crowned by all hearts in a new jubilee;
Here's a health, Carolina, forever to thee!

When performed before or after athletics events, usually only the first stanza is used. Again, when singing the refrain—*Here's a health, Carolina, forever to thee!*—the right arm should be raised with the hand cupped, as if holding a glass of cheer. Sometimes unenlightened souls mistakenly hold the hand open so the gesture resembles a Nazi salute, or else they clench the fist. No true Gamecock fan would do either.

2

Big Thursday

The first 57 games of the football rivalry between South Carolina and Clemson were played in Columbia on Thursday of State Fair Week. An estimated 2,000 spectators braved rain and paid 25 cents each to see the first game on November 12, 1896, at the old fairgrounds on Elmwood Avenue. The kickoff was set for 11 a.m., so as not to interfere with the horse races and other fair attractions.

South Carolina won the first game 12-6, but Clemson won the next four. Schedule conflicts interrupted the series in 1901, and after South Carolina's 12-6 victory in 1902 nearly resulted in a riot, the rivalry was terminated for six years before being resumed in 1909.

The two in-state rivals have met annually since, but Big Thursday was abolished after the 1959 season and replaced by a home-and-home setup that is now played at the end of the season. The first Big Thursday was in November, but dates for the state fair were soon moved up to the middle of October.

Many people believed there was a state law requiring South Carolina and Clemson to meet annually on the football field, but there was no such law—except for one season, when a temporary statute prevented an interruption of the series.

Both schools were members of the Southern Conference, which had adopted a policy banning its members from accepting bowl bids.

Clemson and Maryland had defied the ban after the 1951 season; Clemson accepted an invitation to the Gator Bowl, and Maryland went to the Orange Bowl.

As punishment, the conference banned the two schools from playing any other conference member for one year unless required by law.

The state fair was one of the major attractions of the year in an agriculture-dominated state such as South Carolina, and the fair and the football game presented opportunities for the Clemson student body and supporters to gather in the Palmetto State's capital city.

By the middle 1950s, Clemson had tired of playing annually in South Carolina's home stadium. Enlargement of Clemson's stadium and improved roads fueled the Tigers' push for a home- and-home rivalry. The last Big Thursday contest, a 27-0 Clemson win, was played in 1959.

Despite playing the first 57 games on South Carolina's home field, Clemson holds a big lead in the overall Big Thursday series: 33-21-3.

Big Thursdays & Super Saturdays, a book written in 1982 by former South Carolina sports information director Don Barton, chronicled the first 77 games in the rivalry.

The book's dust jacket states: "It began as somewhat of a side-show to more important activities of the annual State Fair in Columbia, but . . . the annual football game between the University of South Carolina and Clemson University evolved into the state's most exciting and important sports event."

Tickets, Please

The 1946 Big Thursday game was one of the wildest ever, but not because of what happened on the playing field.

Two brothers from New York—Milton and Irving Rosner—printed counterfeit tickets and sold about 4,000 of them. Carolina Stadium had a capacity of about 26,000 then, but more than 30,000 showed up for the game.

When fire marshals declared the stadium full, the gates were ordered locked. Irate fans—some with legitimate tickets, some with counterfeit tickets, and some with no tickets at all but hopeful of seeing the game—broke down two gates and surged into the stadium.

The crowd ringed the sidelines, often spilling out onto the playing field. Several times, play was halted until officials cleared the field.

A riot nearly occurred during halftime, when three young men, apparently Clemson students or supporters, ran onto the field and wrung the neck of a live rooster. A South Carolina cheerleader made a vain attempt to rescue the rooster. The highway patrol and other officers restored order and the game continued.

South Carolina won 26-14.

The Rosner brothers, one of whom had conceived the idea of capitalizing on the popularity of Big Thursday while stationed at Fort Jackson, a U.S. Army base on the outskirts of Columbia, were convicted of forgery and receiving money under false pretenses.

They were guests of the state at the Central Corrections Institute for several years.

3

Cockaboose Railroad

F ans can't ride the Cockaboose Railroad to football games at the university's Williams-Brice Stadium, but they can have a lot of fun once they get there.

Columbia businessman Ed Robinson purchased the unused railroad tracks at the south end of the University of South Carolina stadium and brought in 22 surplus cabooses that he renovated on the outside in garnet and black, the Gamecock colors, and put on the market at $40,000 a pop. The interiors were left for the purchasers to fix up any way they wished.

The entire 22 were sold in a matter of days. Running water, sewer connections, cable television, air conditioning, and heat were added, and the Cockaboose Railroad was up and running for the start of the 1990 football season. The average total investment was about $100,000 per caboose.

Pregame and postgame tailgating never had it so good. Some cabooses are outfitted as bedrooms so owners can stay overnight on game weekends, and some are fixed up for serious partying with the best bar equipment. There is closed-circuit television available to watch the game next door for guests without tickets or for those who are having too much fun to go into the stadium.

The Cockaboose Railroad was the first of its kind in the nation, and Gamecock fans say there's nothing like it in the world. For those big spenders who want to be closer to the action, there are 23 VIP executive suites in the stadium, that has been enlarged a number of times from its initial capacity of 17,600 in 1934 to its current capacity of 80,250.

During the final four years of the 20th century, South Carolina ranked ninth among NCAA Division I-A schools, averaging 78,140 spectators per home game. The 2000 average was nearly 82,000 for six games.

Cockaboxes

Failing health made Jim Price retire as athletics trainer after 30 years on the staff of the University of South Carolina, but he kept busy at home with a small cottage industry manufacturing Cockaboxes.

Jim modified mailboxes to resemble the Cockabooses, painted them in garnet and black and sold them to Gamecock fans. Jim passed away in 1996, but the Cockaboxes scattered throughout Columbia and other places in South Carolina are monuments to his memory.

4

Pranks

S tudent pranks were once a regular occurrence in collegiate athletics, especially in the sport of football. They seem to be rarer now. Students seem to be more mature or sophisticated, or perhaps they have better things to do.

Milking Drill

On November 11, 1961, the Gamecocks prepared to meet Clemson in Carolina Stadium at Columbia.

A couple of minutes before the Clemson team was scheduled to take the field for pregame warm-ups, a squad of "players" trotted onto the gridiron dressed in orange jerseys similar to the Tiger uniforms. The Clemson band struck up the "Tiger Rag," and the cheering section went berserk.

The team lined up for kicking drills, but the punter kept missing the football. Two lines were formed, with half of the "players" holding their hands with thumbs down resembling cows' udders, while those in the other line tugged at the appendages in a milking motion.

Fans of the "Cow College" realized they had been had, but

quick action by security headed off any fisticuffs. The Sigma Nu fraternity had struck. South Carolina won the game 21-14.

Clemson became the "udder university."

Retribution

Clemson claimed a measure of revenge in 1963 when one or more Tiger supporters somehow gained entry to securely locked Carolina Stadium and spread full-strength nitrate of soda to spell IPTAY in six-foot-high letters down the middle of the Gamecock gridiron. IPTAY is Clemson's fund-raising athletic booster club.

The fertilizer turned the grass brown. South Carolina groundskeeper Sarge Frye covered the entire field with green paint to hide the pranksters' handiwork before game time. Clemson won the game 24-20.

Bovine Miss Clemson

Clemson's baseball team came to Columbia in May of 1949 for a two-game series at the old Davis Field diamond on Greene Street, where the Russell House Student Union and parking lot now exist. The hated Tigers had defeated the Gamecocks 6-5 in 11 innings earlier in the season at Clemson.

Several Carolina cheerleaders, led by Don Johnston of St. George, acquired a sickly old cow that had been retired from the herd at a Columbia dairy.

A bedsheet with large lettering that spelled out "Miss Clemson" was draped over the animal's back, and she wore a straw hat festooned with daisies and purple-and-orange (Clemson's colors) ribbon. The old cow was led around the ballpark until she laid down and died.

Carolina won both games of the series.

Another cheerleader involved in that prank was Howard Garfinkel of Walterboro. He had won election as a cheerleader on campus, using the campaign slogan: "There's no Finkel like Garfinkel."

Fertile Bench

When South Carolina's baseball team visited Clemson in 1950, the Tigers were ready in more ways than one.

The old Clemson ballpark had no dugouts, and the teams sat on benches against a backstop that stretched from third base around to first base. The Gamecocks arrived for batting practice, only to find that their bench had been covered with a thick coating of cow manure.

Coach Ted Petoskey was livid and lodged a complaint with Clemson AD Frank Howard. The crusty old Howard grabbed a student manager and ordered: "Boy, git sumpthin' and clean up that sheeut."

The manager used a garden hose to wash the bench down, and the Gamecocks spent the game with wet behinds, standing in manure.

When Clemson was at bat, a group of students stood behind the backstop holding up large white towels. When the Gamecock pitcher delivered the baseball, the outfielders lost the ball in the white background. A complaint to the home-plate umpire evoked little sympathy. An elderly gentleman with a crooked right index finger, he pointed it toward Coach Petoskey and said, "I can't do nothin' about that. Let's play baseball."

Students reached through the backstop wire and attempted to poke peanut shells and lighted cigarettes down the backs of the uniforms of the South Carolina players.

In the middle innings, a Piper Cub aircraft flew in low from the direction of center field. The pilot threw out a live chicken, which perished when it splattered on the infield near second base. Second baseman Jack Mitchell didn't make the catch. The plane was reportedly piloted by Clemson's star fullback, Fred Cone.

Needless to say, the Gamecocks didn't win either of the two games of the series played that year at Clemson.

Where's the Fire?

Tommy Moody, a Gamecock baseball letterman (1970–72), says he heard this story involving George Felton and Ed Lynch, members of the South Carolina basketball squad in the mid-'70s.

It seems Lynch was taking a shower in The Roost, South Carolina's dormitory for scholarship athletes, when Felton procured a fire extinguisher from a hallway and discharged its contents on Lynch's buttocks.

Neither Felton nor Lynch played much basketball under Coach Frank McGuire, but Felton eventually wound up as the Gamecocks' head coach, compiling a five-season 87-62 record between 1986 and 1991.

Lynch had more success on the baseball diamond. He recorded a 15-2 pitching record and was a member of College World Series teams of 1975 and 1977. In professional baseball, Lynch won 47 major league games and pitched nearly 1,000 innings during an eight-year career with the New York Mets and the Chicago Cubs.

He has served as a front-office executive with several major league clubs, including a stint as general manager of the Cubs.

Who Fired That Shot?

Quite a few residents of The Roost were hunters, and some of them kept guns in their rooms. One football player in the early 1970s thought he would play a joke on a teammate whose room was at the end of the hall.

The shotgun blast blew a large hole in the door of the victim's room. From that day forward, all firearms had to be checked with Roost manager Mike Caskey, and the perpetrator was suspended for a semester from the university.

Wrong Number

South Carolina baseball coach Ray Tanner makes full use of his cell phone. On road trips, Tanner is busy making and receiving calls from his front seat on the bus.

The Gamecocks were en route to Auburn, Alabama, for a Southeastern Conference series in March 2000, when Tanner's cell phone rang. The voice on the other end identified himself as a high school coach from Valdosta, Georgia, and asked Tanner if he would be interested in recruiting a left-handed-hitting catcher who stood 6-3, weighed 220 pounds, and was hitting .650 for his high school team.

It took Tanner about a minute to figure out the call was a hoax. Gamecock outfielder Brennan Dees had his own cell phone. He had placed the call from the back of the bus.

Ziggie

Fred Zeigler was the resident clown on the South Carolina football team from 1967 through 1969. He was also a record-setting pass receiver.

Born in the tiny low-country South Carolina town of Reevesville, Zeigler was a walk-on who, according to assistant coach George Terry, had deceptive speed. He was even slower than he looked. About 5-10, he had enormous feet. He also had a great pair of hands, exceptional balance, and a nose for the football.

When head coach Paul Dietzel lamented the dearth of pass receivers before the 1967 season, George Terry told him, "There's a guy on the scout squad who can catch the football."

Zeigler was promoted, earned a scholarship, and over the next three seasons, caught 146 passes—35 in 1967, 59 in 1968, and 52 in 1969—and probably caused Coach Dietzel to age at least 10 years. He was a notorious prankster and practical joker.

Zeigler's 146 career receptions stood as a school record for 18 years and still ranked fourth on South Carolina's all-time list at the end of the 20th century.

Fred Zeigler (USC Sports Information)

As was his habit, Dietzel called on a senior player to say the blessing before each pregame meal, but pointedly avoided naming Freddie before the first nine games of the 1969 season. An indignant Zeigler went to assistant coach Larry Jones and said his feelings were hurt that he hadn't been invited to lead the prayer.

Jones interceded with Dietzel, and Freddie was selected. He bowed reverently and began chanting an Indian prayer ritual. He was never asked to pray again.

Reports began circulating in the news media that Dietzel might resign to accept a post in the administration of President Nixon. Dietzel, who had a flair for the dramatic, called a team meeting to say he would decline the appointment.

When he told his players he assumed they had heard the reports, a voice from the back of the room piped up, "Take the job! Take the job!"

In 1969, when Zeigler was a junior, South Carolina led Virginia 49-28 at Charlottesville, and Dietzel had taken his first team out of the game. As sports information director, I always left the press box and went to the sideline with two minutes remaining in the game. I informed Coach Dietzel that Freddie had caught 11 passes, tying a school record.

With less than a minute to play, South Carolina gained possession on a Virginia fumble. Dietzel sent Zeigler in with the second team and instructed quarterback Randy Yoakum to throw a screen pass to Zeigler on first down. He was tackled for a one-yard loss, but had 12 receptions and a new record.

When I returned to the press box, I learned that the loss on the final catch left Zeigler with 199 yards, a record that stood until Zola Davis had 206 yards against Vanderbilt in 1998. Through the 2000 season, only one South Carolina receiver had exceeded 200 yards in a single game.

Davis caught 14 passes against Vanderbilt in 1998, but the 12 by Zeigler still ties him for the second most in Gamecock history.

Johnny Gregory, a senior receiver in 1968, claims Zeigler should have caught 13 passes in the Virginia game.

"When we broke the huddle," Gregory recalled, "I went to the wrong side. Freddie signaled me to stay there rather than risk a delay penalty. I ran his route and [quarterback Tommy] Suggs threw me a pass that gained 12 yards."

Zeigler caught at least one pass in 29 consecutive games. After graduation he went to law school and is now a prominent Columbia attorney.

Run, Blackie, Run

Blackie Kincaid was a South Carolina halfback in 1949–50, served in the Coast Guard during the Korean conflict, and returned in 1953 to complete his collegiate eligibility. He played for the Washington Redskins in 1954 and in the Canadian Football League with the Montreal Alouettes and the Hamilton Tiger Cats in 1955.

He also earned baseball letters as an outfielder in 1950 and 1954.

I traveled with the baseball team in 1950 as official scorer, and we took a spring-break trip to play at Georgia, Mercer and a U. S. Navy team at the Jacksonville Air Station. We traveled five or six to a car in four automobiles.

Blackie bragged that he could run 20 miles an hour for 10 minutes. First baseman Cy Szakacsi, who was driving, stopped on a rural Georgia road so Blackie could prove his point. Each time he would catch up, the car would speed away, and would then chase it for several miles.

That car arrived in Athens half an hour after the others, and center fielder Kincaid wasn't very effective that day playing on blistered feet.

Coach Ted Petoskey was not pleased.

Rapid Rupert

The influx of G.I. Bill of Rights students after World War II overcrowded the men's dormitories at the University of South Carolina, and three students were billeted in rooms designed to house two.

For the 1948–49 school year, I shared room 109 in Preston Hall with Rupie Drews, a sprinter on the track team, and Don Cox, a 5-9 guard, whose main assignment was to get the basketball to 6-11 center Jim Slaughter. Drews was from Charleston and Cox was from Greenville.

Drews' nickname was "Rapid Rupert," and his eyesight was so bad, his glasses looked like two glass fruit jar lids. Rupie's hobby was sleeping, and if he wasn't in class or on the track, he was in the sack. He had a ritual. He would lie down, carefully place his glasses on the windowsill, and go to sleep. He always donned those glasses upon awakening, before getting out of bed.

Louis Harrelson was from Mullins. He was a heavyweight on the boxing team and a reserve center in football. He did play enough to earn a football letter in 1951, but his nickname was "The Judge" because he spent so much time on the bench.

Louis was also the No. 1 practical joker living in Preston First East. With Rapid Rupert in repose one day, Harrelson sneaked into room 109, stole Rupie's spectacles, doused a wooden chair by the bed with lighter fluid, and struck a match.

Louis yelled, "fire!"—awakening a terrified Rupie, who reached for, but couldn't find his glasses. He leaped out of bed and ran into the wall attempting to find the door, while Louis doubled over with laughter.

The lighter fluid burned off in a few seconds without inflicting serious damage on the chair.

Don Cox remembered another occasion when Jim Slaughter appropriated Rupie's glasses.

"Those glasses were so thick, he couldn't see anything without them," Cox said. "Jim hid the glasses, and Rupie went nuts trying to find them. He couldn't find his way out the door without those glasses."

Rupie Drews had a long career in public education as teacher, coach, principal, and school superintendent at James Island High School in Charleston. He was a pioneer in introducing soccer into the Palmetto State's scholastic sports programs.

This One's Miss December

Chris Boyle and Neil Fox were two catchers from Pennsylvania on South Carolina baseball teams of 1981–84. They were also avid basketball fans and always grabbed seats behind the basket at games in Carolina Coliseum.

As a means of distraction when opposing players were at the foul line, Boyle and Fox would hold up centerfold pages from *Playboy* magazine.

Nocturnal Termite

Tommy Williams was a pretty good infielder on South Carolina baseball teams from 1977 through 1980. He was also a deep sleeper. His nickname was "Termite."

Termite was sound asleep in his room at The Roost, when several baseball teammates and golf team member Steve Liebler lifted the mattress, including Termite, from the bed and transported it to the baseball stadium adjacent to The Roost.

The mattress, with Termite still sound asleep, was deposited at second base. After graduation, Tommy Williams became a successful baseball coach at Lexington High School, where he developed numerous players who advanced to professional baseball or major college programs.

In relating the mattress caper, Steve Liebler recalled, "That was one of those nights when we had been out and had too much fun."

The original Roost had communal bathrooms on each floor, and Liebler remembers a time when a group of athletes decided to build a swimming pool. They erected barriers across the first-floor bathroom doors, stopped up the drains, and turned all the showers on. The first floor of the building was soon flooded.

5
Delay of Game

Kennedy Assassination

The 1963 Clemson game was one of two South Carolina football games that had to be postponed.

On Friday, November 22, as sports information director, I spent most of the day at Carolina Stadium with Chet Forte, producer for ABC-TV, which was scheduled to televise the game. On a quick trip back to the office, I was informed by my secretary that the assassination of President John F. Kennedy had just been broadcast.

I returned to the stadium to find Forte had been told the telecast was canceled; his crew was packing up its equipment. Colleges throughout the nation faced the same dilemma: to play or not to play.

Dr. Thomas F. Jones, president of the University of South Carolina, and Dr. Robert C. Edwards, Clemson's president, conferred and decided to play.

Vince Gargano, a Gamecock football letterman (1949–51) and a classmate of mine, called from Brooklyn, N.Y., to ask about the status of the game. Vince was head coach at Brooklyn's Lincoln High School. From the information I had been given, I assured him the game was on, and he said: "I'm on my way. See you tomorrow."

Clemson sports information director Bob Bradley and I made last-day rounds of the Columbia news media, and we settled down at Swain's Steak House for a meal, when I was summoned to the telephone. President Jones was on the phone. He and Dr. Edwards had had a change of mind and decided the game should be postponed five days, until Thanksgiving Day.

Dr. Jones said he had been unable to find Coach Marvin Bass to advise him of the postponement.

Marvin was at the Heart of Columbia Motel, where the football team spent the night before home games. The "Big Moose" had just finished his bed check when I arrived, and I found him in a rocking chair outside his room.

"I didn't think we would play tomorrow," was his reaction to the news.

Gargano got the news on his car radio about midnight, as he crossed the Virginia–North Carolina border. He continued to Columbia and spent the weekend visiting friends. He didn't make it back on Thanksgiving because his team was involved in high school playoffs.

The Gamecocks and Tigers played their untelevised game, with Clemson winning a close one, 24-20. Many ticket holders had made other Thanksgiving weekend plans, and refunds were offered. For the first time in the history of the Carolina-Clemson series, some tickets were cashed in, and the crowd of 37,414 was about 6,000 below capacity.

That's the only time in the rivalry that the Carolina-Clemson game hasn't been a sellout.

Hurricane

South Carolina's other football postponement occurred in 1951, when a hurricane threatened the eastern seaboard. The game with The Citadel was delayed two days, from Saturday, September 29, to Monday, October 1. South Carolina won 26-7.

6

Close Calls and Travel Troubles

A ll athletic programs encounter travel problems from time to time, sometimes flirting with disaster. Occasionally there are tragedies, such as the plane crash that wiped out the Marshall University football team in the 1970s, and the crash that claimed half the Wichita State football team. The Southern Airways DC-9 involved in the Marshall crash had transported the South Carolina football team a week earlier.

University of South Carolina teams and athletics personnel have been spared disaster, but they have had some close calls and their share of travel delays.

Ninety-Five Others

On Christmas Eve 1971, Basketball Hall of Fame coach Frank McGuire and his team boarded an Eastern Airlines flight for the return home following a 69-59 win over the University of Pittsburgh the night before. Halfway between Pittsburgh and Charlotte, at 32,000 feet, there was a loud boom followed by a winding-down sound in the starboard engine of the DC-9.

A flight attendant assured the anxious passengers there was no problem and the pilot was merely "putting on his air brakes" for the

Coach Frank McGuire (USC Sports Information)

descent to Charlotte. That brought a loud exclamation of "Bull----!" from Allen Sharpe, a cinematographer with Columbia station WIS-TV, who traveled with the team.

The pilot was able to keep the plane on course, powered only by one engine; but as it prepared to land at Charlotte, half a dozen fire trucks could be seen stationed alongside the runway. The plane landed safely, and the basketball party made its connecting flight to Columbia.

Joe Petty, veteran WIS-TV sports director, quipped, as the team departed the crippled DC-9. "I can just see the banner head-line: "Frank McGuire, 95 others, die in plane crash."

Upon my arrival home my son greeted me with "Hey, Dad, I just heard on the radio that a plane made an emergency landing in Charlotte."

My reply? "No kidding."

Borrowed Aircraft

In February 1973, the South Carolina basketball team chartered a propeller-driven Martin 404 from Southern Airways to travel to Toledo, Ohio, where the Gamecocks claimed a 77-74 win over the University of Toledo.

The 40-passenger Martin made a refueling stop on the return trip at Tri-Cities Airport in Tennessee. The plane was about 200 feet off the ground on takeoff, when the flight attendant, in a terrified voice over the intercom, instucted all passengers to check their seat belts.

The pilot made a skillful 180-degree turn, landed the aircraft, and maneuvered it to a halt a few yards from the end of the runway.

"Folks, I apologize for not keeping you informed, but I've been pretty busy up here," the skipper said. "We blew our starboard engine on takeoff."

A glance out the window revealed oil gushing out of the blown engine.

Another Martin was parked at the airport for a scheduled departure the following morning. A phone call to Southern Airways operations in Atlanta resulted in the charter pilot using that plane to continue the flight to Columbia, arriving about 3 a.m. The borrowed plane returned to Tri-Cities before its flight crew, sleeping in a Johnson City hotel, knew it was gone.

Never Backed In

Coach Frank McGuire always occupied the right-hand seat in the front row when the South Carolina basketball team traveled by bus. But on airplanes, he always demanded a seat as far to the rear as possible.

"Nobody ever heard of an airplane backing into a mountain," explained the Irishman, who had a fear of flying.

Snowed Out

Five days after the 1973 blown-engine scare during the Toledo trip, Coach McGuire took the Gamecocks by commercial flight to Buffalo, followed by a chartered bus to Olean, N.Y., to play St. Bonaventure. The Bonnies had lost their previous home game by two points to Virginia Tech, and we were told that St. Bonaventure had never lost two consecutive home games in its ancient gymnasium.

There were also jokes that the Catholic institution always used two priests as the referees. Still, the Gamecocks eked out a one-point victory, 75-74.

Meanwhile, Olean residents were complaining about the lack of snowfall that was hurting business in the nearby ski resorts. A call home to Columbia revealed that South Carolina's capital city, which averages one measurable snowfall every three years, had been hit with an all-time record 14 inches. Some areas of the Palmetto State accumulated as much as 21 inches of snow.

The Gamecocks had another road game, an 84-74 win over Niagara at Buffalo, two days after the St. Bonaventure game. Airports in the southeast had reopened by the time the team arrived home three days after the storm.

Flashlight Landing

In January 1982, Coach Bill Foster booked an ancient 40-passenger Convair from a charter service to take his Gamecock basketball team to Richmond, Virginia, for a game with the Richmond Spiders.

During the approach for landing, the copilot, armed with a flashlight, entered the passenger area, said, "excuse me," leaned over one of the passengers, and shined his flashlight through the window.

The startled passenger's question drew the reply that he was trying to see if the landing gear was down. A warning light had come on, but it sometimes didn't work properly. The plane circled for quite some time to consume fuel and landed as rescue vehicles stood by.

On Top of Old Smokey

The Football Writers Association of America held its 1985 annual meeting at King's Island, Ohio, an amusement park and resort with a Jack Nicklaus–designed golf course about 20 miles north of Cincinnati.

South Carolina AD Bob Marcum had gone to South Bend, Indiana, to visit his daughter and her family. He planned to play golf with some of the writers gathered for the meeting.

The plan was for pilot Joe Baier to fly me to Cincinnati in the athletics department airplane. I was to pick up a rental car and drive to Blue Ash airport—the small field near the meeting site—since no rental cars were available there. After his golf outing, Marcum was to return to Columbia with the pilot while I remained for the writers' meeting and was then to return to Columbia on a commercial flight.

I was reading a newspaper when the plane ran into a thunderstorm at about 7,000 feet over the Smokey Mountains. There was a loud boom and what appeared to be a large fireball off the left wing of the airplane. Joe removed his headphones, turned, and calmly asked, "Did you see that lightning?"

Panic gripped a frightened sports information director, but we landed safely in Cincinnati. Joe inspected the plane and found six small holes, each about the size of a quarter. He covered them with duct tape and completed the flight. I was glad to be on the ground in the rental car.

The lightning had also struck one of the twin-engine plane's propellers. A thorough inspection was made after Joe returned to Columbia, and no major damage was detected.

7

Situations and Personalities

Niagara Falls

Frank McGuire was never one for sightseeing when he took his basketball team on the road. He said he was born and raised in New York City and had never visited the Statue of Liberty or the Empire State Building.

In 1972, however, the Gamecocks were in Buffalo, N.Y., for a game, and McGuire arranged for a bus to take the team to see Niagara Falls. The drive shaft fell off the bus halfway between Buffalo and the Canadian border, and the team was stranded for more than an hour until a relief bus arrived.

Mist from the falls froze into tiny pellets, and when All-America guard Kevin Joyce boarded the bus after viewing the falls, his hair looked as if it was covered with grains of rice.

The Bubbly Group

The Bubbly Group was a gathering of prominent fans who followed Coach Frank McGuire's South Carolina basketball team on road trips.

Sometimes they were referred to as "The Disciples."

One member of the group, Peter Paul Lukas, made wine as a hobby and would often bring some of his product on trips. That's how the traveling fans became known as the Bubbly Group. Lukas owned an equipment dealership in Columbia that sold forklifts. The group included doctors, dentists, bankers, lawyers, and other prominent professionals.

In December 1968, South Carolina defeated Rhode Island, St. Joseph's,, and LaSalle in Philadelphia to win the Quaker City Classic. The 62-59 win in the title game was the only loss suffered that season by LaSalle, which finished with a 24-1 record under Coach Tom Gola.

On the charter flight back to Columbia that night, some of the finest sparkling wine created by Peter Paul Lukas made its appearance, and there was much celebration. The Bubbly Group moniker was probably born that night.

The Bubbly Group numbered anywhere from 25 to 30, down to just a couple, depending on circumstances such as business commitments and the success of the team.

Often on trips, I was asked to recommend the best restaurant for dinner the night before a game. I steered the group to such establishments as Karl Ratches in Milwaukee, and the Original Bookbinder's in Philadelphia; but in Oklahoma City, my reputation for picking the best restaurants was ruined.

Bob Stevens had been South Carolina's basketball coach (1959–62) before going to Oklahoma, and he was still living in the area when Frank McGuire's Gamecocks played at the University of Oklahoma in December 1974. Stevens attended our practice, and I asked him to recommend a restaurant.

He told me Fuzzies was the best, so the Bubbly Group went to Fuzzies. It turned out that Fuzzies was better known for its bar and dance floor than for its cuisine. The food was terrible.

To make matters worse, Peter Paul Lukas commented, "The best thing on the wine list was Mogan David."

Travel delays due to weather sometimes caused problems for members of the Bubbly Group, who were used to traveling with the team on charter flights and returning to Columbia after games in time for business appointments the next morning.

South Carolina eked out a 78-76 win at Virginia Tech in 1971, only to learn that the charter flight that was scheduled to pick the team up at Roanoke had been canceled due to heavy snowfall in the area.

Dr. Charles Crews had surgery scheduled the next morning, and Dr. Bill Salter, a dentist, had patients scheduled. The brother of Rick Aydlett, one of the South Carolina basketball players, who was from Blacksburg, Virginia, drove the two doctors through the snowstorm to the Roanoke bus station, but all the buses were also canceled.

The charter arrived the following afternoon to take the team home. Surgery and dental appointments were postponed.

Cakes

Bobby Cremins was one of many New Yorkers who rode Frank McGuire's mythical underground railroad to Columbia to play basketball at the University of South Carolina. His nickname was "Cakes."

Teammates gave him the nickname because they said his ears were always dirty, caked with dirt.

The son of a longshoreman, Cremins was from the Bronx and attended All Hallows High School, but detoured to Frederick Military Academy in Portsmouth, Virginia, before arriving with the freshman class for the fall semester of 1966. McGuire went to see another prospect in a game involving Frederick and Bullis Prep in Maryland while South Carolina was in College Park to play the University of Maryland.

McGuire was more impressed with Cremins, so Cremins was invited to make a recruiting visit to South Carolina. Assistant Coach Donnie Walsh took the brash youngster to McGuire's home, where a party was in progress. Impressed with the surroundings, Cremins allegedly said to McGuire in his best Bronx accent, "Nice pad youse got here, Frank."

Donnie Walsh took him aside and explained the facts of life to him.

Bobby Cremins in action as a Gamecock sophomore.
(USC Sports Information)

When Bobby left the Bronx for university life, his mother bought him a wool suit and told him she expected it to last four years. "When I arrived in Columbia, the temperature was about 100 degrees," Cremins said. "I never wore that suit again."

After leading the freshman team in scoring and rebounding in 1967, Cremins quickly became the heart-and-soul leader of the varsity. His statistics weren't overly impressive. He scored 589 career points (an average of 7.6 points per game), and although standing only 6-2 and weighing 160 pounds, he pulled down 527 rebounds to average 6.8 rebounds per game.

It was in the leadership department that Cremins excelled on the court. By far the team's best defensive player, he played backcourt, and despite his lack of size, frontcourt as well. He was the team captain in both his junior and senior seasons. The team won 61 games and lost only 17 during his varsity career.

A notoriously poor free-throw shooter when there was no pressure, Cremins rose to the occasion in the clutch games. He had converted only 57 percent and went 5-for-6 from the foul line in a 55-50 road win at Duke his sophomore season. Four days later, at Chapel Hill, he made 13 of 16—including six in a row down the stretch—to spark an 87-86 win over North Carolina.

Cremins brought the basketball up against the Tar Heel press and also grabbed 15 rebounds. When North Carolina pulled to within one point, Tar Heel coach Dean Smith instructed his team to foul Cremins. Bobby kept making both ends of the one-and-one, extending the lead to three points. His final free throw came with five seconds remaining, and the Gamecocks cleared out to avoid fouling. North Carolina scored at the final horn, but still lost by a point.

In the first round of the ACC Tournament, when Cremins was a senior, the Gamecocks held a one-point lead over Clemson with half a minute remaining and the basketball in the hands of Clemson's best shooter, guard Butch Zatazlo. Cremins stole the ball and dribbled away as the clock ran out.

Being from the Bronx, Cremins didn't have much driving experience before he came to college, so he sought out opportunities to improve his skills behind the wheel.

Coach McGuire assigned Cremins and four other players—Corky Carnevale, Dennis Powell, John Roche, and Billy Walsh— to show prospect Henry Wilmore around town. Carnevale was supposed to be the designated driver.

Dennis Powell recalled what happened after Wilmore was delivered to his hotel and the group headed back to campus:

"We dropped Henry Wilmore at the Townhouse Hotel and Bobby insisted on driving. There were nine of us in the car—the five players plus Bobby Fowler, who we called 'Foul Al,' a girl named 'Flash,' and two other guys, Ed Jacobs and Freddie Scafili.

"Cremins lost control of the car rounding a corner on Greene Street and went up the steps of this house and in the front door. The whole porch came down."

Henry Wilmore played his collegiate basketball at the University of Michigan.

On another occasion, Cremins borrowed a car for a date with a student who lived in Capstone House, a dormitory for women on campus. Capstone is on Barnwell Street on a steep hill. Cremins parked on the street, picked up his date, and returned—only to find that the car was missing. Campus and city police were called and stolen car reports were filed.

Two weeks later, the car was found in bushes and a ravine at the bottom of the hill. Cremins had neglected to set the emergency brake, and the car had rolled down the hill, jumped a curb, passed between two houses, and landed in the ravine.

The residents of the two houses were either not at home or didn't hear the car go by.

Dr. Bill Salter related another story about Cremins learning to drive that ended in disaster.

It seems Cremins attempted to back a car out of the garage at a home on Greene Street, but shifted into drive when he thought he was in reverse. The car crashed through the back wall of the garage and dropped into the back yard of a Blossom Street home.

Bobby knocked on the door and said to the lady of the house, "There's a car in your backyard. How do I get it out?"

Dennis Powell remembered another occasion when Coach McGuire was exasperated with the entire team, especially Cremins.

"A lot of us attended summer school," Powell said. "We didn't have to, but we wanted to work at Coach's camp. He was so mad at us that he called everyone in and nailed everybody with something that annoyed him. He was especially mad at Bobby for referring to his father as 'my old man.'

"Coach told Bobby, 'If I ever hear you refer to your father as your old man again, I'll knock your balls on top of your head.'"

Cremins and Corky Carnevale attended a movie together in downtown Columbia and were looking for a ride back to campus, when Bobby spotted a city bus.

"I'll show you how we do it in the Bronx," he told Carnevale as he jumped on the back bumper of the bus. Carnevale followed, but before they arrived on campus, they were spotted by a police-man in a squad car. He turned on his blue light and pulled the bus over. Cremins jumped off and ran, but Carnevale froze—and had to answer to the law.

Carnevale was from Northwood, N.J. His father, Ben— a former coach at the U. S. Naval Academy—was director of athletics at New York University.

Dr. Salter, a dentist, and his wife, Dee Dee, invited Cremins to dinner at the Columbia Country Club. Bobby wore a new suit (not the wool one), but removed his jacket and draped it over the back of his chair in the dining room. Mrs. Salter quietly gave him a lesson in etiquette. Bobby said he removed the jacket so he wouldn't spill any food on it.

Lambert Schwartz was a Myrtle Beach businessman, an avid basketball fan, and a close friend of Coach Frank McGuire. His nick-name was Lambo. Students from many colleges and universities of-ten frequented Myrtle Beach, and South Carolina basketball players were no exception. Bobby Cremins remembers a few hard times at the hands of Myrtle Beach police.

"If they caught us just opening up a beer, they would throw us in jail," Cremins remembered. "We would call Lambo Schwartz and he would come down and get us out."

After graduation, Cremins had tryouts with the Pittsburgh Condors and Carolina Cougars of the American Basketball Associa-tion but was cut by both teams. He played for the Columbia Sertoma Club entry in the national AAU tournament in Carolina Coliseum and accompanied that team to Italy for an international AAU tour-nament.

Bobby went to South America for a year to play basketball in Ecuador, worked as a bellhop at the Waldorf Astoria Hotel in New

York City for six months, and then started a coaching career as an assistant at Point Park College in Pittsburgh. He returned to the University of South Carolina as a graduate assistant, earned a master's degree, and joined Frank McGuire's staff full time.

He moved on to successful stints as head basketball coach at Appalachian State University and Georgia Tech.

At Appalachian State, Cremins compiled a 100-70 record, won three Southern Conference regular-season championships, and one conference tournament title in six years. In 16 years at Georgia Tech, he won two Atlantic Coast Conference regular-season titles and the ACC Tournament four times while compiling a 358-237 record.

John "Ice Man" Schroeder finished his basketball career at South Carolina two years before Cremins joined the varsity. Schroeder, who now lives in Atlanta, closely followed Cremins's career at Georgia Tech. Schroeder said that shortly after Bobby was named head coach at Georgia Tech, he attended a meeting at Myrtle Beach with plans to continue on to Charlottesville, Virginia, to visit a prospect.

When he checked out the cost of a rental car, according to Schroeder, Cremins deemed it too high and instead hitchhiked from Myrtle Beach to Virginia. Schroeder didn't say if the prospect signed with Georgia Tech.

Cremins returned to his alma mater briefly as head basketball coach, but he never took the floor. His tenure lasted about 72 hours.

South Carolina AD Mike McGee introduced Bobby as the new Gamecock coach at a 1993 news conference. Cremins went back to Atlanta, thought it over, and decided to remain at Georgia Tech. Seven years later, he resigned under pressure, despite having led the Yellow Jackets to their best years.

In November of 2000, Cremins returned to South Carolina. He moved from Atlanta to Hilton Head Island. Instead of coaching basketball, he began analyzing basketball on telecasts of college games.

"I love college basketball," he said. "I may coach again. I'm keeping my options open, but right now, I'm a TV analyst."

Eddie Fogler, who became the South Carolina basketball coach after Cremins changed his mind, introduced Bobby when Cremins spoke at a Columbia Tipoff Club meeting in November of 2000.

"The last time I introduced Bobby Cremins was in a bar in Pittsburgh," Fogler quipped.

Bobby Cremins accepting the head basketball coaching job at South Carolina. He changed his mind 72 hours later. (USC Sports Information)

In his speech, Cremins blamed his slow academic start on teammates Skip Harlicka and Corky Carnevale, whom he said made B's and A's without opening any books.

"I was in my second year before I found out I had to go to class," he said. He said that at mid-semester of his first term, he had three F's and one D. Assistant Coach Donnie Walsh called him on the carpet for an explanation.

"I guess I'm spending too much time on one subject," Bobby said he replied.

Cremins said he decided against following through on his decision to return to South Carolina as basketball coach, because after he thought it over, he felt he was betraying the athletes he had recruited to play for him at Georgia Tech.

"I was a Judas and I didn't want to be that," he said.

Freshman Team

On the night that Bobby Cremins led South Carolina to an 87-86 win over Dean Smith's North Carolina Tar Heels, Coach Jack Thompson (no relation to the Gamecock basketball player of the same name) had his swim team in Chapel Hill for a meet the following day.

The South Carolina swimmers desperately wanted to see the basketball game, but there were no tickets available. Thompson had a freshman swimmer who was 6-8. He lined his team up with the tall freshman in the lead and marched up to the players' entrance at the North Carolina basketball arena.

"Freshman team," Thompson announced, and the gate attendant waved him and his team through. The South Carolina swim team watched the basketball game from the baseline, seated on the floor behind the Tar Heel cheerleaders.

Underground Railroad

Bobby Cremins was one of many players from New York City or communities near New York who came to South Carolina to play basketball under Frank McGuire.

The underground railroad first stopped in Chapel Hill when McGuire coached the North Carolina Tar Heels. The entire starting five on the 1957 Tar Heel team that won the NCAA championship hailed from New York.

McGuire's first South Carolina recruiting class, in the fall of 1964, included Jack Thompson and Frank Standard from Brooklyn and two players from New Jersey, Skip Kickey of Union City and Skip Harlicka from Trenton.

Stars on subsequent Gamecock teams included John Roche from Manhattan; Tom Owens and Mike Doyle from the Bronx; Mike Dunleavy from Brooklyn; Tom Riker from Hicksville on Long Island; Kevin Joyce from Merrick on Long Island; Brian Winters from Rockaway Park on Long Island; Jackie Gilloon from West New York, N.J.; and quite a few others.

Stall Ball

Before the shot clock was instituted in college basketball, underdog teams frequently resorted to slowdown tactics and outright stalls in efforts to shorten the games and offset the other team's superior talent.

Coach Chuck Noe came up with the "Mongoose" offense during his short tenure at South Carolina. He reportedly got the idea from Coach Babe McCarthy of Mississippi State. Noe would station three players out near mid-court, with the center in the middle and his two best ballhandlers on either side. Up front, near the baseline, he would station his quickest player and his best corner shooter.

The Gamecocks would hold the ball out near mid-court as long as the defenders didn't come out and apply pressure. If the down-low defenders went to sleep, the quickest Gamecock would break under the baskets, take a quick pass, and score a layup.

The Mongoose effectively neutralized the other team's big man. Since South Carolina played with centers such as 6-4 Bob Haney and 6-6 John Schroeder, while opposing centers were between 6-8 and 7-0, it was a matter of survival. There was no 45-second shot clock at the time, so the ploy worked more often than not.

In a 45-32 win over Furman in December of 1963, Noe employed the Mongoose, and the score at halftime was 19-17, with Ronnie Collins scoring 17 of South Carolina's 19 points. Later the same month, in a tournament at Nashville, Western Kentucky coach E. A. Diddle refused to order his team to come out against the stall, and Western was twice called for a technical foul for not putting pressure on the offense.

Coach Diddle threw his famous red towel high into the air when the second technical was called.

South Carolina won that game 75-60.

In the semifinal round of the 1968 ACC Tournament, North Carolina State went into a stall against Duke at the beginning of the game. The Wolfpack pulled off an upset, 12-10. N.C. State didn't stall in the championship game the following night against North Carolina and lost 76-50.

Bill Curry, the "Mouth of the South," who was the voice of the North Carolina Tar Heel Network, earned a mention in *Sports Illustrated* when he commented on the air that the N.C. State–Duke game "had all of the excitement of artificial insemination."

Dr. Phil Fox, one of the referees in that game, picked up a sportswriter's bag of peanuts from press row and began eating peanuts because of the nonaction.

The nationally ranked South Carolina teams under Frank McGuire were either victimized or nearly victimized several times by stalling opponents.

The halftime score was 4-3 in South Carolina's favor at College Park in January of 1971, and the game was tied 25-25 at the end of regulation. Maryland pulled out a 31-30 upset win in overtime. Two days later, Virginia didn't go into a complete stall, but used slowdown tactics to upset the Gamecocks 50-49.

Clemson held the ball but lost to the Gamecocks 47-44 the same season at Clemson. A year earlier, in the opening round of the ACC Tournament at Charlotte, Clemson nearly pulled off an upset by employing a stall. South Carolina won 34-33.

In the finals of the ACC Tournament the same year, heavily favored South Carolina faced a stall employed by N.C. State. With South Carolina superstar John Roche hobbled by a severe ankle injury suffered in the 79-63 semifinal win over Wake Forest, the Wolfpack stall was parlayed into a 42-39 upset that took two overtimes.

Favored teams sometimes resorted to late-game stalling tactics to protect leads. North Carolina coach Dean Smith perfected the "Four Corners," a variation of Chuck Noe's Mongoose offense, to play keep-away when the Tar Heels had a late lead.

Those Four Corners tactics resulted in the adoption of the shot clock.

A Fighting Rooster

Jeff Denberg, basketball beat writer for *The State*, wrote in 1963 that "The University of South Carolina mascot is a gamecock, and Chuck Noe looks and acts like a fighting rooster."

Noe was perhaps the most intense coach in all of college basketball. He had played basketball and baseball at the University of Virginia and was on his way to the major leagues as an infielder, when a broken leg ended his professional baseball career. He turned to coaching, first in Virginia high schools and later at Virginia Military Institute and Virginia Tech.

South Carolina AD Marvin Bass hired Noe as the Gamecock basketball coach in the summer of 1962. Over the next year and a half, Gamecock basketball was exciting, to say the least. Noe's Mongoose offense kept South Carolina within striking distance of opponents who had far superior talent. He didn't beat a lot of them, but he played them close.

When Coach Vic Bubas brought the nationally ranked Duke Blue Devils to the old Carolina Field House, Noe stationed the pep band directly behind the Duke bench. The trombone player's instrument kept sliding past Bubas's ear. The Duke coach took his team to mid-court during timeouts to escape the noise.

Assistant Coach Dwane Morrison was from Owensboro, Kentucky, and Noe took his team there in December of 1963 to play Kentucky Wesleyan before moving on to Louisville, Noe's hometown, to meet the Louisville Cardinals.

After the Kentucky Wesleyan game, the team was traveling in three rental cars, with Noe driving the first, Morrison the second, and me the third. On a snowy Kentucky mountain road, Noe stopped at a country store. It was about 1 a.m., and the establishment was closed, but the coach had spotted a light inside.

"There's somebody in there," he said. "I need a Pepsi-Cola."

There was an after-hours poker game going on, but the storekeeper agreed to open up for the Pepsis. Johnny Downs was the team trainer. Johnny was a dwarf—3-8 and about 165 pounds. Jim Fox, the Gamecock center, was 6-10.

Johnny walked into the store, followed by Fox, and one of the poker players exclaimed, "My God, it's a circus. They've got a midget and a giant."

Several weeks later, when the Gamecocks played at Georgia Tech, Atlanta sportswriter Furman Bisher wrote a column referring to Noe's team as a circus with its own midget and giant.

Before one game, Noe told Jim Fox to eat a lot of garlic and breathe on the opposing team's center.

South Carolina led the entire game at Maryland, only to have the Terrapins tie the game at the final horn. Convinced he had won, Noe rushed over to the Maryland bench and congratulated Coach Bud Milliken for a good game. Dwane Morrison told him the game was going into overtime and Noe said, "I thought we won by four."

Escorted back to his bench, he was his old self again, coaching brilliantly, and the Gamecocks won by four, 73-69.

Noe once checked out a university motor pool car for a recruiting trip to see a prospect in Delaware. He apparently forgot about the car because he flew home. The car was located several days later, parked at the motel where Noe had stayed.

When South Carolina played Virginia, Noe wanted to defeat his alma mater in the worst way. In 1962, he asked football coach Marvin Bass if he could scout Virginia and devise a game plan. Marvin agreed, and Chuck spent a week as a football coach.

Oddsmakers rated the game a toss-up. South Carolina won 40-6.

Midway through his second basketball season, Noe was hospitalized due to emotional exhaustion and resigned. He recovered, had a successful career as salesman for a firm that specialized in college jewelry, and eventually returned to coaching at Virginia Commonwealth University.

He then became host of a Richmond radio talk show.

R. J.

R.J. Moore is a native of Arkansas who retired from the army at Fort Jackson, opened a service station in Columbia, and became a rabid Gamecock fan. He was an Exxon dealer for many years, and when that oil company squeezed out most of its small dealers, R.J. switched to Phillips 66.

The walls at Moore's 66 are covered with photographs of University of South Carolina athletes. R.J. was once shot while wrestling a gun away from a would-be robber. He wounded the robber, and both of them ended up in a hospital. Moore has survived a stroke and cancer. Nevertheless, over a period of more than 30 years, he missed only one South Carolina football game—home or away.

R.J. Moore closed the 66 station for the Outback Bowl. (Tom Price)

That happened in 1979, when Moore's mother-in-law passed away in Arkansas the day before the South Carolina–Clemson game. On the way to the funeral, R.J. said he "stopped at a liquor store in the middle of this old cotton field in Arkansas."

A friend in Columbia put the telephone next to a radio, and Moore listened to the final moments of the game.

"I was yelling and screaming, and everybody in [the liquor store] was looking at me funny," R.J. said. "I threw $10 on the table to cover the phone call and said, 'We won.'"

The final score that year was South Carolina 13, Clemson 9.

When home games at Williams-Brice Stadium end, R.J. Moore raises the hydraulic lift in his gas station's lube bay to tabletop height, lays plywood over the top, and covers the plywood with tablecloths.

Food and drink are produced, and R.J. proclaims, "It's grease-pit party time!"

A friend named Jake Knotts once gave R.J. a live gamecock. Carolina fans attending one of R.J.'s grease-pit parties fed the bird some beer, and the gamecock became a bit tipsy.

"That bird flew up on the table and commenced to pecking at the cake and other food," R.J. said.

In December 2000, R.J. plastered a sign across the gasoline pumps at his Phillips 66 station: "Closed for the Outback Bowl. Be back January 2."

Frog

Dick Weldon's nickname was "Frog." He was a successful high school coach at Bamberg before he joined the football staff of Coach Marvin Bass at the University of South Carolina. When Paul Dietzel replaced Bass in 1966, Weldon remained a football assistant.

He also coached the 1966 baseball team to a 15-8 record. He was a good coach but never did learn that Division I college left fielders have better throwing arms than high school outfielders. Dick coached third base, and he probably set an NCAA record for having runners thrown out at the plate while trying to score from second base on hard-hit singles to left field.

In the spring of 1966, I accompanied Weldon to Greenville, N.C., for a preseason baseball gathering of coaches, news media, and professional scouts. It's about a 500-mile round trip, and I don't think Dick's car was ever very much under 75 miles an hour. I was holding on for dear life.

We made it without a problem until we passed an elementary school on Rosewood Drive in Columbia, about three blocks from the University of South Carolina athletics offices. Dick was ticketed for speeding in a school zone.

The families of the Gamecock athletics staff often spent a few days in the summer at Wampee, a former plantation on Lake Marion that was operated as a lodge by the South Carolina Public Service Authority (Santee-Cooper).

During one of these sojourns the staff toured Our Lady of Mepkin, a monastery operated by the Trappist order. Mepkin had

Dick Weldon (USC Sports Information)

once been an antebellum plantation owned by Clare Boothe Luce, and she had donated the property to the Trappist order of monks.

The Trappists are a silent order, and the monks do not talk to outsiders—with the exception of one, who serves as a guide who shows visitors around. The monks operate a bakery and raise produce that is sold through stores nearby and in the Charleston area.

Dick Weldon asked the guide if the monks listened to football games on the radio. He was told there were no radios in the monastery.

"Do you mean," Weldon asked, "that when the Carolina Gamecocks are playing the Clemson Tigers, you aren't listening to the game? I can't believe that."

Dick Weldon shared an office with Lou Holtz in 1966–67, when both were assistant football coaches under Paul Dietzel. Thirty-three years later, as South Carolina's head coach, Holtz was the speaker at the first meeting of the Columbia Touchdown Club prior to the 2000 season opener. Weldon was asked to introduce Holtz. Weldon said, "This is like a private being asked to introduce a general."

After the Frog's 20-minute introduction, Holtz commented, "Strom Thurmond took lessons from Dick Weldon on how to filibuster."

For those unfamiliar with South Carolina politics, Thurmond is South Carolina's senior senator who has served longer in the U.S. Congress than anybody else.

Sarge

Sarge Frye may lead the nation in retirements. He retired in 1954, 1977, and 1997, but still can be seen around the University of South Carolina athletics department every working day.

Weldon B. Frye served more than 23 years in the army, participated in the Allied invasion of Europe during World War II, was wounded, and also saw combat experience during the Korean conflict.

His last duty assignment placed him in charge of landscaping and grounds maintenance at Fort Jackson, the large army training base on the outskirts of Columbia. Master Sergeant Frye retired from

Sarge Frye (USC Sports Information)

the army in 1954. University of South Carolina AD Rex Enright hired him immediately.

Sarge did such a good job as athletics facilities groundskeeper that his duties were expanded to include the entire campus. He retired from that position in 1977, but was immediately rehired to maintain the athletics facilities. He retired again in 1997 at the age of 84, but still spends a few hours each day around the athletics department.

"I'm retired but I never have left," is the way Sarge explains it as he shows up about 10 a.m. and 3 p.m. daily to make a pot of coffee and talk over old times.

When asked to explain his longevity, the 87-year-old Sarge answered, "I eat a lot of Little Debbie cakes." He once told an unmarried secretary, "You're never going to catch a man until you learn to make coffee."

Sarge's son Jerry was an end on the South Carolina football team in 1958–60 and a cocaptain of the 1960 Gamecocks. Coach Warren Giese's teams seldom threw the football and almost never threw to the tight end, but Sarge remembers Jerry catching one pass. He thinks it was against N.C. State.

"Jerry caught it on about the 45-yard line," Sarge said. "I was right there on the sideline, and I outran him for 40 yards. He hadn't caught one in I-don't-know-when. I got in front of him, but he gave out and got tackled about the 5-yard line."

Jay Frye, grandson of Sarge and son of Jerry, was a special-teams player on South Carolina's squads of 1983–84. In 1984, South Carolina came from behind to take a 22-21 lead at Clemson with 50 seconds remaining in the game. On the ensuing kickoff, Jay made an unassisted tackle at the Clemson 8-yard line to ensure the victory and a 10-1 regular-season record.

Sarge remembers a Georgia workout the day before a game in Columbia in 1959, and Bulldog coach Wally Butts complaining to him that the stadium grass was too long.

"I told Coach Warren Giese what Coach Butts said, and he told me, 'Don't you dare cut that grass.'"

South Carolina upset Georgia 30–14, the only game the Bulldogs lost that year. Georgia's quarterback was Fran Tarkenton.

There was a time when an invasion by army worms was causing problems with the stadium grass, but Sarge said there was no truth to the rumor that he had a worker stationed at every entrance to stomp the worms to death as they entered.

In 1980, university trustees named the University of South Carolina baseball facility after the longtime groundskeeper, and Sarge Frye Field is his pride and joy.

"We had a couple of big, tall pitchers, Randy Martz and Ed Lynch (in 1977), and I might have pointed that pitcher's mound a little to help them out. They pitched real well," Sarge remembered.

In 1993, the American Baseball Coaches Association named Sarge Frye National Groundskeeper of the Year.

Sarge was standing on a ramp overlooking Sarge Frye Field shortly after the stadium was given his name, when a Gamecock fan and his daughter came by to look over the facility. The little girl asked her dad, "I wonder who the old fellow is that they named this field after."

The father pointed to Sarge and said, "Just ask him."

Basketball coach Frank McGuire invited Sarge to travel with the team to a game at Clemson.

"It was cold as hell," Sarge recalled. "I had a new London Fog coat that cost about $50. I was proud of that coat, but Coach McGuire had a cashmere coat that cost maybe $1,000. When we hung our coats up in the locker room, Coach McGuire took my coat off the hook and placed it over his. He said those damned Clemson people might steal his coat if it wasn't hidden."

Sarge once traveled with the football team to Raleigh for a game with N.C. State and joined the sports information and media group for Friday-night dinner at a restaurant named The Angus Barn. Chateaubriand was ordered for the table, and it was served on a large platter with the sliced beef tenderloin surrounded by a medley of carrots, potatoes, and onions.

Sarge looked at the feast and said, "I could just graze awhile on those vegetables and forget about the meat."

Sarge operated the game clock for basketball games in the old Carolina Field House and in Carolina Coliseum for 33 years, and he claimed he and referee Lou Bello were responsible for Grady Wallace leading the nation in scoring in 1957. Wallace averaged 31.3 points per game.

"When Lou was working, he would come by and ask, 'How many has Grady scored?' When Grady was having a great scoring night, I might have had a slow finger when stopping the clock. Lou would say 'Shoot the ball, Grady.' He could make a game interesting."

Sarge said sometimes he had a quick finger when games got out of hand.

"One time we were leading by about 45 points, so I let the clock run a couple of times, but nothing got by Coach McGuire. He came down to the scorer's table, and said I hadn't stopped the clock when it should have been stopped. He was sharp."

Sarge said Warren Giese was a hard worker who put in a lot of hours when he was head football coach.

"He worked 12 to 14 hours a day and would come in about 7 o'clock every morning and have coffee with me," Sarge said. "When he got fired, he wrote me a letter and said the thing he missed most was not having that morning coffee."

George Terry, who accompanied Coach Paul Dietzel to South Carolina from the U.S. Military Academy, was another who enjoyed early-morning coffee with Sarge.

"He came in early every morning and would go in his office and pick up a big white Bible. He would read it for about 10 minutes and then say, 'Let's go.' The last day he did that, he was real sick, and he died a short time later. Coach Terry was a real gentleman. He was in charge of all the athletic fields, but he wouldn't let anybody use those fields without checking with me first."

Sarge said Coach Joe Morrison would hit golf balls on the football field at Williams-Brice Stadium, digging up a lot of divots, and then tell him, "There's some son of a bitch tearing up this field with a golf club."

"I knew it was him. He would take out a few chunks of grass and try to hit his last one clear out of the stadium," Sarge remembered.

When South Carolina and Clemson played football on Big Thursday each October, the freshman teams would play a night game on "Little Wednesday."

"One year we worked all night after the freshman game, getting the field ready," Sarge said. "When I opened the stadium Thursday morning, I smelled grass burning. It was a frosty morning and you could really smell it.

"Some Clemson people had gotten in and poured ammonium nitrate on the grass to spell out "Clemson." That was before they had grass paint, but I went up on the hill [campus] and got some regular green paint and painted it over. I got it covered up for the game, but come springtime, that fertilizer in the ground went to work, and the new grass came up with the word 'Clemson.'"

A similar situation occurred in the 1960s, when someone used ammonium nitrate to burn "IPTAY" in the middle of the field. IPTAY is Clemson's athletics fund-raising organization.

Pepsodent Paul

Paul Dietzel spent nine seasons (1966–74) as head football coach and director of athletics at the University of South Carolina. He was a super promoter and fund-raiser and had a flair for the dramatic.

Sometimes his enthusiasm was his undoing.

In October 1967, I left the football practice field to pick up Barney Cook, the University of Virginia sports information director, at the Columbia airport to do some promotion work for the weekend game. I heard myself paged at the airport. Coach Dietzel was in a hospital.

Paul Dietzel (USC Sports Information)

Always enthusiastic on the practice field, Dietzel had jumped into the pile to demonstrate a scrimmage play and had torn ligaments in a knee. He underwent surgery that night, and it was believed he would be absent from the sidelines for a while.

At game time Saturday night, however, there was Paul Dietzel, motoring up and down the sideline in a golf cart. South Carolina rallied from behind to claim a 24-23 victory. The golf cart became part of the travel equipment for the remainder of the 1967 season, and Dietzel didn't miss a game or a practice.

Dietzel did miss a game in 1973 at Blacksburg, Virginia, due to health reasons. He came down with diverticulitis and didn't make the trip. Assistant Coach Pride Ratteree directed the Gamecocks to a 27-24 win over Virginia Tech.

My first out-of-town automobile trip with Dietzel was terrifying. We were going to Myrtle Beach for a meeting with Dietzel driving. He always referred to his briefcase as his brains, and while tooling through the tobacco farms in the South Carolina Pee Dee, he told me to hand him his brains.

Traveling about 50 miles an hour, he spread some documents out over the steering wheel and began reading them.

"Coach. Don't you think I should drive?" I asked in a quivering voice.

"I've got it under control," was the answer. I closed my eyes as we sped past the tobacco fields of the South Carolina Pee Dee. Somehow we arrived safely.

A short time after he became athletics director, Coach Dietzel bought a twin-engine Cessna aircraft for the South Carolina athletics department and hired Roger Booco, a retired air force officer, as staff pilot.

Dietzel had been a World War II U.S. Army Air Corps bomber copilot, and he quickly qualified himself to fly the plane. He often took over, with Roger occupying the copilot's seat.

I was advancing a game at Clemson when the team arrived on Friday. I received a telephone call at the hotel from a newspaperman in Winston-Salem, N.C., inquiring about the crash landing of a plane flown by a Paul Dietzel the night before at Monroe, N.C.

I knew nothing about it, but promised to check it out. I approached George Terry, Dietzel's administrative assistant.

"We don't want to talk about that" was Coach Terry's response. I convinced him we couldn't keep it a secret.

It seems two football prospects had visited South Carolina's Thursday practice and were being flown home. The landing gear was either not down or had collapsed on landing, and the plane had slid down the runway until it came to a stop, doing considerable damage. The two prospects signed with the University of North Carolina.

Dietzel had an artistic flair, and he decorated his daily practice schedules with different-colored inks. He became an accomplished water-color painter after retirement. He received permission to use the music from a Broadway play for a new University of South Carolina fight song and wrote the lyrics himself.

The Gamecock logo had been designed by Jack Morris. He was an art major and a halfback on Warren Giese–coached teams in 1959-61. Dietzel felt it looked like an overweight chicken, so he collaborated with the art director of a Columbia printing company to design a sleek new bird in a profile stance. Clutched in the bird's claws were two ribbons; one contained the word "Scholarship," and the other said, "Leadership."

A later administration removed the ribbons, but the bird remains the same some 35 years after its adoption.

Paul Dietzel was a handsome man with a white, toothy smile. While head coach at Louisiana State University, he won a national championship with an undefeated season in 1958.

LSU played Clemson in the Sugar Bowl that season, and Clemson coach Frank Howard referred to Dietzel as "Pepsodent Paul" during media interviews. After leaving LSU, Dietzel coached at Army before coming to South Carolina. Following an upset loss by the cadets to Colgate, a New York City newspaper ran this headline:

"Colgate Brushes Pepsodent Paul."

In his memoir, entitled *Hi Everybody! This is Bob Fulton*, coauthored with Don Barton in 1996, Bob Fulton said Dietzel "will go down as one of the alltime positive thinkers . . . He was handsome—had that Pepsodent smile—and carried the mystique of having won a national championship . . . He could have sold sand to Saudi Arabia."

Coach Dietzel always organized a team skit the night near the end of preseason practice. Players and coaches organized acts that were performed at Drayton Hall, an on-campus theater. Dietzel always choreographed a western theme skit starring his secretary, Emily White, as "Emily Sue, the Desert Rose."

Emily White joined the athletics department staff in 1966. Entering the 21st century, Emily Sue, the Desert Rose was still a member of the athletics department staff, having served as administrative assistant under six athletics directors.

Hofbrau House

Jack Wilson, director of development with the University of South Carolina Alumni Association, was a student trainer during the reign of Paul Dietzel as South Carolina football coach and director of athletics. Wilson recalled one of Dietzel's motivational efforts to inspire the team.

"The team was meeting in the squad room at the Roundhouse [the athletics department headquarters building] and Coach Dietzel called me aside," Wilson said. "He gave me a 100-dollar bill and told me to go across the street to the Dairy Queen and get 65 milk shakes and be back within half an hour."

When Wilson returned with the milk shakes, Dietzel was nearing the climax of his motivational speech. He told about the old German Hofbrau House tradition of raising glasses while singing patriotic songs. Instead of a beer stein, each player raised a milkshake cup and joined in singing the Carolina fight song.

Wilson also recalled the bus trip to Clemson in 1974 for what happened to be the last football game coached by Dietzel in his nine-year tenure at South Carolina.

Two chartered Greyhound buses were normally used for the 135-mile trip from Columbia to Clemson, but Greyhound drivers were on strike. Two campus buses from the University of South Carolina motor pool were pressed into service.

One of the buses had a flat tire on Interstate highway 26 near the town of Joanna, about 50 miles from Columbia. There was no spare, so the caravan was halted for two hours until a replacement tire arrived from the motor pool.

Dietzel always adhered to a strict schedule, never arriving a minute early or a minute late, but the flat tire threw the travel party two hours off schedule.

"I thought he would be very upset," Wilson recalled, "but he was calm and serene, and we arrived at the Clemson stadium at 5 p.m., two hours late for our Friday walk-through."

The following day, Dietzel ended his coaching career with a 39-21 loss to the Tigers.

Blazing a Trail

The South Carolina football team played the University of Houston in the Astrodome in 1973. Coach Paul Dietzel and student trainer Jack Wilson marked arrows on the floor leading from the Gamecock locker room to the field.

The Astrodome was a confusing maze of corridors, and Dietzel was just guarding against the possibility of the team getting lost.

A certain sports information director did get lost trying to find his way back to the press box from the field after the game. He ended up in a room full of workers counting money from concession-stand sales and had to be escorted to the press box by a security guard.

The Houston trip marked Dietzel's only departure from the Friday-night ritual of having the football team watch a movie. At the suggestion of the sports information director, the Gamecocks attended the "Battle of the Sexes" at the Astrodome and saw Billie Jean King defeat Bobby Riggs in a woman-against-man challenge tennis match.

Jack Wilson also remembered that movie star Janet Leigh attended the South Carolina–Houston football game and met Coach Dietzel. He said he had always been a big Janet Leigh fan.

Dietzel's favorite movie to show the team was *Patton*. A projector was part of the travel equipment, with a temporary theater set up at road-game hotels. Once each season, the Gamecock players were treated to—or subjected to—George C. Scott's Academy Award–winning performance as old "Blood and Guts."

Turkey Barbecue

Chicken Amick was a member of the South Carolina legislature who operated a large poultry business near Saluda. He entertained the South Carolina political establishment with a turkey barbecue each year, and members of the athletics staffs at both the University of South Carolina and Clemson University were on the guest list.

Coach Paul Dietzel wanted to fly down to Saluda in the school plane, but Gamecock club director Ed Pitts convinced him to go by automobile, since it was only a 30-mile trip. We arrived at the Amick place at ten till six. Dietzel looked at his watch and noted that the event was scheduled for six o'clock. He made Pitts drive around for 10 minutes so he could arrive at precisely the appointed time.

Tarred Heels

In nine seasons as the head football coach at the University of South Carolina, Paul Dietzel lost 11 more games than he won, but when it came to playing against the University of North Carolina, Dietzel owned the Tar Heels.

Five times the Gamecocks and Dietzel went against the Tar Heels, and five times South Carolina was the winner. The Gamecocks prevailed three times in Columbia, winning 16-10 in 1967, 14-6 in 1969, and 31-23 in 1974. South Carolina won 35-21 at Chapel Hill in 1970, but it was the 1968 game at Kenan Stadium that produced the most remarkable South Carolina victory.

The Gamecocks did everything wrong for three quarters and trailed 27-3. Sophomore Don Bailey returned a kickoff after a Tar Heel field goal 90 yards to the North Carolina 10-yard line, but the Gamecocks missed a chip-shot field goal on fourth down.

On the first play of the fourth quarter, South Carolina quarterback Tommy Suggs threw a touchdown pass to Fred Zeigler, but the two-point conversion failed, and the Gamecocks trailed 27-9. North Carolina fumbled the kickoff, the Gamecocks recovered, and fullback Warren Muir quickly scored. This time the two-point conversion worked, cutting the deficit to 27-17.

On their next possession, the Gamecocks drove 66 yards, and a two-pointer brought the comeback to within two points, 27-25. After holding the Tar Heels, the Gamecocks took over and moved 61 yards, with Suggs scoring on a quarterback keeper.

South Carolina had scored 29 points in 10:01, 22 of those points in slightly more than four minutes.

Final Score: South Carolina 32, North Carolina 27.

No, Bobby! Go, Bobby!

Paul Dietzel's first win as head coach at the University of South Carolina was sparked by one of the most spectacular plays in Gamecock football history.

South Carolina traveled to Raleigh in October 1966 to meet the North Carolina State Wolfpack in the first game in brand-new Carter Stadium, later renamed Carter-Finley Stadium. N.C. State held the upper hand until the Wolfpack was forced to punt in the second quarter. Fearing a fumble, Dietzel had a rule against fielding any punt inside the 10-yard line. The kick sailed over the head of safety Bobby Bryant. Perhaps mistaking the goal line for the 10-yard line, Bryant fielded the football on a high bounce at the two-yard line and turned upfield. Dietzel screamed, "No, Bobby! No, Bobby!" from the sideline.

Bryant got about three key blocks and broke into the clear near the 30-yard line. Dietzel and several thousand Carolina fans began screaming, "Go, Bobby! Go, Bobby!"

The 98-yard punt return, still a school record, triggered a 31-21 Gamecock victory.

Bryant was also an outstanding left-handed pitcher and won the McKevlin Award for the 1966–67 academic year as the top athlete in the ACC. He was the first South Carolina pitcher to strike out a hundred batters in a season.

In one game, he walked the first two batters he faced and then picked both of them off first base. In 1965, he pitched a 13-inning complete-game, 1-0 shutout at Maryland, a game which South Carolina won on a home run by shortstop Donnie Myers, a .220 hitter.

Bryant came to South Carolina from Macon, Ga., as a 6-2, 145-pounder and never weighed more than 172 pounds while a Gamecock. His nickname was "Bones."

Bryant was selected in the baseball draft by both the Boston Red Sox and the New York Yankees; he was also chosen by the Minnesota Vikings of the National Football League. He cast his lot with the NFL.

In 14 seasons with the Vikings, Bryant played on four Super Bowl teams, and when he retired in 1981, his 50-career intercep-

Bobby Bryant (USC Sports Information)

tions were a Vikings team record. When he retired from professional football, he still weighed about 172 pounds.

Bryant was inducted into the University of South Carolina Athletic Hall of Fame in 1979. He is also in the State of South Carolina Hall of Fame and lives in Columbia.

Air Taxi

Fullback Warren Muir was named to the American Football Coaches Association All-America football team in 1969, his senior year.

Warren had played on the plebe team at Army, but when Paul Dietzel left the U.S. Military Academy to coach at South Carolina, Muir—who was from Fitchburg, Massachusetts—transferred to the Gamecock roost.

Muir went home for the Thanksgiving holidays and was to meet Coach Dietzel and me in New York City for a media gathering of the All-America team. I accompanied Dietzel and pilot Roger Booco to New York in the school plane and was scheduled to meet the basketball team for its Dec. 1 season-opening game at Auburn.

I had a Delta Air Lines ticket from New York to Atlanta, but there was no scheduled commercial air service into the small Alabama town of Auburn. There was, however, an air taxi service.

I found the air taxi counter in a remote part of the Atlanta airport and was waiting there when a man dressed in rumpled khaki work pants and a khaki work shirt appeared and asked, "Yawl going to Auburn?"

I thought he was a mechanic. There were four other passengers—two female Auburn students returning from the holiday and two businessmen.

The man who I thought was a mechanic, loaded luggage onto a handcart, rolled it out the door, and loaded it in the back of a station wagon.

"Get in," he said. I thought that was strange. Was he going to drive to Auburn?

He drove to a hangar at the far reaches of the airport and loaded the luggage into a single-engine plane.

It turned out he was our pilot, and when he said, "Get in" a second time, we climbed aboard and took off. We landed at Auburn just as the Southern Airways Martin 404 charter touched down. I joined the basketball team, which went directly to the Auburn Coliseum for a practice.

The Auburn student manager, who was supposed to meet us at the practice site, couldn't be found, but the building was open. However, all the practice basketballs were locked up. South Carolina business manager Ralph Floyd broke a padlock to get to the basketballs, which left the Auburn administration less than pleased.

Floyd paid for the lock, and the Gamecocks won the game the following night, 84-63. Ralph Floyd later became director of athletics at Indiana University, where he served until his death.

The Little Yankee

One day during the summer of 1969, University of South Carolina AD Paul Dietzel asked me to pick him up in my car and drive around Columbia. He wanted some advice, although I believe he had already made a decision.

"What do you think if I hire Bobby Richardson as baseball coach?" he asked.

Bobby Richardson was from Sumter and a folk hero in South Carolina. Signed by the New York Yankees at the age of 17, he was in the major leagues by 19 and was a star second baseman over 11 seasons with the Yanks. He played in seven World Series.

Richardson and his wife, Betsy, had four children. Bobby, tired of the travel, quit professional baseball at age 31, in the prime of his career, to spend more time with his family. He was involved in public relations work with Liberty Life Insurance Co., when he became available to coach the South Carolina baseball team.

Baseball had long been a low-budget sport at South Carolina, coached part time by a football assistant, a physical education professor, or—in the case of Bob Reising—a professor of English. The team had never scheduled as many as 35 games, while the baseball powers were playing 50 to 60 games a year or more.

The Gamecocks were coming off a 12-21-1 season under football assistant Jack Powers in 1969.

I expressed the opinion that the hiring of Bobby Richardson would be a boost to the university's public and media relations, but Bobby had no experience in coaching or recruiting. To be successful he would need a big increase in budget and commitment.

"I'll give him what he needs," was Dietzel's reply.

Richardson's team had a losing first year record, 14-20, in 1970, followed by 18-12 in 1971, 25-16 in 1972, and 25-15-1 in 1973, as Richardson gradually built up the schedule and learned the recruiting ropes.

In 1974, the Gamecocks finished 48-8 and received their first-ever bid to the NCAA playoffs. Richardson's team in 1975 advanced all the way to the College World Series championship game before bowing to the University of Texas. The Gamecocks finished with a 51-6-1 record.

Richardson's qualified for the NCAA playoffs for a third consecutive time in 1976, finishing with a 38-14 record.

In seven seasons, he won 70.6 percent of his games (220-91-2) and built a winning program that is still among the nation's elite.

He resigned after seven seasons at South Carolina to make an unsuccessful run for congress, but returned to coaching a few years later at Coastal Carolina College and Liberty University. He returned to Sumter and lives in the home that he financed with his first World Series check in 1957. During the seven seasons he coached at South Carolina, Richardson never moved to Columbia. Sumter is 45 miles from Columbia, and Richardson made the daily commute.

Phooey on You

Bobby Richardson was deeply religious and devoted a large portion of his time to church work and speaking engagements.

Probably the closest he ever came to using profanity was during a game at Davidson College in 1970. Bobby went out to question a particularly bad call. The umpire had a short temper, and he threatened to throw Bobby out of the game if he didn't get back to the dugout.

Coach Bobby Richardson with two All-America players, pitcher Earl Bass and first baseman Hank Small, 1975 (USC Sports Information)

Just as Richardson reached the dugout, he turned, pointed at the umpire, and said, "Phooey on you."

Major Pipeline

Richardson used his Yankee background and major league connections to recruit several players for the South Carolina baseball team.

Eddie Ford, son of Yankee Hall of Fame pitcher Whitey Ford, was Bobby's shortstop for three seasons (1972–74) and was the first-round draft choice of the Boston Red Sox in 1974. Eddie reached the AAA level in the minor leagues before quitting baseball for law school.

Jamie Chakales (pronounced "Shackles"), son of big-league pitcher Bob Chakales (1951–57), was on Bobby's teams of 1976–77 and played for his successor, June Raines, 1977–78.

Al Worthington, Jr., son of a 14-year major league pitcher, played second base at South Carolina for Richardson as a 1973 freshman before transferring to the University of Alabama. Richardson succeeded Al Worthington, Sr., as head coach at Liberty University.

Phil Rizzuto, Jr., son of the former Yankee shortstop, was a freshman on Richardson's final South Carolina team in 1976. Little Scooter was about 5-8, left-handed, too slow to play the outfield, and too small to play first base. First-year coach June Raines cut him from the squad in 1977.

Disaster had a way of following Little Scooter. While attending summer school, he was driving on Heyward street on a particularly hot day, when his attention was distracted by a couple of comely coeds walking by. A Columbia policeman had parked his motorcycle in the shade of a street-side tree to escape the heat.

Little Scooter ran over the cop's bike.

The Professor

Bob Reising was a scholar who read the classics as well as *The Sporting News.* He taught English literature and was also a pretty good baseball coach.

Reising was from New Haven, Conn., where his father was the assistant police chief, and had played baseball at Michigan State University. He came to the University of South Carolina from The Defiance College in Ohio. Athletics Director Marvin Bass worked out a deal with the English department. Reising would teach literature in the fall and coach baseball in the spring.

Years before Richardson's reign, South Carolina had experienced four consecutive losing seasons and three break-even years in the seven seasons before Reising took over the baseball program. While his two-year success was modest, he had winning records, 15-12 in 1964 and 16-12 in 1965.

In the 35 years between Reising and the end of the 20th century, South Carolina recorded 32 winning baseball seasons, received bids to the NCAA playoffs 15 times, won five regional championships, and advanced to the College World Series five times, finishing second twice. The Gamecocks started the 21st century with a 56-10 record in 2000, their most wins ever.

It might be said that Bob Reising started a winning tradition.

Reising took his first team, the 1964 squad, to a tournament at Fort Stewart, Georgia, cosponsored by the army and Georgia Southern College. The Gamecocks defeated Georgia Southern, Kentucky, and Carson Newman to win the tournament. It was a minor tournament, but it was South Carolina's first baseball championship in its history.

The teams were billeted in barracks at Fort Stewart and were to be fed in the base mess hall. The mess sergeant resented the intrusion and took the position that these civilians weren't going to interrupt the army's meal schedule. He set the baseball teams' meal times as 5 a.m. for breakfast, 10 a.m. for lunch, and 4 p.m. for dinner.

Reising wasn't about to get his team up before 5 a.m., and games were in progress at 4 p.m. He wrecked the budget by taking the team to eat in a restaurant off the base.

Baseball Coach/English Professor Bob Reising.
(USC Sports Information)

Reising was a strict disciplinarian who set an early curfew the night before every game, at home and away. He could be counted on to make several bedchecks each night. He wasn't very popular with his players, but they played hard for him, and he got maximum results out of limited talent.

The home team provided housing on a trip to Wake Forest in 1964, and Reising found his team assigned to rooms in half a dozen dormitories on the Winston-Salem campus, wherever empty rooms were available.

The coach spent half the night patrolling the Wake Forest campus making bedchecks. He played a cat-and-mouse game with first baseman Ronnie Lamb, a halfback from the football team who liked to sneak out after curfew.

The baseball team also slept on folding cots in the old field house at Clemson, in the basketball field house at Virginia, on rickety war surplus bunks in the Duke Indoor Stadium (now Cameron Indoor Stadium), in Byrd Stadium at Maryland, and in several other campus venues before traveling spring sports teams were upgraded to motels.

Quoting Scripture

Wake Forest had an All-America center fielder named Billy Scripture who hit a line drive over the head of South Carolina's center fielder. The ball bounced over the fence for what should have been a book-rule double.

The base umpire signaled "home run," and Reising went out to argue. After much discussion, the base umpire conferred with his twin brother, who was the plate umpire, and reversed his call. Rather than a two-run homer, it was ruled a double, leaving runners at second and third. The side was retired without the Demon Deacons scoring.

South Carolina won the game 11-7.

Bob Reising's favorite expression when a batter was in a slump was, "You swing like you're holding a rolled-up *Sporting News*."

Reising quit at South Carolina when the failing grades of an athlete in his literature class were questioned. He took a graduate assistant's position at Duke University while completing his doctorate. He had accepted the head-coaching job at Furman University for the following year, but the Duke head coach died of a heart attack. Reising became Duke's interim head coach that season, but turned down the job on a permanent basis because he had given his word to Furman.

Reising eventually left coaching for full-time teaching and in 1982, during an NCAA regional tournament, he was spotted sitting in the stands at Sarge Frye Field in Columbia.

He was invited to the press box, where he was interviewed by broadcaster Bob Fulton. He was teaching at Pembroke State University in North Carolina. He said he had driven down to watch the tournament "just to see how the Gamecocks were doing."

South Carolina traveled to Pembroke in 1982, and Bob Reising came to the game, won by the Gamecocks 11-5.

Aloha

In December of 1981, the University of South Carolina took its men's and women's basketball teams and its football team to Honolulu. The Gamecock Club, South Carolina's fund-raising booster organization, chartered several aircraft, and hundreds of fans made the trip.

The men's basketball team flew commercial and preceded the remainder of the party by several days.

It didn't help.

The team lost to Chaminade and the University of Hawaii. Chaminade received some attention a year or so later, when it upset a nationally ranked Virginia team led by 7-foot Ralph Sampson, but South Carolina lost to Chaminade before it became fashionable to lose to Chaminade.

The football team also lost its game to the University of Hawaii, but the women's basketball team prevented a sweep by winning both of its games from the University of Hawaii.

A team of skydivers was scheduled to parachute into Aloha Stadium to deliver the game football just prior to kickoff. Eddie Inouye, Hawaii's sports information director, approached me about 10 minutes before the scheduled parachute entrance and said, "We've got a problem."

The plane had crashed into Pearl Harbor. I believe 12 people— 10 parachutists, and two pilots died in the crash.

The football and women's basketball teams remained in Hawaii for several days after the game, but the men's basketball team was scheduled to leave immediately after the game to prepare for a game against Temple in Philadelphia four days later.

When we arrived at the Honolulu airport, we were told our flight would be delayed because the Los Angeles airport was fogged in, and we couldn't leave until LAX was clear. Four hours behind schedule we took off; but when we got to Los Angeles, LAX was fogged in again.

There were only about 70 passengers on the Pan American Boeing 747, which had more than 400 seats, so we were able to use the middle rows of the wide body as bunks and sleep in relative comfort as the plane flew over the Pacific Ocean.

After more than an hour of circling over Los Angeles, we landed and learned that our Eastern Airlines flight to Atlanta had been canceled due to the weather. We were switched to a Continental flight to Houston, where we made a connection to Atlanta and then to Columbia, arriving 24 hours late.

Another day passed before our luggage arrived—just in time for the trip to Philadelphia.

The Little Kicker

Billy DuPre (1968–70) was South Carolina's first soccer-style placekicker. At 5-5 and 150 pounds, he was also one of the smallest Gamecock football lettermen of all time.

Off the field he wore horn-rimmed glasses and looked more like a mascot or a water boy than a football player.

On October 18, 1969, DuPre kicked a 47-yard field goal with nine seconds remaining at Blacksburg, Virginia, to give South Carolina a 17-16 win over Virginia Tech. Assistant coach Don "Scooter" Purvis, stationed in the coaches' booth near the press box at Lane Stadium, hyperventilated from excitement. He fell to the floor clutching his chest. It was thought that Scooter had suffered a heart attack.

By the time he reached a hospital, Purvis had recovered, but Coach Dietzel decided to send him home in the athletics department's twin-engine Cessna aircraft from the small Blacksburg airport, while the team and travel party bused to Roanoke for a charter flight home. The department plane had taken several assistant coaches to scout Friday-night high school games before dropping them at Blacksburg.

The switch resulted in 96 passengers on the DC-9 charter, which had a 95-passenger capacity. The Southern Airways representative solved the problem by saying the smallest person in the travel party could sit in one of the flight-attendant jump seats.

"DuPre," Coach Dietzel shouted to the game-winning hero. The little kicker flew home strapped in a folding jump seat alongside the charter's working flight attendants, two very attractive young ladies. Billy seemed to enjoy the ride.

The Absent Hero

Dick Harris set NCAA kick- and interception-return records during an All-America football career (1969–71) at the University of South Carolina. In February 1971, his high school in Point Pleasant Beach, N.J., declared "Dick Harris Day," with plans for a parade and a banquet and a ceremony to officially retire his jersey number.

Coach Dietzel planned to fly in the athletics department plane with Harris and Jim Mitchell, Harris's roommate, to New Jersey for the ceremony. Dietzel directed me, as sports information director, to fly commercial to Newark, rent a car, pick up assistant coach Johnny Menger, and drive to Point Pleasant Beach. Menger, the coach who had recruited Harris, was on a recruiting trip to the New York–New Jersey area.

When I left home about 6 a.m. to drive to the Columbia airport, South Carolina's capital city was experiencing the beginning of a rare ice storm. My flight was the last one out before the airport was closed. The weather was sunny and mild in New Jersey, while South Carolina was glazed over with ice.

Dietzel, Harris, and Mitchell never made it off the ground, so Dick Harris was a no-show at Dick Harris Day in Point Pleasant Beach. A telephone hookup was arranged so the honoree could address the banquet crowd, which numbered about 600.

Menger and I filled in as best we could as guest speakers, while the majority of those attending the banquet couldn't understand how South Carolina, located in the middle of the "Sunny South," could be covered with ice, while the weather was so nice in New Jersey.

Dick's older brother, Bobby, was a South Carolina halfback (1965–66). His only touchdown turned out to be the winning score against Clemson in 1965. Bobby received a standing ovation from the crowd when I made mention of that in my speech.

Dick Harris had two returns of more than 90 yards in one game, a kickoff of 96 yards and a pass interception return of 94 yards against the University of Georgia at Athens in 1970. He returned a punt 96 yards against North Carolina that same year.

During his collegiate career, Harris had 162 returns (kickoffs, punts, interceptions) for 2,767 yards and six touchdowns. He averaged 17.1 yards per return.

After graduation, Dick Harris enjoyed a 10-season, all-star Canadian Football League career with Montreal. He moved to Kelowna, British Columbia, where he is a stockbroker. He returned to South Carolina in 1998 for induction into the University of South Carolina Hall of Fame.

Riding the Rails

Ice storms during the 1977–78 and 1978–79 seasons resulted in the Gamecock basketball team traveling by train to two road games.

In December 1977, the team flew to Chicago, only to find that ice on the runway at Champaign had canceled the connecting flight to the twin cities for the game against the University of Illinois.

The City of New Orleans, the reserved-seat train that Willie Nelson sings about, usually left Chicago half-empty; but due to the many flight cancellations, on this particular night, the train was full. Tickets were obtained for the entire travel party, but everyone was scattered throughout the train in half a dozen cars.

Attempts were made to have the cost of the bus that transported the party to the railroad station and the train tickets billed to the University of South Carolina, but both companies demanded cash. It was necessary to take up a collection from everyone in the travel party, including several members of the "Bubbly Group," and enough cash was collected to pay the fare.

The team arrived in Champaign about 3 a.m. with a noon game scheduled. Illinois had a 7-foot freshman center who set a Big Ten record that day by blocking 12 shots, as the Gamecocks were dead on their feet. That kid never played very much after that game.

In February of 1979, an ice storm gripped the entire southeast, and all flights in and out of Columbia Metropolitan Airport were canceled. The Seaboard Coast Line Champion was a train scheduled to leave Columbia about 11 p.m. and arrive in Deland, Florida, about 6 a.m., 14 hours before a scheduled game with Stetson University.

Coach Frank McGuire obtained a parlor car, leaving the remainder of the travel party to make do in coach. The train left Columbia an hour late, about midnight, and didn't arrive in Deland until 8 a.m. With less than a minute remaining in regulation that night, South Carolina had the basketball and a two-point lead. Point guard Kenny Reynolds, attempting to dribble out the clock or draw a foul, was called for traveling when he slipped, fell, and sprained an ankle badly.

Stetson used the possession to tie the score, and South Carolina eventually lost by four points in double overtime. The sprained ankle sidelined Reynolds for the remaining two games on the schedule.

Monk in the Pivot

Walter "Monk" Quinn stood about 5-7 and scored all of 31 points in 24 basketball games during his career (1950–52) at the University of South Carolina.

In February of 1951, the Gamecocks were in Washington, D.C., to meet George Washington University. The game was tied at the end of regulation and went into overtime. Players kept fouling out, and with two minutes remaining, South Carolina was down to three players.

Quinn pointed to the George Washington center and said, "I'll take the big guy. You two guard the other four." George Washington won 89-80.

Our Ump

Frank McGuire canceled South Carolina's basketball series with Clemson for five years, between 1972 and 1977, in a dispute over the treatment he and his team received from the Clemson crowds.

Clemson baseball coach Bill Wilhelm in 1974 attempted to do the same thing, but was told by Bill McClellan, his athletics director, that he had to schedule at least one game a year with the Gamecocks.

Wilhelm reluctantly agreed, but with the stipulation that the first game had to be at Clemson, and South Carolina had to furnish one of the umpires. Bill Cummings, a veteran umpire from Columbia, was assigned to work the game.

I was driving to Clemson for the game when I saw Cummings about 40 miles from Columbia alongside his broken- down automobile on Interstate 26. He threw his umpiring gear into the trunk of my car, and we completed the trip.

Coach Bobby Richardson had used Earl Bass and Greg Ward, his top two pitchers, in a doubleheader at Florida State two days earlier, so sophomore left-hander Tim Lewis drew the starting assignment at Clemson.

With Bill Cummings calling the balls and strikes, Lewis pitched a shutout, winning 3-0. Lewis completed his collegiate career in 1976 with a 36-6 record, a school record at the time; he rose to the AAA level in the New York Yankee organization but never quite made it to the major leagues.

Cummings apparently wasn't the first umpire to hitch a ride with the Gamecocks. Kenneth "K. K." Ouzts (pronounced "Oots") umpired most of South Carolina's home games during the 1950s and 1960s. Occasionally he was assigned to work Gamecock road games.

Larry Jewell, an All-Atlantic Coast Conference infielder (1955–57) recalled that several times during his playing career, K. K. Ouzts played cards with players on the team bus while en route to away games.

Ouzts, who lettered one year in baseball at South Carolina (1934) before quitting college to play professional baseball, was a railroad engineer who ran a switch engine on tracks near the South Carolina baseball stadium. For many years after he quit umpiring, he would blow several long blasts on the air horn of his diesel engine as his train rumbled past the South Carolina baseball field when games were in progress.

Bill Ouzts, the older brother of K.K., was a star pitcher (1931–33) for the Gamecocks, practiced law for many years, served on the Columbia City Council, and was mayor pro tempore.

What's the Score?

The South Carolina and Clemson baseball teams played each other four times during the 1997 season. The Gamecocks won the first game, 11-3, at Clemson under first-year coach Ray Tanner, but were routed on their home field, 15-1, and lost the second game played at Clemson, 12-9.

When the Tigers came to Sarge Frye Field on April 23, Tanner's Gamecocks needed a win to gain a split in the season series.

The game began at 7 p.m., and Phil Kornblut, who hosted a statewide talk show from 6 to 8 p.m. on the South Carolina Radio Network, called the press box about 7:15 to check on the score.

"Clemson leads 5-0 in the top of the first inning with no outs," he was informed.

"You've got to be kidding" was Kornblut's reaction.

He called back at 7:45 and was told that South Carolina led 7-5 with no outs in the bottom of the first inning.

"Now I know you're kidding," Kornblut said. As soon as he signed off his show at 8 p.m., he headed for the ballpark.

He arrived in time to see South Carolina send 16 batters to the plate in the fifth inning. The Gamecocks didn't have to bat in the bottom of the ninth, but they scored in every other inning, with run totals ranging from one in the sixth to 12 in the fifth.

The final score: South Carolina 38, Clemson 16.

The 38 runs were a school record, as were the 54 runs totaled by both teams. Designated hitter Ryan Bordenick and center fielder Mike Curry had six hits apiece, tying a 66-year-old school record. Nine runs batted in by Bordenick tied another record. Outfielder Derick Urquhart's three doubles tied another record.

South Carolina had 30 hits, including seven doubles, one triple, and seven home runs, and eight Clemson pitchers combined to walk 14 Gamecock batters and hit one.

The series was cut to two games a year in 1998, resulting in loud protests from fans. South Carolina coach Ray Tanner and Clemson coach Jack Leggett restored the series to four games before the 2001 season. Clemson holds a wide lead in the series, which dates back to 1900.

Costen Conversion

A freak play that turned into a touchdown resulted in a South Carolina win over Clemson in the 1961 "Big Thursday" football game at Carolina Stadium.

Clemson led 14-13 in the fourth quarter and seemed on its way to a clinching touchdown when Billy Gambrell intercepted a Tiger pass at the Carolina 36-yard line. The little two-way back returned the interception 28 yards to the Clemson 36.

The Gamecocks moved to the Clemson 26-yard line, where fullback Dick Day slashed off tackle but dropped the football. The fumbled ball skidded laterally across the field, and neither team reacted immediately to the fumble.

After what seemed an eternity, South Carolina quarterback Jim Costen scooped up the errant football—and with the stunned Tigers watching—sped 24 yards to the goal line. Gambrell ran for a two-point conversion to make the final score 21-14.

Who Fired That Gunnels?

Offensive skill players usually dominate the headlines, but linebacker Bobby Gunnels was the featured star of South Carolina's 1965 football victory over Clemson.

South Carolina led 17-10 late in the fourth quarter, when Clemson began a drive and moved to the Gamecock 21-yard line. On third down and nine, quarterback Thomas Ray was sacked for a nine-yard loss. On fourth down, however, he completed a 19-yard pass for a first down and then threw a touchdown pass to pull Clemson to within one point with 40 seconds remaining in the game.

Bobby Gunnels (USC Sports Information)

Clemson appeared to be going for a tie by lining up for the PAT. The Tigers faked the kick, and holder Jimmy Addison threw a pass intended for Bo Ruffner and a two-point conversion that would have won the game for the Tigers. Linebacker Gunnels deflected the pass, and it fell incomplete, preserving a 17-16 victory and clinching a tie for the Atlantic Coast Conference championship.

The next morning, the banner headline in Columbia's morning newspaper, *The State,* read: "Gunnels Flags Down Two-point Pass to Save 17-16 Gamecock Win for First Grid Crown. South Carolina and Duke tied for the Atlantic Coast Conference championship."

Several months later, the ACC stripped South Carolina of its share of the championship due to alleged recruiting irregularities.

Fire Ants and Black Magic

The University of South Carolina's colors are garnet and black. Garnet is a dark red color. The 1980 Gamecock football team was called "Fire Ants and Black Magic."

Head coach Joe Morrison always wore black clothing on the sidelines, and the defensive team, in its garnet home jerseys, swarmed to the football "like a bunch of fire ants."

Defensive coordinator Tom Gadd applied the nickname after the 1983 upset win over Southern California. While grading film, he said the defense "looked like a bunch of fire ants getting after the football."

When asked by news media why he always wore black, Morrison replied, "I opened the closet. It was hanging there. It was clean and it fit."

The Fire Ants won their first nine games in 1984 and rose to No. 2 in national rankings before being upset by Navy in their 10th game. The Gamecocks defeated Clemson to finish the regular season 10-1, but lost a close decision to Oklahoma State in the Gator Bowl for a 10-2 final record.

It was the first time that a South Carolina football team had won more than eight games in one season.

Old Dependable

Joe Morrison's nickname was "Old Dependable" during a 14-year National Football League career with the New York Giants. At one time or another, he played six offensive and two defensive positions.

When he retired as a player, Morrison held a Giants career record with 395 pass receptions for 4,993 yards, was second in touchdowns with 65, and seventh in rushing yards with 2,474. When he retired as a player, he became head coach at the University of Tennessee–Chattanooga without any experience as an assistant.

The Giants retired jersey No. 40.

Morrison quickly built UT–Chattanooga into a Southern Conference power, then moved to the University of New Mexico. Frustrated by not receiving a bowl bid after leading the Lobos to a 10-1 record in 1982, he was lured to South Carolina by Bob Marcum, the AD at the time.

South Carolina finished with a 4-7 record in 1982 under Coach Richard Bell and wasn't expected to be much better in 1983, faced with a schedule ranked second-toughest in the nation. The Gamecocks finished 5-6, with the highlight being a 38-14 upset of Southern California.

When asked if he was afraid to face such a tough schedule, which included a game with Notre Dame, Morrison replied, "Heck, no. I've never seen Notre Dame or Southern California except on television. I'm looking forward to seeing them."

Joe Morrison (USC Sports Information)

A year later, when South Carolina's regular-season record was 10-1 in Morrison's second season, the Gamecocks defeated the Fighting Irish at Notre Dame, 36-32. Morrison was named National Coach of the Year.

Morrison took the Gamecocks to three bowl games in six seasons, but lost all three. He lost 21-14 to Oklahoma State in the 1984 Gator Bowl and also lost to Louisiana State in the 1987 Gator Bowl for an 8-4 record, and to Indiana in the Liberty Bowl in 1988, when the final record was again 8-4. The Gamecocks were 5-6 in 1985 and 3-6-2 in 1986, before earning bowl bids in Morrison's final two seasons.

Athletics Director Bob Marcum had signs made for the doors of the offices in the Roundhouse, South Carolina's athletics administration building. Morrison took the sign bearing his name and title of head football coach off his door and reinstalled it on the door to the men's restroom at Jerry Kelly's Restaurant and Bar, his favorite Columbia watering hole.

When the South Carolina State Fair was in session across the street from Williams-Brice Stadium, Morrison would send equipment manager Jim Shealy and assistant strength coach Sid Kenyon over to the fairgrounds each day to purchase a foot-long hot dog and a lemonade for the head coach's lunch. Morrison picked up a case of food poisoning from a bad frankfurter one day and had to excuse himself three times that afternoon from football practice.

A friend of Sid Kenyon's grandfather distilled moonshine whiskey, and Sid's granddad sent a bottle of the white lightning as a gift to Coach Morrison.

After sampling the moonshine, Morrison said to Kenyon, "Sidney, a man could get used to this moonshine. It makes my regular Scotch taste rather tame."

In February 1989, less than six weeks after the Liberty Bowl, Morrison suffered a fatal heart attack while playing racquetball.

It Ain't Broke

Joe Morrison employed a two-quarterback system for most of the 1984 football season, with Allen Mitchell the starter and Mike Hold coming off the bench.

Mitchell was the star of several of the wins, but Hold had a knack for coming up with the spectacular play.

Hold didn't play in the season opener and appeared only briefly against Duke, but in the third game, his 62-yard pass completion to Ira Hillary set up the winning touchdown, which Hold scored, in a 17-10 win over Georgia. Hold also scrambled 33 yards to score at Notre Dame in a 36-32 comeback victory.

At his weekly news luncheons, reporters began asking Morrison if he would bench Allen Mitchell and make Hold the starter.

"No," he always replied. "Allen Mitchell will start, but Mike Hold will play. If it ain't broke, don't fix it."

Hold continued to come off the bench to make big plays, and South Carolina won its first nine games and was ranked second in the nation, but at Navy, both Mitchell and Hold had bad days, and the Gamecocks were upset 38-21.

The following week, in the final regular-season game, Hold started against Clemson and went all the way. He rallied the Gamecocks with a fourth-quarter, 86-yard drive and scored the deciding touchdown in a 22-21 victory.

"We started Mike, because we thought he was quicker and had a better arm," Morrison explained in his postgame news conference. In the game, however, Hold completed only six of 24 passes, while piling up 75 rushing yards.

Mitchell also didn't leave the bench in the Gator Bowl, which South Carolina lost 21-14 to Oklahoma State.

Pass the Napkins

Joe Morrison's first contract to coach football at the University of South Carolina was written on a paper napkin.

The story began during a basketball game in Carolina Coliseum, December 1, 1982. AD Bob Marcum telephoned the coliseum during a 71-67 Gamecock win over Western Carolina and directed me to come to his office in the Rex Enright Athletics Center immediately after the game. He fired head football coach Richard Bell at 11:00 that night. Bell, in his only season as head coach, had recently completed a 4-7 season.

I was scheduled to accompany the basketball team the following day to Tempe, Arizona, for the Fiesta Classic Tournament, while assistant sports information director Mike Nemeth was to accompany the women's basketball team to Detroit, with graduate assistant Rob Matwick manning the office in Columbia.

Marcum's quick decision on firing Bell indicated he had a replacement in mind, and I felt it would be wise to remain in Columbia over the weekend. Nemeth accompanied the men's basketball team to Tempe and Matwick went to Detroit with the women.

About 9 a.m. on Sunday, Marcum telephoned my home and asked me to meet him at the restaurant in the Carolina Inn in 30 minutes. When I entered the restaurant, I spotted Joe Morrison in a back booth.

After introductions, Marcum said Morrison had agreed to become South Carolina's new football coach. Marcum used a ballpoint pen to write a simple contract on a paper napkin. He and Morrison signed it. The University of South Carolina legal staff drew up a more detailed, formal contract the following day.

Taxi!

One of my most embarrassing moments in nearly 31 years as sports information director occurred near the end of the 1962 football season, my first as SID at the University of South Carolina.

I flew to Detroit on Wednesday to advance a game scheduled against the University of Detroit. When I checked in to my hotel, there was a message from Walt Doherty, the Detroit SID, that read: "Tom, I'm in trouble. Grab a cab and meet me at the sports department of the *Free Press*."

I had never been to Detroit before, and he had said to grab a cab, so I jumped into a taxi in front of the hotel and said, "Take me to the *Free Press.*"

"What?" the driver asked.

"The newspaper. The *Detroit Free Press.*"

The driver made a 180-degree turn, went about half a block and said, "Here we are."

I think the meter read about 60 cents.

I located Walt Doherty in the sports department attempting to mend some fences. It seems Walt had had a couple of drinks with a sportswriter after a weekly media luncheon, and the writer asked Doherty's opinion of Detroit's effort to beef up its football schedule with games against Army, Arizona State, South Carolina, and others.

Not realizing the writer was looking for a story, Walt said he thought the University of Detroit should stay in its own league and play opponents that reside closer to home.

The headline in the *Free Press* read: "SID Says UD Should De-emphasize."

The athletics director and the football coach, Doherty's bosses, weren't happy, but the comment was vindicated a few weeks later when the University of Detroit announced it was dropping football for financial reasons.

Walt Doherty moonlighted as the public-address announcer for Detroit Pistons basketball games at Joe Louis Arena, and I accompanied him to a game with the San Francisco Warriors to see Wilt Chamberlain play. It was the week before Thanksgiving, and the evening's promotion was a drawing for 350 frozen turkeys.

I had one of the lucky numbers, the only thing I had won since high school. What would I do with a 10-pound turkey for three days before returning to South Carolina?

Walt took it home and gave it to his landlady.

In mid-November there wasn't much grass remaining on the field at Detroit's little football stadium, and the temperature was about 33 degrees at kickoff. A light rain was falling and the field was sideline-to-sideline mud.

The little press box seated about 20, and there was a trapdoor leading to the roof, where South Carolina radio announcers Bob Fulton and Johnny Evans broadcast the game from inside an unheated tent. Their only illumination was a small light bulb similar to those found in refrigerators.

Although business manager Frank Johnson was on the trip, the Detroit athletics director handed me a check to cover South Carolina's guarantee. It was for $35,000.

Deacon Dan

Sophomore quarterback Dan Reeves, at 18 the youngest starting quarterback in the nation, had spotted a flaw in the Detroit defense during film study and told Coach Marvin Bass that a surprise quarterback sneak would result in a sizable gain against that alignment.

South Carolina gained possession at the Detroit 42-yard line following a poor punt, and on the Gamecocks' first scrimmage play of the game, Reeves quarterback-sneaked 42 yards untouched into the end zone. South Carolina went on to a 26-13 win.

Reeves was probably the smartest football player that I knew at South Carolina. I called him "Deacon Dan." Although a college quarterback, he was an undrafted free agent who played seven years as a running back with the Dallas Cowboys. He led the NFL in touchdowns his second season.

Broadcaster Bob Fulton said this about Dan Reeves: "He was highly intelligent, fiercely competitive, a serious student of football, and a positive thinker."

Dan also liked to eat steak. During the summer before his senior season, he drove to Columbia from his home in Georgia for some promotional photographs. Coach Marvin Bass told me to take Dan to lunch at the Market restaurant. I ordered the luncheon special, while Dan consumed a double filet mignon.

Reeves's roommate as a player with the Dallas Cowboys was Walt Garrison. Garrison wrote the foreword for *Reeves: An Autobiography*, Dan's life story coauthored with Dick Connor and published in 1988.

Garrison said, "Rooming with Dan was damn near like rooming with one of the coaches, because he probably helped me learn more about football than the coaches did. . . . "

As head coach of the Denver Broncos, the New York Giants, and the Atlanta Falcons, Reeves has taken teams to the Super Bowl four times.

When he became head coach at Denver, Reeves hired Marvin Bass, his coach at the University of South Carolina. When Dan left Denver and moved to the New York Giants, Marvin retired and returned to South Carolina with his terminally ill wife, Audrey.

After Audrey passed away, Bass rejoined Reeves with the Atlanta Falcons and, although more than 80 years of age, was going strong in an advisory capacity.

The weight room at Williams-Brice Stadium was renovated in 2000 and named the Marvin Bass Weight Room, chiefly through contributions from players, coaches, and administrators who had served with Bass at the University of South Carolina. About $105,000 was raised for the project.

The largest single contributor to the weight-room fund was Dan Reeves.

Reeves played one season of baseball at the University of South Carolina, in 1964, and on several occasions demonstrated perhaps the best throwing arm of any Gamecock outfielder.

In a tournament at Fort Stewart, Georgia, a Georgia Southern batter hit a sinking line drive to right field. Reeves attempted a diving catch, but the ball rolled behind him. Reeves got up, chased the ball down, and threw the runner out at third base as he attempted to stretch the hit into a triple.

In a game at Columbia, South Carolina led N.C. State 8-7 with one out and the tying run on third base in the top of the ninth inning. A Wolfpack batter hit a deep fly ball to right field, and it appeared the runner would tag up and score after the catch to tie the game. Reeves threw him out at the plate to complete a double play and end the game.

Little Brother

Bill Bradshaw remembers his freshman days as a scout-squad quarterback scrimmaging against the Gamecock football varsity.

Facing him across the line of scrimmage was a huge, very aggressive nose guard named Emanuel Weaver.

On every play, Bradshaw said Weaver would knock him down, pick him up, and say, "I'm sorry, little brother."

By the time he reached his senior season, Bradshaw had switched positions to wide receiver and was a mainstay on the 1984 "Fire Ants and Black Magic" team that won 10 games. When South Carolina scored with 54 seconds remaining in the final regular-season game to defeat Clemson 22-21 for a 10-1 record, Bradshaw did a perfect back flip in the end zone, landing on his feet.

Under the anti-celebration rule adopted several seasons later, that would probably have drawn a 15-yard penalty.

The Stoic

The dictionary defines stoic as indifferent to passion and emotion and calm and unflinching under suffering and bad fortune.

James Seawright, an All-America linebacker on South Carolina's "Fire Ants and Black Magic" football team of 1984, was a stoic. He seldom spoke unless spoken to.

After winning their first five games, the Gamecocks traveled to South Bend, Indiana, to take on Notre Dame. During a Friday workout in Notre Dame Stadium, Dr. Bill Smith—the team dentist—asked Seawright if he realized he was walking on hallowed ground.

"What does that mean?" Seawright asked.

"This is where the Four Horsemen rode," Smith explained. "This is where Knute Rockne coached."

"Means nothing to me, because they're all dead," Seawright responded. The following day, South Carolina defeated Notre Dame 36-32, with James Seawright leading the defense.

Mr. Death Valley

Tiger supporters like to call Clemson Memorial Stadium Death Valley, although Marvin Bass once referred to it as Bird Paradise after his Gamecock football team won a football game there.

Many years ago, a rock brought from Death Valley in California was presented to legendary Clemson coach Frank Howard and mounted atop the bank at one end of the gridiron, which now is named Frank Howard Field.

During a workout the day before the 1982 game at Frank Howard Field, several South Carolina players were examining Howard's rock, when the crusty, old retired coach approached.

"Hey, there, you Gamecocks. Did you know this field was named for me?" Howard asked.

Sophomore defensive back Earl Johnson, who was from Florida and unfamiliar with the old coach's fame, retorted, "You must be Mr. Death Valley."

Mink Jackets

Charlie Bradshaw, father of South Carolina receiver Bill Bradshaw, was a star quarterback at Wofford College and a teammate of receiver Jerry Richardson, who played for the Baltimore Colts and became the owner of the National Football League's Carolina Panthers.

Charlie Bradshaw, Jr., played quarterback at Wofford the same time that Bill played at South Carolina. Charlie, Sr., who along with business partner Richardson had built a fortune in the fast-food restaurant franchising business, worked out a plan with his wife so they could see both sons play.

If one of the teams played a day game and the other a night game, both parents would see the day game and fly by private plane to the night game. Occasionally, however, Wofford and South Carolina played at the same time. On such occasions, one parent went to the Wofford game and the other went to the Carolina game.

One weekend, both schools had night games, and on Saturday morning I received a telephone call at home. As sports information director, I was the telephone-company contact for installing phone lines in the press box and radio booths.

Charlie Bradshaw had seats in a VIP box, adjacent to the press box, and he asked if I had any objection to his having a telephone installed at his seat. A Spartanburg radio station broadcast the Wofford games, but the Terrier games were not broadcast in the Columbia market.

Bradshaw said the marketing man with his company had attempted to clear time with a Columbia station to take a feed of the Wofford broadcast, but with no success. He wanted the phone to listen to the broadcast from Spartanburg while watching the South Carolina game.

I had no problem with the request if it could be worked out with the phone company. There were telephone installers and maintenance men on duty at the stadium, but the phone company's business office—which assigned numbers and issued installation orders—was closed on Saturdays.

Half an hour later, Charlie called back and said never mind. His marketing man had found a Columbia station that cleared time for the broadcast, and so Charlie took a radio to the Carolina game.

For the remainder of the 1984 football season, Wofford had a radio outlet in Columbia sponsored by a hamburger chain, and a marketing man's job was safe.

Mr. and Mrs. Bradshaw displayed a touch of mink during a chilly November night game in Williams-Brice Stadium. They were dressed in matching mink Eisenhower jackets.

A Bohunk's Memory

For many years, members of the South Carolina scout squad—those freshmen, scrubs, and redshirts assigned to simulate opposing teams in practice against the varsity—were referred to as bohunks.

Rick Hipkins, who lettered as an offensive lineman in 1969–70, recalled a day in the life of a bohunk in 1967.

"I remember a skinny guy with glasses coming into the huddle and drawing a play in the dirt for us to run," Hipkins said. "We scored on the first-team's defense."

Head coach Paul Dietzel, supervising the practice from a hydraulic tower, shouted something down to the little assistant.

"Again, this guy gets into the huddle and draws another play, and it goes for a long gain. Over the hydraulic whine of the tower coming down, Dietzel said on his electronic bullhorn, 'Darn it, Lou. That's not how that play was designed.'"

"I'm telling everyone that I played for Lou Holtz when he coached at South Carolina in 1967," Hipkins said.

After two years on the Dietzel staff, 1966-67, Holtz moved for one season to Ohio State as an assistant before becoming head coach at William & Mary, North Carolina State, The New York Jets, Arkansas, Minnesota, and Notre Dame.

Thirty-two years after leaving, Holtz returned to South Carolina in December 1998 as head football coach.

Holtzisms

Lou Holtz won 216 football games in 27 years at five other universities and then spent one year with the New York Jets of the National Football League and two seasons as a television analyst before becoming South Carolina's head coach before the 1999 season. His reputation for quick wit and one-line retorts rivals his fame for winning football games.

Holtz took over a program that was coming off a 1-10 season, with a 10-game losing streak that stretched to 21—longest in the nation.

South Carolina defeated New Mexico State 31-0 in the opening game of 2000, Holtz's second season and fans—mostly students—tore down the goalposts. A week later, South Carolina upset ninth-ranked Georgia 21-10 and the goalposts were again destroyed.

Columnist Gene Sapakoff of the *Charleston Post and Courier* noted that the public-address announcer had warned, "Fans are not allowed on the field," as the final seconds ticked off in the Georgia game.

"Who was he kidding?" Sapakoff asked.

A Greenville travel agency displayed a sign that read, "Now booking USC bowl trip."

"I've been here two years. We've won two games and we're on our third set of goalposts," Holtz quipped during his Monday media luncheon following the Georgia game.

"I'm glad it wasn't best two out of three," he said in analyzing the win over the Bulldogs.

On a Gamecock player who appeared certain to down a punt at the Georgia 1-yard line, only to have the football roll through his legs, and into the end zone for a touchback: "He looked like he was playing Putt-Putt golf."

A few more words of wisdom from Holtz:

Asked about bowl talk after opening the 2000 season 2-0: "I've never known a football team that went to a bowl with two wins."

Pressed on the subject, Holtz replied, "We'll probably go to the Toilet Bowl in Flushing, N.Y."

On what will happen when the Gamecock football program begins to win consistently: "We're going to need fire hoses to keep the people out."

Lou Holtz (USC Sports Information)

Asked if he were superstitious: "No. Some people carry a rabbit's foot for luck. It isn't lucky for the rabbit."

On talkative linebacker Marco Hutchinson: "Marco should be a ventriloquist. He talks enough for two people."

On pregame pep talks: "I give the same locker-room talk every week. The players have it memorized. I can see them mouthing the words."

His weekly in-season routine: "Win Saturday. Enjoy Sunday. Teach Monday. Practice Tuesday. Execute Wednesday. Perfect Thursday. Get ready Friday. Win Saturday."

Asked if his alma mater, Kent State, scheduled any Big Ten teams when he played there: "The Humane Society wouldn't allow it."

Holtz said when he was a player at Kent State he wanted to win the Heisman Trophy because "I would have been the first third-stringer to win it."

On wide receiver Corey Alexander: "Corey Alexander is so fast, he could race across the room, turn off the light switch, and be back in his seat before the lights went out."

On his team's lack of depth in 1999: "We could never get on Noah's Ark. We didn't have two of anything."

In 1999, after watching his team in practice, Holtz said, "We either must improve our tackling, or we need to find some way to have it outlawed."

"We'll be stronger in the kicking game, or I'll be incinerated for murder."

More on the kicking game: "The only things wrong with our kicking game are the ball doesn't go through the uprights, and when we punt, it doesn't go far enough."

In his postseason assessment following the Outback Bowl, Holtz said, "In our kicking game, the execution was good, with the exception of the kicker, and sometimes we should have executed him."

On the Southeastern Conference schedule that has the Gamecocks playing Tennessee and Florida on back-to-back weekends each season: "I don't know what they are paying us to play those games, but I doubt if the guarantees will cover the hospital bills."

On living in a university city and being near young people: "I don't want to live in a town where the average age is deceased."

On winning: "Winning improves class attendance. When we win, the players want to go to class and be congratulated by classmates."

After the Gamecocks defeated Mississippi State for a 4-0 record in 2000, following the 21-game losing streak in 1998 and 1999: "We can play with anyone in the country. I didn't say which country."

Sophomore tailback Derek Watson fumbled twice in the Mississippi State game, and sportswriters asked if Watson might be benched. "I'm married to him," Holtz replied. When told of the statement, Watson said, "If I fumble again, he might start cheating on me."

Holtz stuck with Watson, and the sophomore ended the regular season with 1,066 rushing yards and 12 touchdowns—11 of them rushing and the other when he blocked a punt on special teams and recovered it for a touchdown against Florida.

On trash talk and bulletin-board material, Holtz observed: "Never let your mouth write a check that your body can't cash."

More on trash talk: "Seniors trash talk because they're going to be gone. The others have to play next year."

On why he has only one chair in his home office: "Anyone who comes in has to stand and doesn't stay long."

Asked if an injured player would travel to a road game: "We don't take tourists."

On the need for players to give their all: "We need somebody to jump on the hand grenade to save the group."

On playing Alabama in Tuscaloosa: "I feel like they had a lottery and we lost."

On why he doesn't read newspapers: "They'll make you think you are better than you are or they'll make you think you are worse than you are."

On competing in the Southeastern Conference: "You had better be ready to play every day or you'll spend a lot of time in the whirlpool."

At the end of the 2000 season, nine of the 12 teams in the SEC were invited to play in bowl games, an all-time NCAA record. South Carolina met Big Ten-member Ohio State in the Outback Bowl on New Year's Day in Tampa. Among the eight other SEC bowl teams, the Gamecocks defeated Georgia, Mississippi State, and

Arkansas; they lost to Tennessee 17-14 in the final minute and led conference-champion Florida 21-3, before succumbing 41-21.

Louisiana State, Auburn, and Mississippi—the other SEC bowl teams—were not on the 2000 South Carolina schedule.

The SEC went 4-5 in those bowl games. South Carolina, Georgia, Louisiana State, and Mississippi State were winners while Florida, Mississippi, Auburn, Arkansas, and Tennessee were losers.

Holtz advised the 1,000 fans and players who attended the football team's season-ending banquet January 13, 2001: "When you look into the mirror and find you are ugly, don't blame the mirror." He also noted that "loyalty is an absolute necessity to your teammates."

On tackling Jared Lorenzen, Kentucky's 275-pound quarterback, Holtz opined, "It's like trying to bring down the Statue of Liberty."

On missed tackles: "There are only four ways you ever miss a tackle. We showed no partiality to any of the four phases. I think we covered all of them."

Holtz was head coach at Arkansas from 1977 to 1983. The Razorbacks routed his first South Carolina team 48-14 in 1999, so Holtz had a special incentive going into the 2000 game with Arkansas.

"After the way they pummeled us last year, if we can win this game, I will personally tear down the goalposts," he said, but quickly added (to deter fans who had destroyed goalposts after two other wins), "I don't need any help."

South Carolina defeated Arkansas, 27-7, but the goalposts remained standing. Holtz explained that he "took a look at those suckers and then at my arms and decided against it. I would have been there all day."

The president of the South Carolina student body presented Holtz with a piece of one of the destroyed goalposts at the team's season-ending banquet.

Late in the Arkansas game, defensive back Andre Goodman picked up a Razorback fumble at the South Carolina 10-yard line and had a clear path to the goal line 90 yards away, but for some reason stepped out of bounds at the South Carolina 15-yard line.

"That was my fault," Holtz told the news media. "I didn't do a good job of explaining why the white lines are there."

Goodman appeared at one of the "Lunch with Lou" sessions and was asked by a fan why he stepped out of bounds after picking up the fumble.

"If you find out, let me know," Goodman answered.

Earlier in the season, Goodman had returned an interception 70 yards against Georgia.

The win over Arkansas raised South Carolina's 2000 record to 6-1 and made the Gamecocks bowl-eligible. Holtz was asked if South Carolina was in the driver's seat for a bowl bid and a possible conference championship.

"We're not in the driver's seat, but we are in the car," he replied.

After the team's record moved to 7-1 a week later following a win over Vanderbilt, a writer asked Holtz again if the team had advanced to the driver's seat. "We stayed in the car," he said, adding, "We put on new tires."

Lou Holtz (USC Sports Information)

At the Monday news luncheon before the 2000 home game with Tennessee, Sports Information Director Kerry Tharp announced that four Congressional Medal of Honor recipients would be recognized during halftime. Holtz remarked, "We need those four to help us out."

Despite a 30-14 win at Vanderbilt, Holtz expressed disappointment with his team's level of play and told the press, "We're lacking in fundamentals. We'll go out today and run some fundamental plays. Tomorrow, we'll talk about the mutiny." After a particularly poor practice, he said of his players, "They couldn't even drown in a pool if they tried."

Star Gamecock sophomore running back Derek Watson originally committed to the University of Tennessee before signing with South Carolina. Prior to the game with Tennessee, Holtz predicted, "Derek Watson is the poster child in the Tennessee locker room this week."

South Carolina's improvement from an 0-11 season in 1999 to 7-1 after eight games in 2000 was the largest single-season turnaround in Southeastern Conference history. Holtz received most of the credit, but he demurred, saying, "The horse does the work, and you tip the coachman."

Looking back over the 2000 season, Holtz said, "This season is a miracle. We're witnessing a miracle here. I believe in miracles." The miracle was temporarily put on hold when Tennessee scored with 26 seconds remaining to defeat the Gamecocks 17-14, dropping their record to 7-2.

South Carolina went to Gainesville with a chance to clinch a berth in the SEC championship game and converted two blocked punts into a 21-3 first-quarter lead, before Florida scored 38 unanswered points to win 41-21. The Gators defeated Auburn 28-6 in the SEC title game in Atlanta. South Carolina lost its third straight decision, 16-14, when Clemson kicked a field goal with three seconds remaining. The Gamecocks finished regular-season play with a 7-4 record.

The invitation to the Outback Bowl—where South Carolina would meet Ohio State—marked the sixth time that Holtz had guided a team to a bowl game in his second season as head coach. Previously, he had done so at William and Mary, North Carolina State, Arkansas, Minnesota, and Notre Dame. The Outback was the

21st trip to postseason play for Holtz, whose previous record in bowls was 10-8-2.

South Carolina was making its 10th bowl appearance. The Gamecocks had lost their first eight, but finally emerged victorious, defeating West Virginia in the 1995 CarQuest Bowl at Miami.

"When I was a kid in grade school growing up in East Liverpool, Ohio; when I was attending Kent State University; and when I was an assistant coach at Ohio State under Coach Woody Hayes, never in my wildest dreams did I imagine I would be coaching the University of South Carolina against my home-state university," Holtz said.

Having coached at Ohio State and having attended to college in Ohio, Holtz said meeting the Buckeyes on New Year's Day was a very special occasion for him.

On the prospect of South Carolina taking more than 30,000 fans to the Outback Bowl, Holtz commented, "I hope our fans will leave enough people in this state to guard the banks, and the rest of them will come to Tampa."

South Carolina's allotment of Outback Bowl tickets was just under 28,000, and the Gamecock ticket office had to refund orders for more than 3,000 tickets. South Carolina sold out its allotment in less than a week. Some Gamecock fans obtained their tickets through sources in Tampa, ensuring that more than 30,000 followers of the garnet and black would be among the 66,655 fans in Raymond James Stadium on New Year's Day.

South Carolina's record turnaround from 21 consecutive losses to a 7-4 season and a bowl bid earned Holtz recognition from the American Football Coaches Association as Region Two Coach of the Year. He was one of five finalists for AFCA National Coach of the Year honors. Holtz had previously been named a regional Coach of the Year at N.C. State (1972), Arkansas (1979), and Notre Dame (1988).

Holtz also made a clean sweep of SEC Coach of the Year honors. He was named by *The Sporting News,* the Associated Press, and his fellow SEC coaches.

The *Football News* chose Holtz as its National Coach of the Year.

Holtz put the honors in perspective, saying, "I think it's great to be named coach of the year, but all you have to do is realize Mike

DuBose was named coach of the year last year, and now he's unemployed."

DuBose was fired by Alabama a year after being named the SEC's top coach.

"One day you're drinking the wine and the next you're picking the grapes," Holtz said.

Holtz said his philosophy was "trust everybody, but still cut the cards."

On why his players do not have their names on the backs of their jerseys: "When they go to the NFL, they can do that. Here, I think that they play for each other and the University of South Carolina. And it also helps program sales tremendously."

Holtz temporarily suspended that rule when the Gamecocks took the field for the Outback Bowl wearing new jerseys with individual names inscribed on the backs. The players were allowed to

Lou Holtz (USC Sports Information)

take the jerseys home with them as mementos. When the 2001 season begins, however, there will be no names on the backs of South Carolina football jerseys.

South Carolina went into its final 2000 conference game—against Florida in Gainesville, where the Gators had not lost to an Eastern Division team since the SEC split into divisions—with a chance to win the division and advance to the conference championship game in Atlanta.

"Not everybody will want to make this trip," Holtz said. "Florida has never lost to an Eastern Division team in the swamp. We're very capable of being embarrassed. I explained that to [our players]. We'll find out if they were paying attention."

However, he amended his pessimism by adding, "We have a chance, about as much chance as Ralph Nader has of being elected president. At least we're on the ballot. We're not a write-in, but they probably spelled our name wrong. We're proud to have gotten into this game. It is big."

On playing in "The Swamp," where Florida almost never loses, Holtz commented, "You don't need to lose your last dollar to Rockefeller."

Although South Carolina was 7-2 going into the Florida game and 5-2 in conference games after an 0-11 season in 1999, Holtz said, "Where we are is not where we want to be. We're going into as difficult an environment as we can. We have a wonderful opportunity in one difficult environment, but we should relish it."

However, he warned, "If we go to a bonfire, and everybody brings a gallon of gasoline, it could get out of hand."

That's just about what happened in Gainesville. The Gamecock offense drove to a touchdown and blocked two punts, returning both for touchdowns, to grab a 21-3 lead in the first quarter. The Gators then scored 38 unanswered points to clinch the SEC East and a berth in the conference championship game with a 41-21 victory.

There were numerous bizarre plays. After South Carolina returned two blocked punts for scores, Florida faked a punt and ran for a 26-yard gain. A Florida pass bounced off the helmet of a South Carolina defender and into the hands of a receiver to set up a touchdown. Another Florida pass was deflected by a South Carolina defender, but a Gator interior lineman caught it on the rebound and lumbered into the end zone for a touchdown.

Holtz likened his team's reaction to Florida's second-quarter blitz to "a deer caught in the headlights of an automobile."

On what happened in Gainesville the weekend after election day: "And you thought the presidential-election count was the only wacky thing going on here in the Sunshine State. I can understand why the election is all fouled up in Florida.

"We knocked Florida down and they got up. Florida knocked us down, and we didn't get up."

Before the Florida game, Holtz likened the excitement of a big game to his college days: "When I had a date in college, I got excited. That didn't happen very often. The SEC championship goes through Gainesville. We really and truly have a chance. There's not one name engraved on a ticket to Atlanta (and the SEC title game)."

Before the Clemson game, Holtz was asked what his main concern was with Clemson's running and passing quarterback, Woody Dantzler, who had been slowed by a leg injury.

"That he will play," was the reply.

Holtz commented on living in a Columbia neighborhood populated by both South Carolina and Clemson fans.

"It's like the Viet Cong and the Vietnamese," he said. "You can't tell who's who."

He said Clemson fans don't have their cars marked and "if somebody is rude to you, you walk away and you say that must have been a Clemson fan."

Although South Carolina scored with less than a minute remaining to take a 14-13 lead, Clemson used a 50-yard desperation pass completion to set up a field goal with three seconds left in the game to claim a 16-14 victory. South Carolina ended regular-season play with a 7-4 record, a remarkable turnaround from 0-11 in 1999 and 1-10 in 1998.

Before the season, Holtz was reminded of the winless 1999 season and kidded by some of his golfing buddies who asked him if he had bought a 7-11 store and changed the name to 0-11.

Although South Carolina is a small state, its high schools have produced many collegiate football stars. Holtz said, "South Carolina has more great football players per capita than any state in the union."

On whether he would seek a contract extension and a raise: "Money is not important to me. Maybe I didn't word that right. I made more money outside of coaching. I never wanted the most money in the world. I also didn't want to be real poor."

On another occasion a similar question was raised and Holtz answered, "I have a lifetime contract. That means I can't be fired in the third quarter if we're ahead and moving the ball."

Three days after the 2000 Clemson game, athletics director Mike McGee announced Holtz would receive a raise and his five-year contract would be rolled over. All assistant coaches received 10 percent raises. The staff received another raise after the Outback Bowl victory over Ohio State.

On reasons for South Carolina's turnaround 2000 season: "Expectations, attitudes, standards. If there were one word, it would be expectations. I have tried to raise their expectations. We have some talented people. I just don't want them to undersell themselves."

His goals for South Carolina's football program, Holtz said, are to win a conference championship, go to a bowl, win a bowl game, win a national championship, and graduate all seniors.

Two members of the Outback Bowl selection committee, Bernie Epstein and Roger Nanney, came to Columbia for a media luncheon and news conference at one of the local Outback restaurants. For Nanney it was a trip home. He is a University of South Carolina graduate and grew up near Moncks Corner.

One of Roger Nanney's relatives, Denise Nanney of Spartanburg, was the first woman basketball player to score more than 1,000 points at the University of South Carolina. She tallied 1,577 in 98 games from 1974 to 1977.

Holtz was asked at that gathering his feelings on playing against Big Ten power Ohio State.

"I'd rather be playing Vermont," he quipped.

A Columbia radio station gave away a free trip to the Outback Bowl, and Holtz was asked to draw the winning name. He playfully announced, "The winner is Mrs. Beth Holtz." When the laughter died down, he announced the name of the real winner.

Holtz said his players approached their first bowl appearance with excitement and anticipation, "like when I went into military service. I was excited and eager, but if I had known what was ahead, I might have been up in Canada."

He said if the team had a good week of practice, the players would go home December 21 and reassemble after Christmas, but "if not, Santa's going to have a hard time finding them."

After the bowl win over Ohio State, an 8-4 final record, and ranking in the nation's top 20, Holtz vowed, "We're going to take this sucker to another level."

He noted that 19 players who started against Ohio State in the Outback Bowl would return for the 2001 season. As for recruiting needs, he said, "We need a game breaker, a kick returner, a wide receiver, and a kicker."

On his own personality after a successful season: "I'm the same guy I've always been—controversial, moody, temperamental."

On recruit signing date, February 7, 2001: "It's like giving birth to a baby. Is it a lawyer? Is it a doctor? Is it going to discover a cure for AIDS? Is it going to end up in prison?"

Holtz said he had accomplished most of the 107 things he set out to do in his lifetime, but "I still haven't been on an African safari. I took a camera to the zoo once, but I don't think that counts. I'm still looking for someone slower than me so I can run with the bulls at Pamplona."

ESPN analyst Beano Cook, commenting on the many upset victories by Holtz-coached teams, said, "He's a better underdog coach than he is a favorite coach.

Discipline

While Lou Holtz is famous for his one-liners and comedy routine, he has a serious side and is a strict disciplinarian.

In 1977 he suspended three of his top players before meeting an already-favored Oklahoma team and oddsmakers gave Arkansas no chance in the Orange Bowl. The Razorbacks won 31-6.

Sophomore tailback Derek Watson was suspended for violating team rules before South Carolina met Ohio State in the 2001 Outback Bowl. Watson had rushed for 1,066 yards during the 2000 season and had led the SEC in all-purpose yards with 1,834. His rushing yardage for the season ranked third in the powerful SEC.

Watson was the main kickoff return man with 537 yards and a 21.5 average, not counting a 92-yard return against Mississippi State that was nullified by a penalty. He returned three punts and caught 21 passes. He also blocked a Florida punt while playing on special teams and recovered it for a touchdown. He scored 11 rushing touchdowns, and his 12 TDs led the Gamecocks in scoring.

There was little doubt that Watson was South Carolina's best football player, and when news of his suspension was announced in the media, South Carolina went from a five-point underdog to a seven-point underdog against Ohio State.

Holtz moved versatile sophomore Ryan Brewer from wide receiver back to his old tailback position, and the former Ohio high school "Mr. Football" more than took up the slack. He rushed for 109 yards in 19 attempts, caught three passes for 92 yards, returned two punts 18 yards, and scored all three South Carolina touchdowns as the Gamecocks upset the Buckeyes, 24-7.

Brewer donned wristbands for the Outback Bowl game. On one of them he wrote "No Regrets," and on the other "To the End." He explained afterward, "I wanted to play with no regrets and go all the way to the end. It's something I did in high school. I wanted to get myself a little pumped up for this game."

Brewer was a unanimous choice for the Outback Bowl's Most Valuable Player. As a freshman in 1999, he played tailback and rushed for 163 yards in 35 attempts. He also caught six passes, returned kicks 175 yards, and punts 143 yards.

As a sophomore Brewer played primarily as a wide receiver and returned punts, but he did carry the football 14 times from tailback during the regular season and netted 66 yards with no touchdowns. He returned 26 punts and 184 yards and was the team's second-leading pass receiver with 33 catches for 326 yards and one touchdown.

His Outback Bowl performance raised his 12 game totals to 175 rushing yards for a 5.3 average, 36 pass receptions for 418 yards, and 28 punt returns for 202 yards, totaling 795 all-purpose yards.

Brewer had an extra incentive to excel against Ohio State. A native of Troy, Ohio, he grew up an Ohio State fan but wasn't offered a scholarship by the Buckeyes. In fact, Ohio State showed little interest in Brewer, considering him too slow and too small to play in the Big Ten.

How big is he? The South Carolina media guide and game rosters listed Brewer as standing 5 feet 10 inches and weighing 210 pounds. Some print media accounts described him as 5-8, 190. When asked, sports information director Kerry Tharp said, "He's probably about 5-9 and 195."

Lou Holtz is from East Liverpool, Ohio and was a 150-pound center/linebacker at Kent State University. He was asked at the Outback Bowl postgame news conference if there were similarities in his playing days and those of Brewer.

"Ryan Brewer would be greatly offended if you compared him to me," Holtz answered. "That's really a low blow. I'll tell you what kind of athlete I was. I signed a non-aggression pact with the other team. You don't hit me, and I won't hit you."

South Carolina's rushing offense netted 218 yards and yielded no quarterback sacks against an Ohio State defense that had held opponents to an average of fewer than 100 yards per gamed, and Holtz was asked if the Gamecock offensive line had done a good job against the Buckeyes.

"We'll let them eat dinner," he replied.

When photographers took a long time setting up photos of the Outback trophy presentation, Holtz quipped, "We can do a painting quicker."

His assessment of South Carolina's performance: "I felt we were ready to play. We were a good football team today; better in every way. We beat a fine football team. Now we have to take it to a new level."

On several players dumping the traditional ice water on him as the game ended: "I wish different people had picked it (the cooler) up; the ones who tend to drop (fumble) it."

The Gamecocks stayed overnight in Tampa before returning to Columbia the day after New Year's, and Holtz was asked if his team rules were still in effect.

"We will have a curfew tonight," He answered. "It's 6 a. m., and I expect them to honor it."

Holtz said he would send the Outback Bowl game ball to the Lou Holtz Hall of Fame museum in East Liverpool. The team re-

Ryan Brewer accepts the 2001 Outback Bowl Most Valuable Player Trophy. (USC Sports Information/Gregg Martin)

turned to Columbia the morning of January 2, but Holtz and his wife, Beth, were not aboard the chartered plane. They went to their home in Orlando for a few days of rest and relaxation.

About 1,500 Gamecock fans braved near-freezing temperatures to meet the charter at Columbia Metropolitan Airport. The game's MVP also was not on the flight. Ryan Brewer went directly home from Tampa to Troy, Ohio, for a few days with his family before returning to South Carolina for the spring semester.

The biggest postseason question mark regarding South Carolina football was the future of suspended star tailback Derek Watson. Holtz addressed that question at the final news conference, several days after the team returned from Tampa.

He said the suspension was for the bowl game only and that Watson would be welcomed back, as long as he adhered to team rules.

"I welcome him. I want him back," Holtz said. "Derek Watson is a great football player. He's as good a running back as I've ever coached anywhere. Derek Watson could put this team on his shoulders and carry it. Derek Watson will either fill up NFL stadiums or sweep them out. It's up to him."

Assistant coach Buddy Pough spoke with Watson at his home in Williamston, and Watson also spoke with Holtz by telephone. A sports information office statement said Watson "expressed a deep amount of remorse and was looking forward to getting back in school and getting his life turned around."

Watson attended the team banquet on January 13 and was one of 22 players who received a special "Winners" award for grading out a winner in at least two-thirds of the games he played in. He told a newspaper reporter he felt he had "let my teammates down" and was looking forward to resuming his college football career.

Spring semester 2001 classes began the second week of January, with spring football practice scheduled February 22–March 31, wrapped around a nine-day spring break.

Holtz granted All America defensive back Sheldon Brown and defensive end John Stamper, both redshirt juniors, permission to try out for Coach Ray Tanner's 2001 Gamecock baseball team, provided they didn't miss any of the football squad's early morning running that began in late January.

He said there shouldn't be a conflict because, "I don't think there are many baseball practices at six o'clock in the morning."

South Carolina was the only unranked football team that played in a New Year's Day 2001 bowl game, and the 24-7 victory over Ohio State vaulted the Gamecocks into the final top 25. The final Associated Press poll, selected by the news media, ranked the Gamecocks 19th while the *USA Today/ESPN* poll selected by a board of coaches, placed South Carolina 21st.

Holtz quipped that the final polls proved that members of the news media are smarter than coaches.

Kiss of Death

Losing bowl games to teams from South Carolina has become the kiss of death for head coaches at Ohio State University.

One day after losing the 2001 Outback Bowl game 24-7 to South Carolina, Ohio State fired head coach John Cooper. In 13 seasons with the Buckeyes, Cooper compiled a 111-43-4 record but was only 2-10-1 against archrival Michigan and 3-8 in bowl games. Ohio State bought out the three remaining years on Cooper's contract for 1.8 million dollars.

Woody Hayes, Ohio State's all-time leading coach with a 28-year record of 205-61-10, was fired after losing to Clemson in the 1978 Gator Bowl. Hayes was fired for punching a Clemson player who intercepted a Buckeye pass late in the game to seal the Clemson victory.

The loss to South Carolina also left Cooper with an 0-8 record in head-to-head meetings with Lou Holtz. Although South Carolina and Ohio State had never met previously in football, Cooper coached seven seasons at Tulsa and lost seven consecutive games to Arkansas teams coached by Holtz.

The Outback Bowl victory broke an 0-4 Holtz string against Ohio State with all of the losses coming while Holtz coached at other schools.

Although born in West Virginia, Lou Holtz grew up in Ohio, and earlier in his career he indicated that one of his life's ambitions was to be head football coach at Ohio State. When he left Arkansas to coach at Minnesota, there were reports of a clause in his contract that would have allowed him to leave without penalty to coach at either Notre Dame or Ohio State.

After serving two seasons, 1966-67, at South Carolina as a young assistant coach under Paul Dietzel, Holtz spent a year at Ohio State under Coach Woody Hayes before landing his first head coaching job in 1969 at William & Mary.

Therefore, immediately after the Ohio State job came open on January 2, 2001, the Holtz name was one of the first projected into speculation as the successor to John Cooper.

Holtz, who celebrated his 64th birthday January 6, 2001, quickly put the rumors to rest.

"I am not looking for anything other than trying to build this South Carolina program and then riding off into the sunset, or being carried off," he said. "If I were younger or in another part of my career, I would be flattered and honored to even be considered. But I'm not the right person for the job, and my heart is at South Carolina."

No Holtz Barred

The presence of Lou Holtz and South Carolina's remarkable turnaround in 2000 attracted the most national and regional media attention for South Carolina football since the Fire Ants and Black Magic season of 1984.

South Carolina has always been closely covered by the Palmetto State media, but stories about the Gamecocks and their 63-year-old head coach began showing up more and more frequently in national and regional newspapers and on web sites and television networks.

A story bylined by Ward Gossett, Assistant sports editor of the *Chattanooga Free Press*, began in this manner:

"Lou Holtz doesn't run onto a football field. He doesn't really walk either. His gait is a cross between a limp and a totter, one that screams loudly for wheel chair assistance.

"His red Gamecock hat with the faded black bill is pulled down low over pointy ears. Occasionally, he jams his hands into his pockets of crisply pressed khakis. His black coaching shoes are gleaming. He looks more the part of a retired field maintenance man than head coach in the Southeastern Conference.

"Looks are deceiving, aren't they? That's a mistake a lot of people make."

Wayne Drehs pointed out in a column on ESPN.com that after three games South Carolina had already scored six more points than it did in all of 1999 and sophomore running back Derek Watson, "the heart of the new-look offense," had 28 more yards than he did in 1999.

Drehs wrote that Holtz had always been an old school coach known more for pounding the football at opposing defenses than for wide-open schemes.

"But that's changing," Drehs concluded, thanks to help from his son, assistant head coach and offensive coordinator Skip Holtz and a staff that featured five other assistants with head coaching or coordinator experience.

"Holtz has embraced the wide-open offense, and the results are staggering," Drehs concluded.

Skip Holtz said his father told the staff the Gamecock offense was broken and asked, "How do we fix it?"

"Even on defense," Skip said, "where we were pretty good last year (1999) we decided that if the offense isn't going to be great, we better change the defense too . . . My dad isn't one to let any grass grow under his feet."

Regarding the changes, Lou Holtz was quoted by Wayne Drehs, "To a certain extent, yes. I guess I've modernized. But there wasn't much of a choice."

Michael Murphy of the *Houston Chronicle* wrote these words:

"Out of the frying pan and into the blast furnace. That was basically the feeling when Lou Holtz came out of 'retirement'— the relative comfort of a television analyst gig—and took over the woeful South Carolina football program."

Murphy went on to say that Holtz was not a man to back down from a challenge and remained convinced his team was on the verge of breaking through.

"I believe if you create the right attitude you can win anywhere," Murphy quoted Holtz midway through South Carolina's turnaround season. "We're not winning because of me. Trust me. We have a plan. We try to follow the plan."

Murphy concluded the plan has produced results everywhere Holtz has coached, taking each of six teams to a bowl by his second season.

Ken Denlinger, writing in the *Washington Post* noted many fans were wearing tee shirts bearing such slogans as "Cock A. Doodle Lou," and "Got Lou? We Do."

Denlinger interviewed one fan who said, "They were kind of lenient on Lou last season (0-11) because he's God. Lou Holtz is God. But if that losing streak had carried over in a large way they would have gotten rid of him. Trust me."

Denlinger said ego was a factor in the success of Holtz and he quoted the coach as saying, "If I go to a banquet, I want to be the speaker. If I go to a wedding, I want to be the groom. If I go to a funeral, I want to be the corpse,"

George Diaz of the *Orlando Sentinel* said Holtz, "The charming leprechaun with the impish smile is working magic again."

After South Carolina defeated Mississippi State *New York Times* writer Joe Drape said Holtz detractors had claimed, "When he showed up to coach South Carolina two years ago, it was perceived as a ticket-selling stunt by a football program that had been more P. T. Barnum than Bear Bryant and as a desperate encore for a once-golden talent lost without the applause."

"So where is that crazy, old and addled Lou now?" asked Drape, and then answered his own question. "Back in the polls at No. 23 with an undefeated South Carolina (4-0) team that demonstrates how Holtz, 63, has always had a plan and is about to make it work again."

Holtz and the South Carolina team also received high praise from media in the Gamecocks' back yard. Columnist Scott Fowler wrote in the *Charlotte Observer* after South Carolina's 7-4 season:

"My choice for college football's coach of the year this season drinks 24 Diet Cokes per day and has lost his three most recent games.

"Lou Holtz—South Carolina's crinkly, cranky elf of a coach —has done the best job in the country in 2000."

Fowler added that Holtz's "comic style sometimes overshadows his true talent: resurrection."

By leading South Carolina to the Outback Bowl in his second season, Holtz became the only coach in NCAA history to take six different programs to postseason games. South Carolina's improvement from 0-11 to 7-4 was the greatest turnaround in Southeastern Conference history and the second-best ever in the NCAA.

Charlotte *Observer* writer Stan Olson said, "We thought he'd had it, didn't we? We thought that Lou Holtz, college football's one-time program savior/miracle worker, had pulled off his last magic trick . . . . We were wrong."

In another story, Olson pointed out that an average of 78,272 fans crowded into Williams-Brice Stadium for each home game during the 0-11 season of 1999, and the average in 2001 was 81,904, nearly 2,000 above the stadium's seating capacity of 80,250.

The 224 wins by Holtz in 29 seasons placed him 11th on the all-time collegiate victory list and third among active coaches.

Lunch With Lou

When Lou Holtz came to South Carolina, he started a tradition of having lunch with Gamecock fans the day before home games with proceeds from the luncheons going to worthwhile projects.

Holtz brings three players and each of them addresses the crowd before the coach talks and answers questions submitted by fans. Crowds for the Lunch With Lou sessions were large even during the 0-11 season in 1999, but swelled to overflowing in 2000.

Lunch With Lou before the Tennessee game, the final home game of the 2000 season, drew a crowd of more than 900.

Master of Ceremonies Todd Ellis, a Columbia attorney and former star quarterback, called Lunch With Lou, "the second hottest ticket in town," next to the six home games, all of which were sellouts.

Share the TV

Lou Holtz remembers being invited to dinner by Coach Bear Bryant while visiting Tuscaloosa, Alabama, for a clinic when Holtz was football coach at N. C. State.

The dinner was at a country club and there was

*Lou Holtz
(USC Sports
Information)*

115

an NFL exhibition game featuring former Alabama quarterback Ken "Snake" Stabler on television. Bryant called ahead and arranged for a private dining room and a TV set.

"People kept peering into the room," Holtz remembered. "When I went to the bathroom I asked someone why people kept peering into the room."

It seems Bear Bryant had commandeered the establishment's only television set.

Did You Know

South Carolina 2000 senior wide receiver Jamie Price was a three time All-American in track and field. He ran the anchor leg on the 2000 Gamecock 4x100 relay team that won an NCAA title.

Wide receiver Brian Scott walked on to the 1999-2000 South Carolina basketball team and played in three games.

Freshman All-America defensive back Deandre' Eiland set a national record in the 55-yard dash with a time of 7.70 seconds while competing for Tupelo High School in Mississippi. He also ran a 13.48 in the 110-meter hurdles.

South Carolina ended the 2000 regular football season ranked first in the Southeastern Conference and seventh nationally in scoring defense. The Gamecocks allowed an average of 15.8 points per game. In total defense South Carolina was fourth in the SEC and 16th nationally.

South Carolina scored 259 points in 11 regular-season games in 2000. That nearly tripled the 87 points scored by the 1999 team. The Gamecocks had 34 plays of 25 yards or more in 2000, the longest being an 81-yard return of an interception for a touchdown against Tennessee by linebacker Kalimba Edwards.

The longest pass completion was 78 yards for a touchdown from Phil Petty to Ryan Brewer, also against Tennessee. The longest rushing gain was 68 yards for a touchdown by Derek Watson against Clemson. Watson had nine plays—rushing or receiving— that gained 25 yards or more, including touchdown rushes of 68, 65, 61, 58 and 34 yards.

Watson's longest kickoff return that counted was 53 yards. He had a 92-yard return against Mississippi State nullified by a penalty. Watson's 1,066 yards rushing were the most ever by a South Carolina sophomore, topping the 1,022 yards by Harold Green in 1987. Green went on to a ten-year National Football League career with the Cincinnati Bengals, St. Louis Rams and the Atlanta Falcons.

Watson also was credited with a 35-yard punt return against Florida when, playing on special teams, he blocked a punt and recovered in the end zone for a touchdown.

Offensive lineman C. J. Frye is the son of South Carolina head track and field coach Curtis Frye and has a twin sister, Curtell, who participates in track and field at the University of Virginia. Their dad has won National Coach of the Year honors.

The father of tight end Kyle Crabb was a starting linebacker on South Carolina's 1969 Atlantic Coast Conference championship football team. Greg Crabb earned three letters 1969-71.

The father of defensive back Kevin House played ten years in the National Football League. Kevin House, Sr., was a wide receiver with the Tampa Bay Bucs and the Los Angeles Rams. Playing in the Outback Bowl was a homecoming for Kevin, Jr., who attended Chamberlain High School in Tampa.

The father of wide receiver Willis Hamm, Jr. was formerly director of athletics at South Carolina State University.

Running back Andrew Pinnock was named "Mr. Football" in Connecticut in 1998 as a senior at Bloomfield High School and wide receiver and punt return specialist Ryan Brewer was named Ohio High School Player of the 1990s by *Ohio Prep* magazine and "Mr. Football" in 1998 at Troy High School.

Defensive back Andre Goodman's hobby is writing poetry.

Sophomore linebacker Pat Fleming opposed his brother in the 2001 Outback Bowl. Henry Fleming plays offensive tackle for Ohio State. The Fleming brothers are from Manning, S.C.

Freshman Ohio State linebacker Jason Bond came to the Outback Bowl with two South Carolina connections. His father, Brett Bond, was a South Carolina football letterman, 1977-79, and his uncle, Mike Vargo, lettered with the Gamecocks, 1980-81.

South Carolina's average attendance of 81,904 for six home games in 2000 was 102 percent of the Williams-Brice Stadium seating capacity of 80,250. Final NCAA figures on the ranked South Carolina's home attendance 12th in the nation. Seven of the top 11 came from the Southeastern Conference.

Fade to Glory

Eric the Red was a Viking folk hero. One play made walk-on quarterback Erik Kimrey a Gamecock folk hero in the fourth game of the 2000 football season.

South Carolina trailed Mississippi State 19-13 late in the fourth quarter but was driving when quarterback Phil Petty threw an incomplete pass on third down and ten from the Mississippi State 25-yard line. Petty was knocked down on the play and suffered a sprained ankle.

Kimrey, who had played sparingly in the first three games of his third collegiate season and not at all in 1998 and 1999, had four career pass completions with one interception in eight attempts, all in a mop up role against New Mexico State.

When Coach Lou Holtz called on him to replace the injured Petty, Kimrey said, "Coach, I can throw the fade route."

"When a player tells me he can do something, I'm all for that," Holtz said, and he waved Kimrey into the game.

Receiver Jermale Kelly ran the fade route, and Kimrey lofted a perfect pass over MSU defender Kendall Roberson. Kelly raced into the end zone and the extra point gave South Carolina a 20-19 lead. The Gamecocks recovered a fumble and kicked a field goal and held off a fierce Bulldog drive to win 23-19.

An interview with *Sports Illustrated* followed, and Kimrey's math professor asked for his autograph. A television news crew showed up at his home in the suburban town of Irmo. National radio networks requested live telephone interviews.

Coach Lou Holtz put the touchdown pass in perspective.

"I'm very proud of Erik Kimrey," Holtz said, "but he made one play. Others in the game played 60 minutes. It's a team game."

Kimrey started a week later against Alabama and did a creditable job but, despite the ankle injury, Petty played most of the second half and threw two touchdown passes, but South Carolina lost 27-17. Kimrey was the backup to Petty for the remainder of the season and saw very little game action. Final season statistics showed he played in seven games, started one and completed 18 of 31 passes for 200 yards and one touchdown.

That one TD was a biggie.

Kimrey was an all-state quarterback at Dutch Fork high School near Columbia but wasn't heavily recruited. His coach at Dutch Fork was his father, Bill Kimrey, who was a journeyman pitcher on South Carolina's 1975 College World Series runner-up baseball team.

Erik enrolled at South Carolina as a walk-on in the fall of 1998. He didn't rate a biography in the 1999 South Carolina media guide, and his only mention was on a supplemental roster of "squad members." His first name was misspelled "Eric".

His biography in the 2000 Media guide contained these two entries:

1999: Squad member.

1998: Squad member who was redshirted.

There were seven quarterbacks listed on South Carolina's 1999 roster. Six of them played during the 0-11 season. Kimrey was the seventh.

Center Philip Jones had this reaction to his roommate's newfound fame: "It's just a fairy tale. I'm so happy for him. He's worked so hard. Nobody deserves it any more than he does."

During the postgame celebration after the game-winning TD pass, nose tackle Cleveland Pinckney, the anchor of the Gamecock defense, whispered in Kimrey's ear, "Brother, that was big time."

Kimrey described his role as backup quarterback as "the best job, because you're a cheerleader, until something happens."

Perseverance

Fifth-year senior Jason Corse was a study in perseverance with the South Carolina football program.

Corse is from Lake Forest, Illinois, and walked on as a 186-pound tight end and placekicker as a freshman in 1996. He was assigned to the scout squad and wasn't invited for two-a-day practices with the main squad the following season. In 1998 and 1999 he also wasn't invited to two-a-days but each year reported as a walk-on when classes began.

Corse was invited to report for two-a-days as a fifth-year senior in 2000 and won the job as kickoff specialist. Coach Lou Holtz said one of his early-season kicks was short, and the opposing team made a substantial runback with Corse making a touchdown-saving tackle.

"After that collision, Jason started kicking them into the end zone for touchbacks," Holtz said.

Corse was one of the players invited to speak at one of the Lunch With Lou sessions and said he caught a lot of passes thrown by quarterback Erik Kimrey while on the scout squad, "before Erik became a superstar."

The reference was to Kimrey's moment of glory when he threw the winning touchdown pass against Mississippi State.

Corse also was assigned the placekicking duties the final three games of the regular season and made all seven of his extra- point tries. However, he missed both of his field-goal attempts. In the Outback Bowl, Course kicked three extra points and made one of two field-goal attempts.

Goalposts Down

If goalpost manufacturers showed extra profits on sales to Southeastern Conference member schools and other football programs during the 2000 football season, they should pay a commission to the University of South Carolina.

South Carolina ended its 21-game losing streak—the longest in the nation— in the 2000 season opener with a 31-0 victory over New Mexico State. Exuberant fans tore down the goalposts.

A week later, ninth-ranked Georgia came to Williams-Brice Stadium in Columbia, and South Carolina ended a string of 18 consecutive conference losses with a 21-10 upset. Again, the goalposts came down.

When Louisiana State upset Tennessee in Baton Rouge, Tiger fans ripped the goalposts down. A week later, Georgia ended a string of nine consecutive losses to Tennessee by defeating the Vols in Athens. Bulldog fans tore down the goalposts.

Unbeaten Auburn fell to Mississippi State in Starkville, and Mississippi State fans ripped down the goalposts.

One one goalpost came down Nov. 2, when LSU defeated Alabama in Baton Rouge for the first time in 31 years.

Assaults on the goalposts weren't strictly confined to the Southeastern Conference.

Ball State, the last team that South Carolina defeated before beginning its 21-game losing streak, inherited the nation's longest string of consecutive losses when South Carolina won its season opener. Ball State's losing string also stretched to 21 games before the Cardinals upset Miami of Ohio on the road, 15-10.

Ball State students wanted to tear down the goalposts in their home stadium to celebrate the road victory, but a work crew beat them to it. The crew dismantled the goalposts and put them in storage. They were reassembled in time for Ball State's home game October 14, 2000, against Eastern Michigan.

When Ball State won 33-14, extending its winning streak to two games, the goalposts were torn down and dumped into a duck pond near the stadium.

At Clemson, in upstate South Carolina, some fans attempted to destroy the goalposts when the Tigers, a three-touchdown favorite, survived a scare and edged N.C. State by a touchdown in an ACC battle. Security guards shooed them away, and the goalposts at one end of the stadium were merely knocked askew.

Even Oklahoma, which has won several national championships, saw its goalposts destroyed when the Sooners upset top-ranked Nebraska on the last Saturday in October 2000. The Oklahoma student body destroyed the goalposts again when the Sooners defeated Kansas State in the Big 12 championship game to end the regular season as the only undefeated team in NCAA Division I-A. The Sooners went on to defeat Florida State in the Orange Bowl to be recognized as national champions.

Never before had so many goalposts, at approximately $5,000 a pair, succumbed in a single season.

Valid Victorian

Lars Cederquist came from Sweden to play golf under Coach Puggy Blackmon at the University of South Carolina. He brought with him impeccable academic qualifications, including a perfect score on the mathematics portion of the Scholastic Aptitude Test.

Lars was on track to receive a master's degree in mechanical engineering by the time he completed his four years of collegiate golf eligibility in 2001. He was a straight-A student.

When he completed his bachelor's degree requirements after three years, Cederquist was asked to submit a résumé and photograph for consideration as class valedictorian. *Valedictorian* was a word not familiar to Cederquist in his native Sweden.

The envelope he submitted was marked, "Need for Valid Victorian."

Blackmon's parents live at Hilton Head Island, and when the Gamecocks played there in a tournament, they entertained the team with a seafood cookout. Lars was chowing down on the boiled shrimp, a delicacy he hadn't experienced in Sweden, when a teammate detected a crunching sound.

"Lars," he said, "you're supposed to peel the shrimp before you eat them."

"Lay Down, Dawgs"

In Athens on September 4, 1993, Georgia led South Carolina 21-17, with the Gamecocks threatening in the dying moments. South Carolina had used all of its timeouts.

Quarterback Steve Taneyhill passed to tight end Boomer Foster for a first down at the Georgia 2-yard line. Three line smashes by tailback Brandon Bennett, wrapped around a Georgia offside penalty, moved the football to the 1-yard line.

After the third try, veteran Georgia broadcaster Larry Munson pleaded, "Lay down Dawgs. Lay down Dawgs. Don't get up," hoping the clock would expire before South Carolina could run a fourth-down play.

With no time for a huddle, Taneyhill screamed, "Same play!" as the Gamecocks hurriedly lined up. Bennett leaped over the line and into the end zone with two seconds remaining on the game clock.

"The great back goes over the top. He scores and breaks our hearts," Munson told his radio audience.

Leading 23-21, South Carolina decided not to kick the extra point and risk a block and two-point return. Taneyhill downed the football.

Seven years later, in September of 2000, Georgia—ranked ninth in the national polls—came to Columbia. South Carolina had broken its 21-game losing streak against nonconference rival New Mexico State the week before, but was still saddled with a Southeastern Conference losing streak of 18 games.

Remembering Larry Munson's words on the 1993 Georgia broadcast, a Columbia man had "Lay Down Dawgs" painted in large letters across the front of his home.

South Carolina won in an upset, 21-10.

Many Hats

The late Frank Johnson wore many hats as a member of the University of South Carolina staff, but is best remembered as head basketball coach, a post he held for over 14 and a half seasons (1941-42; 1946-58), with time out for World War II military service.

He also coached freshman football and served as business manager and assistant director of athletics. After leaving the athletics department, Johnson served as a fund-raiser in the university's development office.

Despite the burden of other duties and working with one of the lowest budgets in the area, Frank fell just one game shy of breaking even in his career—he won 174 games and lost 175. He also coached an NCAA-scoring champion in Grady Wallace, who averaged 31.25 points per game in 1957 to edge out Joe Gibbon of Mississippi, Elgin Baylor of Seattle, Wilt Chamberlain of Kansas, and Chet Forte of Columbia for the national title. They averaged between 28.9 and 30.05 points per game.

Frank was a little flaky and often made statements similar to those later made famous by New York Yankee catcher Yogi Berra. The players nicknamed Johnson "Punchy," but never called him that within earshot, except one time by accident.

The basketball team was in Chapel Hill for a game with the North Carolina Tar Heels. Several players were in a hotel elevator when Harry Stewart, a football tackle and walk-on member of the basketball squad who had been the object of some criticism from Johnson, declared, "Damn that Punchy Johnson!"

At that moment, the elevator door opened, with Johnson waiting to enter. He heard the remark and said to Stewart, "You're not dressing for the game tonight. You can go to the movie."

"But Coach," Stewart answered, "I've already seen that movie."

Stewart sat out the game.

Once when giving a scouting report on the University of Georgia, an upcoming opponent, Frank told star center Jim Slaughter he had to be aggressive in defending the hook shot of Georgia's 6-8 Bob Schloss.

"Hell, he's never made one," the 6-11 Slaughter commented.

"Yes, he has, too," Johnson replied. "He made one last week against Georgia."

Don Cox recalled a trip to North Carolina when he, Chuck Prezioso, and Slaughter were riding in a car driven by Johnson when the coach was stopped by a North Carolina highway patrolman for speeding in the town of Apex. Prezioso was another football player who also played basketball He was from Rockford, Illinois, the hometown of both Johnson and Rex Enright, South Carolina's athletics director and head football coach.

"Coach Enright loved Prezioso, and he could get away with anything and he knew it," Cox remembered. While Johnson was debating the speeding charge, Prezioso shouted from the background, "Lock him up! We've lost 10 games in a row. If he's locked up, maybe we can win a game."

Johnson paid a $50 fine, which Cox remembered was a lot of money in 1949, but placed a telephone call to the South Carolina highway commissioner before the basketball game.

At halftime, a North Carolina trooper sought out Johnson and returned his $50.

Cox recalled that Prezioso once swiped Johnson's hat, threw it on the floor, stomped on it, and then returned it to the spot where Johnson had placed it. When the coach picked up his battered hat, Prezioso said, "Coach, you've got to have that hat cleaned and blocked. It's a mess."

In the recruitment of Grady Wallace from Pikeville Junior College in Kentucky, Johnson brought in almost the entire Pikeville team, including head coach Walt Hambrick, who became Frank's assistant and replaced him as head coach for the 1958-59 season. Hambrick lasted only one year as head coach, leaving with a 4-20 record. He became a full-time physical education professor and later served as athletics director at Coastal Carolina College.

Johnny Gramling, a star quarterback (1951-53), played under Johnson on the 1950 freshman football team.

The freshmen were making a trip to Miami to play the University of Miami freshmen, Gramling recalled, and Johnson posted a travel squad list and announced, "Those who are not on the travel squad are not making the trip."

One of Frank's duties as assistant AD was scheduling, and South Carolina booked football games against the University of Detroit for 1962 and 1963. It's not clear which end made the mistake, but South Carolina had the 1963 game on one date and Detroit had it on another—in Detroit—the same date the Gamecocks were scheduled to play Tulane in Columbia.

The dilemma was solved when Detroit dropped football after the 1962 season, but, that left South Carolina a game short on its 1963 schedule. Memphis State University was added to fill the void.

Ted

Coach Ted Petoskey's hemorrhoids were the undoing of first baseman Cy Szakacsi and outfielder Red Wilson during a 1950 series against the Jacksonville Navy baseball team.

The South Carolina team was billeted in a barracks at the Jacksonville Naval Air Station. Ted had a curfew, but he always went to bed early and never made a bedcheck. Cy and Red went out for a night on the town.

Ted was having a particularly uncomfortable night and was up roaming the barracks in the wee hours when the night owls came home.

They did a lot of extra running for that.

Ted Petoskey was a three-sport star at the University of Michigan and the top athlete from the town of Petoskey, Michigan. It was said he was so good they named the town after him.

Petoskey was a star end and captain on the Michigan football team when the center was future president Gerald Ford. He also excelled in basketball and baseball and played professional baseball for a number of years, including two "cups of coffee" in the big leagues—six games in 1934 and four games in 1935 with the Cincinnati Reds.

He was hitless in seven at-bats in 1934, but batted .400 in 1935, when he went 2-for-5.

Petoskey was South Carolina's baseball coach for 12 seasons—1940-42 and 1948-56—compiling a 113-118-1 career record. He also coached the Gamecock basketball from 1935 to 1940, winding up with a 37-67 record. During his career at South Carolina, he also served as an assistant football coach. Petoskey coached a short time at Wofford College between his World War II service and his Gamecock assignments. During his stint at Wofford, and in a game against South Carolina, he allegedly had his pitcher throw a shaved potato to a Gamecock batter, According to the legend, the umpire called it a strike.

After leaving the University of South Carolina staff, Petoskey served as recreation director and coach at the Central Correction Institution, South Carolina's state penitentiary. He said he liked coaching the cons because "all of our games are at home."

On several occasions, the South Carolina baseball team scrimmaged against CCI. Whenever a foul ball went over the fence, a chorus of "I'll go get it" was heard from the prisoners in the stands.

A Gamecock batter once disputed a third strike, and Petoskey yelled out, "You'd better not argue with that umpire. He's doing life for murder."

The Happy Hungarian

John "Cy" Szakacsi was from Fairport Harbor, Ohio. He came to the University of South Carolina as a G.I. Bill of Rights student after World War II. From 1947-50, he earned three basketball letters as a guard—scoring 525 points in 59 games—and three letters in baseball (1948-50). He was a pitcher for two seasons and batted .330 as a first baseman his senior year.

We called him the Happy Hungarian.

Just about everyone had trouble with Cy's surname, pronounced Sa-KOTCHEE. The first day of one semester, the professor in his English course was attempting to take roll call. She was a young lady, not much older than the G.I. veteran students in the class.

After she made several attempts without coming close, Cy blurted out: "Sa-KOTCHEE, Sa-KOTCHEE. What's the matter? Can't you speak English?"

Szakacsi remained in South Carolina after graduation and coached more than 650 basketball wins at several high schools in the Columbia area. He is now in the State of South Carolina Athletic Hall of Fame.

Coach Pig Farmer

After World War II military service, Harry Parone came south from his native Connecticut to play baseball and basketball at the University of South Carolina. He earned four baseball letters as an outfielder from 1946-49 and was one of the last of the great two-handed set shooters on the basketball court, lettering in 1949.

Parone's first job after graduation was as athletics director and head coach of all sports at tiny Dentsville High School on the outskirts of Columbia. His salary was $3,000 a year.

"My classroom was in a tar-paper shack, and my locker room was in the tar-paper shack next door," Parone recalled. "We kept pigs in a pen next to the locker room. Sometimes the odor was a little tough to take in the spring."

Whenever funds ran short for his athletics program, Harry would sell a pig.

There were no showers in the locker room, and athletes had to sprint across the campus to another building to shower.

"One lady who lived nearby complained to the principal about naked boys running across the school grounds. "Sometimes I was one of them," Parone said.

Parone said there was no fence around the football field, and paid admissions to the football games were on an honor-system basis.

"We set up a table and charged 25 cents for students and 50 cents for adults," he said.

Parone used $250 of his annual budget to buy an ancient bus that transported his teams to away games. The school had no gymnasium, so all basketball games were played on the road, and the team practiced on an outdoor court when it couldn't borrow a court from another school.

"We operated that way for five years before we finally built a gym," he said.

Parone coached football, baseball, golf, boys' and girls' basketball, boys' and girls' track, boys' tennis, girls' volleyball, and soccer. His football teams won three state championships.

After 10 years at Dentsville, Parone became athletics director for Richland County School District Two. The district's football stadium is named Harry Parone Stadium. He was inducted into the South Carolina Coaches Association Hall of Fame in 1995.

Mr. Weaver

Emanuel Weaver was a massive lineman from New Orleans who came to the University of South Carolina after two years at a junior college and was a letterman on the 1980 and 1981 football teams.

He was also the first Gamecock player permitted to wear an earring.

South Carolina played the University of Pittsburgh in the 1980 Gator Bowl, and the official parties of both schools attended a seafood buffet at Jacksonville Beach. My wife, Margaret, was behind Weaver in the buffet line. She had never seen a man wearing an earring and asked me, "Is he gay?"

I told her I didn't think so, but I certainly wasn't going to ask him.

Coach Jim Carlen was once asked what he called Emanuel Weaver. His reply was: "Mister Weaver."

The Gamecocks consumed a lot of seafood but fell short of the lobster-eating record. One of the Gator Bowl hosts said that in a previous year, a dozen lobsters were polished off by a Clemson lineman.

Weaver sometimes suffered from allergies while at South Carolina, and one time on the practice field, he had an allergy attack that resulted in fluid forming in his ear tubes, which affected his hearing. The big lineman feared he was going deaf, and student trainer Sid Kenyon was assigned to drive Weaver to a hospital in an old station wagon. Kenyon recalled that the driver's-side sun visor on the old vehicle kept flopping down during the trip.

Weaver produced a pocketknife, opened it, and while an anxious Kenyon looked on fearfully, Weaver used the knife to tighten a loose screw and said, "You help me, I'll help you."

"He got my attention when he pulled out that knife," Kenyon said. "Everybody was kind of scared of him anyway. He was kind of intense."

Emanuel Weaver played for the Cincinnati Bengals in 1981-82. His NFL career was shortened by injury. He is now a deputy sheriff in Somerset County, N.J.

*Emanuel Weaver
(USC Sports
Information)*

Lombardi Time

Rob DeBoer was a delightfully naïve youngster from Omaha, Nebraska, when he arrived in South Carolina to play baseball and football. The reason he chose S.C. was that football recruiters at the University of Nebraska told him he would not be allowed to play baseball there. He had grown up a Cornhusker fan.

DeBoer was named all-state in both football and baseball at Burke High School in Omaha but was considered by scouts a better prospect for professional baseball than for football.

Jeff Churchich, a former South Carolina catcher (1985-86), lived in Omaha and contacted baseball coach June Raines, who alerted the football staff. That's how Rob DeBoer became a two-sport star at the University of South Carolina.

As a freshman, Rob gained 700 yards for the football team before making his first trip with the baseball team in February 1991. The Gamecocks opened the season at the University of Jacksonville in Florida. The team checked into its hotel about 6 p.m. the day before the game and was due to depart at 6:30 for practice.

Rob was five minutes late, and when he boarded the bus, pitching coach Randy Davis told him: "Rob, you've got to get on Lombardi time."

"What does that mean?" DeBoer asked.

"Don't you know who Vince Lombardi was?" Davis replied.

"Sure," retorted DeBoer. "He was that guy from Notre Dame."

"No, no, Rob. Vince Lombardi was the famous coach of the Green Bay Packers."

"I knew that," replied DeBoer. "I was thinking of that other guy from Notre Dame. Rock Ka-nootney."

During April of his freshman season, DeBoer and the South Carolina baseball team played a series at Wichita State University. The flight home involved a change of planes at Dallas–Fort Worth. During the flight from Wichita to Dallas, DeBoer removed his shoes, and his feet swelled to the point where he had difficulty putting his shoes back on.

"When you fly, your feet get bigger," DeBoar explained to his teammates.

*Rob DeBoer
(USC Sports
Information)*

DeBoer lettered four seasons (1990-93) as a fullback; as of the 2000 season, he ranked 14th among Gamecock rushers with 1,810 career yards. He averaged 4.7 yards per attempt. His best game occurred during his freshman season—104 yards against The Citadel.

He was a cocaptain of the 1993 team.

In baseball, DeBoer had a .283 career batting average as a catcher/designated hitter in 159 games (1991-94), and slugged 15 home runs. He was drafted in the sixth round by Toronto after his junior season, but turned down the Blue Jays' offer and returned for his senior seasons in football and baseball.

Drafted by the Oakland Athletics after his senior season, DeBoer played five seasons of professional baseball, reaching the AA level at Huntsville in the Southern League. He returned to Columbia, and after a brief fling in the investment business, opened an athlete's training facility named Rob DeBoer's Athlete Factory.

Crazy Yankee

Steve Taneyhill was one of the most colorful athletes ever to play football at the University of South Carolina. He was also one of the best and played from 1992 to 1995.

During his four seasons at quarterback, Taneyhill compiled 8,380 yards in total offense. He completed 753 of 1,245 passes for 8,782 yards. He threw 62 touchdown passes and had 21 games in which he passed for more than 200 yards.

Taneyhill wore an earring and had long hair tied in a ponytail. A Columbia store that specialized in sports souvenir items did a thriving business selling small football helmets with a blond ponytail sticking out the back.

Taneyhill would practice his golf swing with an imaginary club during pauses in the action and would hit fungoes with an imaginary baseball bat after each Gamecock touchdown. He autographed the Tiger paw in the middle of Clemson's Memorial Stadium after a South Carolina victory.

Taneyhill also wore a bandana beneath his football helmet, and in 1995, following South Carolina's 65-39 win at Mississippi State, a frustrated Bulldog fan screamed, "Hey, Taneyhill! What's that on your head?"

"Your wife's panties," the brash quarterback from Altoona, Pa., yelled back.

When Brad Scott replaced Sparky Woods as head coach, Taneyhill cut his hair and led South Carolina to a 24-21 win over West Virginia in the 1994 Carquest Bowl at Joe Robbie Stadium in Miami. It was South Carolina's first bowl victory in nine tries.

After graduation, Taneyhill became the coach of an eight-man football team at a small private high school in upstate South Carolina. A sportswriter once asked Taneyhill how he would like to be remembered by South Carolina fans.

"That crazy Yankee quarterback" was his answer.

Steve Taneyhill (USC Sports Information)

Mistletoe

Billy Laval was a feisty little guy who weighed about 135 pounds. He was also the only football coach at the University of South Carolina who served for more than one season and who never had a losing record.

Laval coached the Gamecocks for seven seasons (1928-34) and always won at least one more game than he lost. His best record was 6-2-2 in 1928, the year he took the Gamecocks to Chicago to meet the University of Chicago and Coach Amos Alonzo Stagg.

At the time, Chicago was a member of the Big Ten Conference. Laval won 6-0 before 35,000 fans, by far the largest crowd that the Gamecocks had ever played before.

Auburn was unbeaten, untied, and under consideration for the Rose Bowl in 1932, when South Carolina, under Laval, tied the Plainsmen (as Auburn was then known) 20-20 on December 3 at Birmingham. Auburn stayed home on New Year's Day. Laval's football record at South Carolina was 39-26-6.

He also coached baseball for seven years and enjoyed six winning seasons and had a career mark of 89-33-1. His .728 winning percentage is the highest of any South Carolina baseball coach who coached more than one season. Laval's only losing baseball team compiled a 7-8-1 record in 1928, and his best diamond team was 17-3 in 1933.

Four players from a Texas state championship high school team strengthened South Carolina's basketball roster for the 1932-33 season. Laval was also athletics director and, perhaps sensing a good hoops season, took over the basketball team from A. W. "Rock" Norman. South Carolina finished with a 17-2 record and won the Southern Conference championship.

After one season, Laval reinstalled Rock Norman as coach, and the team was undefeated until the Southern Conference Tournament, when several players came down with the mumps. South Carolina lost to N.C. State in the tournament's first round and finished with an 18-1 record.

Laval had a successful career at Furman University before being hired by South Carolina.

When he was named head coach at Furman, Laval told school authorities he was a baseball man and didn't know much about football. He studied up on the game and defeated South Carolina four consecutive times. South Carolina trustees took this position: If you can't beat him, hire him.

After leaving the Gamecocks, Laval coached at Emory and Henry before ending his career at little Newberry College in South Carolina.

While coaching at Newberry, Laval was the speaker at a meeting of the Columbia Touchdown Club. He concluded his remarks by saying, "If you don't like what I have said here today, you will notice as I leave the room that I have mistletoe tied to my coattails."

Brandi Laval, great-granddaughter of the old coach, is a University of South Carolina graduate and administrative assistant to Gamecock baseball coach Ray Tanner.

A Boy Named June

June Raines was a 30-year-old freshman when he enrolled at the University of South Carolina in the fall of 1967 after a 10-year career as a minor league catcher, during which he said he was often provoked into fights because of his "girl's first name."

Raines spent a year as an indifferent student at Furman University before signing a professional contract with the Cleveland Indians. He played in every classification of minor league baseball from Class D at Selma, Alabama to AAA at Portland, Ore., during his eight seasons with the Cleveland organization and two with the Washington Senators.

He was called up to the American League once when two Cleveland catchers were injured. He spent five days warming up pitchers in the bullpen before being sent back to the minors without getting into a major league game.

"The best five days of my life," is the way Raines remembered it.

He also had fond memories of catching a no-hitter by Luis Tiant at Burlington in the Carolina League and also catching "Sudden" Sam McDowell. Tiant later won 229 games in a 19-year major league career, and McDowell went on to a 15-year big-league career in which he won 141 games.

Raines said he was a good catcher, but one thing kept him out of the big leagues.

"It was called a slider," he said.

His career batting average in the minors was something like .212.

Raines was a student assistant coach and earned bachelor's and master's degrees in four years before returning to professional baseball as a minor league catching instructor and manager with the Philadelphia Phillies organization.

When Bobby Richardson resigned after the 1976 season to make a run for congress, Raines returned to South Carolina. His 20-year tenure, 1977-96, is by far the longest of any University of South Carolina baseball coach.

Raines won 763 games, took the Gamecocks to the NCAA playoffs 11 times, won four regional championships, and advanced four times to the College World Series. His first Gamecock team in 1977 finished second, losing 2-1 to Arizona State in the championship game of the World Series.

He was inducted into the University of South Carolina Athletics Hall of Fame in 2000.

In 1979, June Raines took his South Carolina baseball team to Greenville, N.C., for a two-game series with East Carolina University. His only assistant coach—Johnny Hunton—was on a recruiting assignment and could not make the trip.

Raines was pitching batting practice and failed to duck behind the protective screen when outfielder Paul Hollins hit a line drive that struck the coach between the eyes. He went down in a heap. An ambulance hurried Raines to a hospital, and the team was left with no coach.

After a team meeting, it was decided that third baseman John Marquardt would run the team on the field, and pitcher Hal Gaalema would handle pitching changes. Senior southpaw Jeff Twitty had an 0.76 earned-run average that season—second best in the NCAA—and was the team's closer.

In the bottom of the ninth inning, South Carolina led 3-2, but an East Carolina batter reached first base as the potential tying run. Gaalema—who later became statistics coordinator for Atlanta Braves cable telecasts—walked slowly to the mound in his best imitation of Casey Stengel, with both hands shoved into his back pockets.

The plate umpire walked out and said, "Coach, what do you want to do?"

Gaelema pointed dramatically toward the bullpen, tapped his left forearm, and said, "Give me my left-hander."

The left-hander was the only pitcher in the bullpen. Twitty retired the side to earn one of his 10 saves that season.

Bob Fulton and I were broadcasting the game, and Fulton suggested we not mention the injury to Coach Raines until we received a report from the hospital, so as not to alarm his wife, who was probably listening to the broadcast back in Columbia. Several times, however, Bob mentioned "third-base coach Hal Gaalema," which no doubt made his family wonder why Raines wasn't coaching third base.

About the seventh inning, we received word that X rays were negative and Raines had been sent to the hotel. After the game, we found him sitting in the hotel bar drinking a beer and groaning, "Boy, my head aches."

We kidded him that doctors had X-rayed his head and found nothing.

Raines was back on the field for the second game of the series, which South Carolina lost 5-4 in 10 innings, when Twitty, who allowed only four earned runs in 47 2/3 innings that season, gave up a game-ending two-run homer.

After dropping a three-game series at Auburn in 1992—one of the losses in extra innings, and the finale by a 6-0 shutout—Raines was so upset, he told the team he was walking back to Columbia. He walked down the middle of the road, and every time the team bus driver attempted to pass, Raines stepped in front of the bus. After about a mile, he boarded the bus for the trip back to Columbia.

Twitty Bird

On the recommendation of East Carolina coach Hal Baird, Jeff Twitty was drafted in the 25th round by the Kansas City Royals in 1979. One year later, he was called up to the team that won the 1980 American League pennant.

Twitty pitched 22 innings in 13 games and compiled a 2-1 record. He was sent back to AAA the following spring and never pitched in the major leagues again, but he wears a World Series ring. He was the winning pitcher in his first major league appearance.

Twitty returned to the University of South Carolina and was graduate assistant pitching coach under June Raines while earning a master's degree. In 1985, ESPN televised a South Carolina–Ohio State game from Sarge Frye Field, and one of the announcers was Jim Kaat, whose 25-year major league career overlapped Twitty's brief stint with the Royals.

Kaat was asked if he remembered Twitty.

"Oh, Conway," Kaat replied. "Sure, I remember Conway." In the majors, Twitty was nicknamed for the country music singer, but his nickname while pitching for the University of South Carolina was "Bird," for the cartoon character Tweety Bird.

Twitty became the head coach of a small school in Florida, St. Leo College, before joining the University of New Orleans as pitching coach. He eventually left coaching and moved back to South Carolina.

The Pearl

Earl Bass is considered by many to be the best pitcher ever to compete for the University of South Carolina. His nickname was Earl the Pearl.

Bass had a 5-1 record as a freshman in 1972, was 12-1 in 1974, and 17-1 in 1975. In 1973 he pitched only eight and a fraction innings before being sidelined for the season with tendinitis in his right elbow.

Bass lost to UCLA in the Riverside tournament in California his freshman year, lost without allowing an earned run when teammates committed a modern school-record nine errors against Georgia Southern in 1974. He also lost the final game of his collegiate career, pitching on two days' rest, to the University of Texas in the championship game of the 1975 College World Series.

Earl Bass had a flair for the dramatic and might have been considered a little cocky. Before batting gloves became popular, Earl wore a golf glove on his left hand. He played a lot of first base when he wasn't pitching, and the designated hitter rule had yet to be adopted, so Bass wore the glove when he batted. He also wore it when pitching, inside the fielder's glove on his left hand.

South Carolina played at South Alabama in 1974, and South Alabama Coach Eddie Stanky (who had a reputation for seeking any edge available to intimidate an opponent during his long major league playing and managing career) objected to Earl's golf glove. Earl slowly peeled off the glove, stuck it in his back pocket and told Stanky, "I'm still going to whip your ass."

Bass proceeded to pitch a complete-game 9-2 win, and Stanky rushed out and embraced the Gamecock pitcher, saying, "You're my kind of ballplayer."

Earl Bass made his only relief appearance of the 1975 season with one out in the sixth inning against North Carolina State in the championship game of an NCAA regional tournament in Columbia.

Earl had pitched six innings of an 11-3 win over The Citadel two days earlier. South Carolina led 4-3 when Bass relieved Tim Lewis. N.C. State had one run in and two runners on base. Bass retired 10 consecutive batters before walking Gerry Feldkamp with two outs in the ninth inning.

With the potential tying run on base and the winning run at the plate, first baseman Hank Small called time and walked over to the mound. Bass told him, "Get your ass back over to first base and put your glove in your pocket, because this guy is mine."

He struck out pinch hitter Dave Moody to end the game and send the Gamecocks on their first trip to Omaha and the College World Series.

Bass was granted a medical redshirt by the NCAA for his injury season of 1973 and could have returned in 1976 for another collegiate season. However, he was drafted and signed by the St. Louis Cardinals and began his professional career at the AAA level.

The Cardinals' AAA team was based one season in New Orleans and played home games in the Super Dome. The team was then moved to Springfield, Illinois, and played in a high school stadium. Earl, who enjoyed the nightlife, described New Orleans as "heaven" and Springfield as "the pits."

The tendinitis in his elbow reoccurred, and Bass was released before reaching the major leagues. He was inducted into the University of South Carolina Athletics Hall of Fame in 1989 and the State of South Carolina Athletics Hall of Fame in 2000.

Bass was named first-team All-American by the American Baseball Coaches Association in 1974 and 1975. Also in 1975, he was runner-up to Arizona State shortstop Jerry Maddox for the Lefty Gomez Plate, presented by *Collegiate Baseball* to the best amateur baseball player in the United States.

Bass is now a wine salesman, calling on retailers throughout the United States. He lives in Surfside Beach, S.C.

Dandy Randy

Randy Martz was a 6-4 drop-back quarterback from Elizabethton, Pennsylvania, when he was recruited to play football at the University of South Carolina. He was also a pretty good pitcher, but was not drafted by professional baseball when he graduated from high school.

A short time after he enrolled, the South Carolina football staff switched from a pro-style offense to the veer, an offense that required a mobile, running quarterback. Except for a brief stint at tight end, Martz spent three seasons on the scout squad running the opposition's plays against the varsity in practice.

Football coach Jim Carlen had a policy that did not permit his quarterbacks to play baseball, so Martz did not try out for the baseball team his first two years. When workouts for the 1977 baseball season began, Carlen told Coach June Raines, "If you want that

Martz boy, you can have him, but he won't help you because he's no athlete."

Martz made 16 starts for the Gamecocks that spring, compiled a 14-0 record, and pitched South Carolina to within one win of the College World Series championship.

In his two no-decisions—an 8-8, 11-inning tie at the University of Tampa and a 7-6 loss to South Alabama in the NCAA regional tournament—South Carolina had the lead when Martz left the game. In 138 2/3 innings, Martz compiled a 1.98 earned run average. He was named to every All-America team and won the Lefty Gomez Plate as the nation's best amateur baseball player.

The Chicago Cubs made Martz their first-round draft choice in 1977 after he had played one year of college baseball. He pitched three seasons with the Cubs and one game with the White Sox and won 17 major league games before an arm injury ended his career. In 1982, his best major league season, he won 11 games for the Cubs.

South Carolina was on a spring trip to Florida when Randy Martz was involved in his first no-decision. The Gamecocks held a three-run lead when Raines took Martz out. Tampa tied the score, and the game went into extra innings.

After 11 innings, the two umpires, both University of Tampa graduate students, walked off the field, although there was enough daylight for another hour of play.

Game called due to darkness, they explained to Raines. It turned out they had meal tickets to eat in the University of Tampa dining hall, which was scheduled to close in 15 minutes. Records list that game as an 8-8 tie.

The second no-decision of Martz's collegiate career was against South Alabama in the opening game of the 1977 NCAA regional tournament in Columbia. South Carolina led by three runs after six innings, but South Alabama had four consecutive left-handed batters due up.

Coach Raines relieved righty Martz with southpaw Scott Thomas, reasoning that Randy would be available to pitch again in the short four-team tournament. All four left-handed South Alabama batters hit safely, and the Jaguars rallied to win 7-6.

Martz hit a South Alabama batter. After going to first base, the batter called time and was limping around, attempting to shake off the pain.

141

South Carolina had to win four consecutive games in the losers' bracket to win the regional and advance to Omaha and the College World Series. Martz pitched a complete game in the championship game and struck out 13 Wake Forest batters in a 6-1 win.

South Alabama coach Eddie Stanky went out to check on his player, and on his way back to the third-base dugout, he detoured close to the pitcher's mound. Always one to seek an edge by intimidating an opponent, Stanky said to Martz, "You'd better be glad we're using the DH (designated hitter), because if you came to bat, we'd stick one in your ear."

Bob Fulton, the radio voice of University of South Carolina sports for more than 40 years, spent one year (1954) broadcasting major league baseball with the Mutual Network's Game of the Day. Fulton said Stanky, then manager of the St. Louis Cardinals, refused to give his starting lineup to the media until he exchanged lineup cards at home plate a few seconds before the start of each game. The National League later adopted a rule requiring that lineups be released to the media half an hour before game time.

Stanky managed the Cardinals from1952 to 1955 and the Chicago White Sox, from 1966 to 1968. In 1977, while at South Alabama, he was named manager of the Texas Rangers, but quit after one game to return to college coaching. The baseball stadium at the University of South Alabama is named Eddie Stanky Field.

Randy Martz graduated from the University of South Carolina with a degree in journalism and now lives in East Alton, Ill.

Mookie

At the beginning of the 1976 fall semester at the University of South Carolina baseball, coach June Raines walked into the sports information office with a young prospect and said, "I want you to meet Willie Wilson."

The young man, William Hayward Wilson, spoke up and said, "Coach, in Bamberg they call me Mookie."

Mookie Wilson was one of six brothers who played baseball at Bamberg-Ehrhardt High School. The little Class A school won something like eight consecutive South Carolina state championships with one or more Wilson brothers in the lineup.

A center fielder, Mookie was drafted in the 10th round by the Los Angeles Dodgers after two seasons at Spartanburg Methodist Junior College, but enrolled at the University of South Carolina instead of signing with the Dodgers.

He led the Gamecocks to the championship game of the 1977 College World Series and was the only unanimous choice for the CWS all-tournament team among a field of candidates that included such future big leaguers as Bob Horner and Hubie Brooks of Arizona State and South Carolina pitchers Randy Martz, Jim Lewis, and Ed Lynch.

Black players in the deep south were still rare in 1977, and Mookie was subjected to some racial slurs, especially when the Gamecocks played at Mercer. A group of students sat on blankets or towels on a bank behind the center-field fence and invited him to a watermelon cutting after the game.

As if he were following a movie script, Mookie hit a 10th-inning home run that landed among the hecklers, as South Carolina won 4-3. Mookie stopped while walking to the locker room after the game and said, "Darn. I forgot my watermelon."

In his only Division I collegiate season, Mookie batted .357, stole 33 bases, and hit eight home runs. He moved up from the 10th round to the second round of the 1977 draft and was chosen by the New York Mets. He turned down the original offer by the Mets, but scout Wayne Brittain went to Bamberg armed with a better deal, and found Mookie fishing on a riverbank, where he signed his first contract.

A right-handed hitter until he reached the AAA level of professional baseball at Norfolk, Mookie became a switch hitter. He compiled a .274 career average in 1,403 major league games over 12 seasons with the Mets and the Toronto Blue Jays. He stole 327 bases during his major league career and hit 67 home runs.

Mookie played in four league championship series, two each with the Mets and Blue Jays, and one World Series. He gained everlasting fame when he hit the ground ball that went through the legs of Bill Buckner for an error that allowed the Mets to come from behind and win the 1986 World Series over the Boston Red Sox.

While playing at Jackson, Mississippi, in the Class AA Texas League, Mookie and his wife, Rose, were married in a home-plate ceremony before a home game. He said Rose "always wanted a big diamond, and that was the only way I could get her one."

While with the Mets, Mookie lived in Lakewood, N.J., and he and Rose founded a girls' club for teenagers from low-income neighborhoods. "Mookie's Roses" were featured on a CBS television program and in *USA Today*. They decided to sponsor a girls' club because Rose said that all youth charities underwritten by professional athletes were for boys.

After retiring as a player, Mookie Wilson became the Mets' first-base coach and managed a team in the Arizona Fall League in 2000. His stepson, Preston Wilson, is a major league outfielder with the Florida Marlins.

Mookie's youngest brother, Phillip, played two seasons at the University of South Carolina and reached the AAA level with the Portland Beavers in the Minnesota Twins' organization. Another brother, John, played at one of South Carolina's regional campuses, USC-Aiken, and reached the AA level in the Mets' minor league system.

Wilson never explained why his nickname was Mookie, except to say his grandmother gave him the name. As things turned out, it was good that he rejected the name Willie, applied by June Raines; a contemporary of his named Willie Wilson was a star outfielder with the Kansas City Royals while Mookie Wilson was with the Mets.

Always a free swinger, Mookie was encouraged by Raines to be more patient at the plate. His answer was, "Coach, if it's white and moving, I'm swinging at it."

The Killer B's

A trio of junior right-handed pitchers whose surnames began with the letter B combined to win 39 games as the 2000 University of South Carolina baseball team compiled a 56-10 record and registered more wins than any other NCAA Division I baseball team.

They were called the "Killer B's."

Kip Bouknight led the way with a 17-1 record; Peter Bauer's record was 13-2;, and Scott Barber's total was 9-2, including a school-record 15 saves, as he doubled as the No. 3 starter and closer. The Killer B's combined to pitch 374 2/3 innings, representing more than 63 percent of the team's total of 592 2/3 innings. The combined earned run average of the three aces was 2.95.

Bouknight and Barber are native South Carolinians, while Bauer hails from Maryland.

Bouknight's ERA was 2.81 in 144 innings, Barber's was 2.96 in 106 1/3 innings, and Bauer's was 3.11 in 124 1/3 innings. Bouknight struck out 143 batters, Barber fanned an even 100, and Bauer missed the century mark by one, fanning 99. Bauer walked only 36, Bouknight 34, and Barber, 20, (a 5:1 strikeout-to-walk ratio).

South Carolina won the Southeastern Conference championship with a 25-5 league mark, topping the previous record for most conference wins by one. The Gamecocks won a regional title, but were denied a trip to the College World Series when Bauer and Barber lost to Louisiana Lafayette after Bouknight won the first game of the super regional.

Bouknight won four National Player of the Year awards, including the prestigious Golden Spikes Award and the Rotary Smith Award presented by the Houston Rotary Club. He was named SEC Player of the Year in baseball, as well as the SEC Male Athlete of the Year. He and Barber were first-team All-SEC honorees, while Bauer was named to the second team.

All three of the Killer B's were named to the 2000 All-Region team selected by the American Baseball Coaches Association. Bouknight was named to every All-America team selected, and Barber and Bauer were third-team selections by the ABCA. Bauer was voted the Most Valuable Player in the regional tournament in which South Carolina defeated Wake Forest to advance to the super regional.

In the June 2000 free-agent draft, Bauer was a second-round selection by the Toronto Blue Jays, and Barber was picked in the sixth round by the Arizona Diamondbacks. Bouknight, despite his dominating collegiate statistics, wasn't drafted until the 21st round by the Oakland Athletics. Some of the pro scouts said he wasn't tall enough at an even six feet and 192 pounds.

Bauer was 6-7 and 247 pounds. Barber was 6-4 and 203. Both of them signed six-figure contracts, with Bauer's figure reportedly $800,000.

Bouknight, a Southeastern Conference honor roll student with a 3.8 spring semester 2000 grade-point average on a 4.0 scale, postponed professional baseball for at least a year to return to Coach Ray Tanner's Gamecock team for his senior season, needing just one victory to tie the school career mark of 36 wins set by left-handed pitcher Tim Lewis from 1973 to 1976. He was also on the verge of setting records for career innings and strikeouts.

Geography Lesson

Edmond Wilson was a 6-10 freshman when the South Carolina basketball team was scheduled to play in the Great Alaska Shootout at Anchorage in November of 1990.

Edmond wanted to know where Alaska was, so team trainer Brainard Cooper produced an atlas and opened it to a map of the United States. Due to space limitations, Hawaii and Alaska were shown in cutouts to the west of the contiguous 48 states and below Seattle.

Cooper explained that the team would fly from Columbia to Atlanta to Seattle to Anchorage.

Looking at the map, Wilson asked why it was necessary to fly all the way up to Seattle when Anchorage appeared to be just off the California coast.

A three-year letterman (1991-93), Wilson played in 69 games and scored 320 points.

Homesick

Bobby Giles played a season of basketball at the University of South Carolina before entering the U.S. Army Air Corps in 1943, where he served on bomber flight crews.

Bobby Giles, Jr., said one of his father's duties, as the youngest member of the bomber crew, was to kick bombs that stuck in the bomb bay until they were loosened and fell on the target.

When World War II ended and the football season was about to begin in 1945, Giles was awaiting his discharge at Greensboro, N.C., when legendary Duke University coach Wallace Wade recruited him for the Blue Devil football team.

Giles stayed at Duke a few days before returning home to Columbia for a weekend that turned into a lifetime. Feeling a little homesick, he contacted South Carolina coach Rex Enright. Giles was an outstanding fullback/linebacker for three seasons (1945-47) and added two basketball letters (1946-47) to the monogram he had earned in 1943.

Giles had a long career in education and coaching, winning state championships in football, basketball, and baseball at tiny Olympic High School in Columbia before consolidation reduced Olympia to middle school status.

He is in the South Carolina Coaches Hall of Fame.

While homesickness returned Bobby Giles, Sr., to the University of South Carolina, his son went all the way to Provo, Utah, for his college education. Bobby, Jr., was recruited by South Carolina for baseball. Instead, he played at Brigham Young University and returned to South Carolina, where for many years he umpired college and high school baseball games and refereed women's basketball games.

Almost a Gamecock

South Carolina football coach Rex Enright recruited Charlie Justice when he was discharged from the navy in 1946, and Justice committed to becoming a Gamecock.

On a visit to Columbia, Justice—a newlywed—arranged for an apartment and was taken to the Columbia Hotel by Enright assistant Frank Johnson. The following morning, Enright and Johnson went to the hotel to take Justice to breakfast, only to find he had checked out.

It seemed a couple of University of North Carolina recruiters had spirited him away about midnight. He became one of North Carolina's all-time greatest players and starred with the Washington Redskins of the National Football League.

He Was a Gamecock

Jim Pinkerton played high school football with Charlie Justice at Hendersonville, N.C. Home in North Carolina for a weekend in 1946 while stationed at Charleston, awaiting discharge from the U.S. Marine Corps, Pinkerton saw his old teammate, who told him he was planning to play football at the University of South Carolina.

In anticipation of being a teammate of Justice's again, Pinkerton stopped off in Columbia and arranged to enroll at South Carolina. Justice wound up in Chapel Hill, while Pinkerton earned four Gamecock letters (1947-50) as a football end and four more (1946-49) as a third baseman on the baseball team.

Pinkerton was a successful high school football coach before becoming commissioner of the South Carolina High School League.

Nice Duds

George Wright played center on the University of South Carolina football team (1948-49) and was elected president of the student body. His roommate was Bayard Pickett, a defensive back who lettered three seasons (1948-50). Former teammates tell this story about the roommates.

During a light rainfall one day, Wright was walking across the University Horseshoe between classes when he spotted Pickett wearing a raincoat belonging to Wright.

"Bayard, what are you doing wearing my raincoat?"

Pickett opened the coat to reveal the clothing underneath and replied, "I didn't want to get your suit wet."

Wright married Beth Fillingim, South Carolina's May Queen of 1949. Two of their children, Bryant and Alice, were Gamecock cheerleaders. Another son—Van Earl Wright—became a well-known sportscaster with Cable News Network and Fox Sports Net. Several years ago, Van Earl was recognized as the outstanding young alumnus of the University of South Carolina College of Journalism.

A marine corps veteran of World War II, Pickett returned to the marines as an officer after graduation.

The Rockford Files

Rex Enright was from Rockford, Illinois, and he used his hometown as recruiting territory while serving as an assistant coach at the University of Georgia and as head football coach at the University of South Carolina.

Enright graduated from the Notre Dame School of Law, where he became a star fullback following the departure of the Four Horsemen. Enright spurned a legal career to become a football coach.

While an assistant at Georgia, where he also served briefly as head basketball coach, Enright went back to Rockford to recruit Frank Johnson, who became a three-sport star—football, basketball and baseball—for the Bulldogs.

In 1938, Enright was named head football coach and director of athletics at the University of South Carolina. Frank Johnson graduated from Georgia in 1936 and coached at his alma mater and the University of Mississippi before joining Enright's staff at South Carolina in 1940.

Frank was a jack-of-all-trades, serving as freshman football coach, head basketball coach, business manager, and assistant athletics director for many years.

Enright brought several athletes from Rockford to South Carolina, including Stan Stasica, Pat Vella, and Chuck Prezioso.

Stasica was Enright's first Rockford recruit and perhaps the best, but he played only one season of varsity football at South Carolina. After the 1941 season he entered the military, and when World War II ended, he completed his collegiate career at the University of

Illinois. After his one football season at Carolina, Stasica was named to the All-Southern Conference first team.

He also played basketball, appearing in 21 games and scoring 212 points for a 10.1 average.

Vella earned a football letter as a quarterback in 1949 and Prezioso was a three-year football letterman (1949-51). He also played on the golf team and earned one basketball letter, in 1950, when he scored 193 points in 22 games.

Prezioso was a fullback until a chronic knee injury limited his gridiron activity to placekicking and kept him off the basketball court. Two of his sons became Gamecock athletes. Chip lettered with the golf team, and David was a linebacker (1975-77). David was cocaptain of the football team his senior season.

David Prezioso was not recruited by major schools out of high school due to his size and first enrolled at Presbyterian College. According to reports, he was asked to leave that institution after mounting a groundskeeper's tractor one night and driving it up the steps of the school's administration building.

He transferred to South Carolina, walked on to the football team, and developed into a star despite his lack of size. He was a cocaptain of the 1977 football team.

A certain sports information director once coached a Little League baseball team in Columbia. His best two players were Chip and David Prezioso.

Rex

Webster's *New World Dictionary* defines the word *Rex* as: "King: The official title of a reigning king."

Rex Enright was king of the University of South Carolina football program for 15 years. Although his career coaching record was five games short of breaking even (64-69), Enright was so beloved, that trustees named the athletics department office building and adjacent practice facilities "The Rex Enright Athletics Center" and an oil painting of Enright hangs in the building's lobby.

The Rex Enright Athletics Center was completed shortly after Enright retired from the sidelines in 1956 to become the full-time athletics director. Due to its circular construction, the building has been long referred to as "The Roundhouse."

One reason for Enright's popularity was his ability to defeat arch rival Clemson in the annual "Big Thursday" game played during State Fair Week in Columbia each October.

After losing his first three games, in 1938-40, to the Tigers, Enright engineered an 18-14 upset in 1941. The Gamecocks took an 18-0 lead, then withstood a furious Clemson comeback. Clemson won in 1942 to put the Enright record at 1-4 against the Tigers before he took a three-year leave of absence to serve in the navy during World War II.

Enright returned in 1946 and coached the Gamecocks for 10 more seasons, through 1955. During that span, his record against Clemson was 7-2-1, with the second loss coming in his final season. Clemson fielded some of its greatest teams during this period.

The only Gamecock loss in the first nine years of this era occurred in 1948. South Carolina held a 7-6 lead with less than a

Rex Enright (USC Sports Information)

151

minute to play, but a blocked punt resulted in a Clemson touchdown and a 13-7 win. Clemson went on to an unbeaten, untied season and defeated Missouri in the Gator Bowl.

Clemson came into the 1950 Big Thursday game unbeaten, untied, and unscored upon, but had to come from behind in the closing moments to claim a 14-14 tie after South Carolina halfback Steve Wadiak had reeled off 256 yards on 18 rushes, an average of 14.2 yards per carry. Clemson finished the season unbeaten but once tied and defeated Miami in the Orange Bowl.

Clemson's 1951 team, which lost to Miami in the Gator Bowl, suffered a three-touchdown loss, 20-0, to Enright's Gamecocks on Big Thursday. Enright was the major reason that Frank Howard, Clemson's otherwise successful football coach for 30 years, had a losing record against South Carolina. Howard was 13-15-2 against the Gamecocks.

Following one loss to the Gamecocks, Howard greeted members of the news media at the locker room door and said, "Come on in, gentlemen, and claim the body."

After he led South Carolina to a 6-2-2 record in 1947, which included a 21-19 win over Clemson, boosters chipped in and presented Enright with a new Cadillac. When halfback Steve Wadiak became a superstar a couple of years later, cheerleaders chanted during games, "Give the ball to Wadiak. Enright needs a new Cadillac."

It was said that in the postwar years, three things could be counted on from Rex Enright every season: He would beat someone he wasn't supposed to, lose to someone he wasn't supposed to, and beat Clemson.

Even while serving in the navy, Rex Enright was looking out for the football program at South Carolina.

Commander Enright was stationed at the Jacksonville Naval Air Station when a group of Jacksonville civic leaders announced plans for a New Year's Day 1946 bowl game (which would eventually become the Gator Bowl). South Carolina and Wake Forest had played to a 13-13 tie during the 1945 season, so Enright suggested a rematch in the bowl game.

The bowl committee bought the idea, and South Carolina, despite a 2-3-3 regular-season record, received its first-ever bowl bid. The Gamecocks had beaten Presbyterian and Camp Blanding (a military team), and had tied Clemson, Miami, and Wake Forest, while losing a close game to Maryland and being blown out by Duke and Alabama.

Wake Forest won the rematch in the inaugural Gator Bowl, 26-13. Johnnie McMillan coached South Carolina's first bowl team, and Enright returned from the navy to resume his head-coaching duties in 1946.

Twenty after Four

South Carolina held a precarious 20-14 lead over West Virginia late in the fourth quarter in November 1953. Fog rolled in as daylight was ebbing at Morgantown, and Gamecock football Coach Rex Enright couldn't read the scoreboard clock.

Enright grabbed a student manager by the arm and said, "Son, go find out what the time is."

The youngster sped off and returned in a few seconds to report, "Coach, it's twenty minutes after four."

The Cadillac

Steve Wadiak never played high school football. The school he attended in Chicago didn't field a football team, so Wadiak competed on the wrestling team and played baseball.

Wadiak played a season of service football while in the navy and joined a Chicago sandlot team after being discharged.

Chicago Bears guard Bill Milner played two seasons at South Carolina (1941-42) before entering the military and then completed his collegiate career at Duke University. Milner spotted a sandlot game in progress one day and stopped to watch. He was impressed with the performance of a 19-year-old halfback and was surprised to learn the youngster was interested in playing college football.

Milner contacted Gamecock coach Rex Enright, and Wadiak enrolled at South Carolina in January 1948. Freshmen were eligible for the varsity due to the Korean War, and Wadiak rushed for 420 yards his rookie season. His nickname quickly became "The Cadillac."

The 998 yards Wadiak gained in 1950, his junior season, remained a school record until Kevin Long and Clarence Williams topped 1,000 yards in 1975.

In four years at South Carolina, Wadiak set a career rushing record—broken nearly 30 years later by Heisman Trophy winner George Rogers—of 2,878 yards. His freshman-season average of 8.2 yards per carry was still a school record in 2000, and Wadiak's 5.3 yards per career rush ranked among the top 10. His average of 79.9 rushing yards per game was third on the all-time list.

In 1950 Clemson brought to Columbia an undefeated, untied team that hadn't given up a point. The Tigers had to come from behind for a 14-14 tie after Wadiak had rushed for 256 yards in only 18 attempts. That record stood for 23 years, until Jeff Grantz rushed for 260 yards against Ohio University in 1973. Wadiak's one-game total is still third best in Gamecock history. Brandon Bennett rushed for 278 yards against East Tennessee State in 1991.

When Wadiak was drafted by the Pittsburgh Steelers after his senior season, the Canadian Football League was in a bidding war with the National Football League. Former Wake Forest coach Douglas "Pea Head" Walker was the coach at Toronto and made a strong effort to sign Wadiak.

Wadiak was within a few days of deciding between the NFL and the CFL when he was killed in a traffic accident early in 1952.

His No. 37 became the first jersey number in any sport to be retired by the University of South Carolina.

Take the Wind

The South Carolina football team upset West Virginia 20-14 at Morgantown in 1953 to deny the Mountaineers an undefeated regular season.

When West Virginia came to Columbia for the second game of the 1954 season, Gamecock coach Rex Enright knew the Mountaineers would be bent on revenge, and it would be important for South Carolina to get off to a good start.

A stiff wind was blowing at game time, so Enright told Captain Harry Lovell, "If we win the toss, take the wind. That means they will probably kick off to us."

He shouldn't have added the sentence that mentioned "kick off."

South Carolina won the toss and a confused Lovell blurted, "We'll kick off." The West Virginia captain said, "We'll take the wind."

South Carolina kicked off into the wind. West Virginia had opening field position near midfield and turned that advantage into a 26-6 victory.

The Option

The week before losing to West Virginia at Columbia in 1954, South Carolina opened its season at West Point, N.Y., against an Army team that was coming off a 7-1-1 season in 1953 and was generally regarded as the best team in the East. The Cadets were ranked anywhere from eighth to 23rd in four national polls.

Army had lost its home opener just three times in 64 seasons, and its overall record in Michie Stadium was 130-11. South Carolina was a substantial underdog.

South Carolina scored first, but soon trailed 14-7. Sophomore quarterback Mackie Prickett entered his first collegiate varsity game with the Gamecocks at their own 4-yard line. He engineered several first downs, but the Gamecocks eventually faced a fourth-and-1- while still in their own territory.

The limited substitution rules of the day precluded sending in a specialist, so the coaching staff signaled from the sidelines for a punt. Instead, Prickett broke the huddle in a running formation and ran the option play for a first down while Enright nearly had a heart attack. Prickett continued the 96-yard drive that tied the score at 14 at halftime.

South Carolina dominated the second half, rolling up 446 rushing yards, to pull a major upset, 34-20.

Sophomore halfback Mike Caskey wore a plastic mask attached to his helmet to protect a broken nose and crushed cheekbone suffered in an earlier injury. In a sidebar, United Press International writer Oscar Fraley called Caskey "The Masked Marvel."

Stanley Woodward, a nationally syndicated columnist, raved over the blocking of Gamecock fullback Bill Wohrman, saying "This character did not merely screen the Army backs, he dynamited them."

Both Prickett and Wohrman are members of the University of South Carolina Athletic Hall of Fame.

Downfield

South Carolina led Clemson 13-8 late in the fourth quarter of the Big Thursday game of 1954, but the Tigers were driving toward a possible winning touchdown.

A pass was completed to halfback Joe Paglei, but official Ray Moore threw a flag. He said Paglei had gone out of bounds, making him an ineligible receiver, and had come back in bounds to catch the football.

On the next play, Clemson completed a long pass to the South Carolina 10-yard line. Again, Ray Moore threw a flag. He said Clemson lineman Dick DeSimone was illegally downfield. The drive was halted, and South Carolina took over with less than a minute remaining in the game. Quarterback Mackie Prickett turned that minute into an eternity for Coach Rex Enright.

Enright sent a reserve lineman into the game with these instructions: "Tell Mackie to use swing pass blocking but run the football and stay in bounds" to keep the clock running.

The messenger confused the instructions and told Prickett, "Coach said to throw the swing pass."

Prickett rolled out to the right and completed a 12-yard pass to Carl Brazell for a first down as time expired. Enright breathed a sigh of relief.

Clemson coach Frank Howard told official Ray Moore as he left the field, "Buddy, you better be right when I look at the film."

Van Newman, sports editor of the *Columbia Record*, obtained the game film and had one frame that showed DeSimone clearly downfield. The photo was blown up and published in the Monday-afternoon newspaper.

After studying Clemson's game film, Howard telephoned Moore and said, "Buddy, you were right on both calls."

Ray Moore lived in Columbia. His profession: Salesman of BC headache remedies.

Minute Forty-Five

South Carolina was scheduled to play Virginia November 1, 1952, at Foreman Field in Norfolk in the annual Shriner-sponsored Oyster Bowl football game.

Coach Art Guepe had his finest team at Virginia, and the Cavaliers had lost only to Duke while South Carolina had a 3-2 record. The Cavaliers were heavy favorites.

I was South Carolina bureau manager for United Press at the time and normally covered home games of South Carolina or Clemson. Both were on the road and out of state this particular weekend, so I planned a trip to Norfolk as a spectator. However, the Richmond UP bureau learned I was coming and asked me to cover the game. I hitched a ride to Virginia with Don Barton, the South Carolina sports information director.

For three-and-a-half quarters, the game went as predicted, with Virginia holding a 14-0 lead, and South Carolina unable to generate much offense.

Shelley Rolfe, a Richmond sportswriter, commented, "If South Carolina had the ball with first down on the 2-yard line, do you think they could score?"

South Carolina coach Rex Enright sent his second-team quarterback, Dick Balka, into the game. A transfer from Notre Dame, Balka threw two incomplete passes before hitting Lockhart McLendon for a 28-yard gain. Next came a 17-yard completion to Walt Shea, followed by a 25-yard touchdown pass to Clyde Bennett. The extra point cut Virginia's lead to 14-7.

Virginia fumbled the kickoff and Bob Korn recovered for South Carolina at the Cavalier 6-yard line. On the second play, freshman halfback Mike Caskey scored, and the point after tied the game. Caskey was eligible due to a rule allowing freshmen to play on varsity teams due to the Korean War.

A clipping penalty against Virginia on the kickoff backed the Cavaliers up to their 6-yard line. On the next play, quarterback Charlie Harding was hit by Gamecock tackle Gene Witt and fumbled. The ball rolled into the end zone, and South Carolina guard Bob King recovered it for a touchdown.

Three touchdowns in one minute and 45 seconds. Final score: South Carolina 21, Virginia 14.

Don Barton went over to Shelley Rolfe and asked, "Does that answer your question?"

Ballots collected at the end of the third quarter had chosen Virginia end Tom Scott as the game's MVP. South Carolina's whirlwind comeback dictated a revote, and Dick Balka was announced as the game's MVP.

After filing our stories, Don Barton, Jake Penland, sports editor of *The State*, *Columbia Record* sports editor Van Newman; broadcaster Bob Fulton; and I were walking to Barton's car when we passed a group of unhappy Virginia fans.

We overheard one of them say, "I never did like that Guepe. They should fire his ass."

Virginia won the remainder of its games to finish with an 8-2 record, and Art Guepe left to become head coach at Vanderbilt.

The South Carolina team was traveling back to Columbia by train, and we stopped by the railroad station before heading back to South Carolina in Barton's car.

Rex Enright was in a jovial mood after the big victory and insisted that Barton take the media group to Washington to see the Redskins play the Pittsburgh Steelers the following day, so we set out for the nation's capital.

While passing through Portsmouth, Barton was stopped by a motorcycle policeman for driving 18 miles an hour in a 15-mile zone. He was let go with a warning.

In northern Virginia, shortly before we reached the District of Columbia, a Virginia highway patrolman turned on his blue light. As the officer approached the car, Barton handed him his driver's license before he was asked to by the patrolman.

"I see you have been stopped before," the officer commented.

"Everybody knows to show a driver's license when stopped," Barton retorted. We could envision the five of us spending the night in jail.

Barton was let off with another warning, however, and we saw the Steelers beat the Redskins on Sunday before traveling all night and arriving in Columbia just in time to report for work on Monday.

Cloud of Dust

Warren Giese had only one losing season in five years (1956-60) as head football coach at the University of South Carolina. He used an ultraconservative ball-control offense that seldom employed the forward pass.

He explained that when you throw the football, three things can happen, and two of them are bad: The pass could be completed, but it could be also be incomplete, or, worse yet, intercepted.

During his tenure, the leading receiver at South Carolina never caught more than 12 passes in a season. Julius Derrick led the team with six receptions in 1957, and Jimmy Hunter caught nine in 1959. Alex Hawkins, a halfback, was the team's leading passer in 1957 when he completed 9 of 12 attempts.

The halfbacks, Hawkins and King Dixon, threw more passes than the quarterbacks. They usually threw to each other—Dixon to Hawkins or Hawkins to Dixon.

Giese believed it was better to take 10 minutes off the clock by driving 80 yards in 20 plays than by completing an 80-yard pass, because "the other team can't score if it doesn't have the football."

His offense was referred to as "four yards and a cloud of dust." The only problem with his philosophy was that one broken play, penalty, or other mistake would upset the four-yards-per-play schedule.

A 32-year-old assistant coach at the University of Maryland when he replaced the retired Rex Enright at South Carolina before the 1956 season, Giese wasn't expected to win many games his first year. He was a native of Milwaukee, Wisconsin, and at the time the youngest NCAA Division I head football coach in the nation.

When Duke came to Columbia for the second game of the Giese era, South Carolina hadn't defeated the Blue Devils in 26 years, since a 20-0 win in 1930. There was a scoreless tie in 1947.

Duke's quarterback was Sonny Jurgensen, who would become a National Football League all-star with the Washington Redskins.

The South Carolina defense, helped out by its ball-control offense that squeezed out one touchdown, shut out Duke 7-0. The Gamecocks went on to compile a 7-3 record. University trustees became so excited they tore up Giese's contract and made him a tenured professor.

Giese studied NCAA statistics and often used them to defend his conservative philosophy in debates with reporters during his weekly media luncheons. Football was still a run-oriented game, and most of the top 10 teams in passing statistics had losing records. Also, the rules limited substitution.

Limited substitution required players to play both offense and defense and made it difficult to use kicking specialists. When the two-point conversion rule was adopted in 1958, Giese had figures to show that two-pointers would be successful 40 percent of the time, while traditional PAT kicks succeeded 65 percent of the time. He argued that more could be gained by going for two, so he never again attempted a placekick.

His philosophy also effectively eliminated the field goal for the Gamecocks, because there was no experienced placekicker to convert three points when needed. During the five years Giese was head coach, he never attempted a field goal.

South Carolina's records for two-point conversions, set during the Giese era, may never be broken. Quarterback David Sowell and fullback Phil Lavoie each made three two-pointers against Virginia in 1959. Halfback Alex Hawkins scored six two-pointers during the 1958 season, and Lavoie tied that record in 1959. The Gamecocks scored four two-pointers against Virginia in 1959 and 13 for the season.

Giese's records after the 7-3 1956 campaign were 5-5, 7-3, and 6-4, including two more wins over Duke; the only defeat inflicted on Georgia's 1959 Orange Bowl team, 30-14; and a 27-21 upset of a Texas team that went to the Sugar Bowl.

Fans became bored with the grind-it-out style of play, and Giese only defeated arch rival Clemson once in five tries, 26-6, in 1958. When he had his first losing season, 3-6-1 in 1960, Giese was replaced by Marvin Bass. Bass was a former Giese assistant who had left for a year to join the staff of Coach Bobby Dodd at Georgia Tech.

Giese had taken on the dual role of director of athletics following the death of Rex Enright in 1960. After being relieved of his coaching duties, he remained in the role of AD for another year before becoming a full-time professor and head of the University of South Carolina Department of Physical Education in 1962.

He also earned his doctorate from Florida State University.

While ultraconservative with his game strategy, Giese was an innovator when it came to using electronic gadgetry in an effort to gain an edge. He had his quarterbacks sleep with a "Dormaphone" under their pillows. That gadget was a type of tape player that softly recited the plays and game plan for the quarterback to absorb as he slept.

A television set enclosed in a sideline tent was connected by cable to a camera at press-box level so the players and coaches on the sideline could have a high-level view in analyzing the action on the field. Giese's closed-circuit TV was the forerunner of other innovations such as the use of Polaroid photographs of formations, play diagrams sent by fax to the sidelines, etc. The NCAA has outlawed most of such gimmicks as unfair advantages.

Giese ran for public office as a Republican and served as a state senator for many years in South Carolina.

Warren Giese held closed practices that barred all outsiders, including the news media. Jake Penland, veteran sports editor of *The State*, Columbia's morning newspaper, who had had free run of the practice field under Coach Rex Enright, was ejected from Giese's first practice session.

Penland continued to cover the South Carolina games, but always sent an assistant to the face-to-face interviews and frequently attacked the coach in his columns. Penland taped a photograph of Giese to his toilet bowl at home.

Giese used Capital City Park, the Columbia minor league baseball venue, as a practice site before the Clemson game because the high wooden fence afforded more security than the practice fields at the Rex Enright Athletic Center. He noticed some movement inside the baseball scoreboard and sent security guards to check it out.

They burst in on a couple involved in a lover's tryst.

After shutting out Warren Giese's South Carolina teams 7-0 in 1956 and 13-0 in 1957, Clemson coach Frank Howard told the news media, "If ole Geezie ever scores on me, I'll tip my hat to him."

After South Carolina scored four touchdowns in its 26-6 victory over Clemson in 1958, Howard opened his postgame press conference by saying, "My head sure got sunburned today."

Accidental Touchdown

King Dixon had an accident on the way to a touchdown with the opening kickoff against the University of Texas.

The little halfback came down with a virus the night before the 1957 night game in Austin. Dixon had diarrhea throughout the day, and there was doubt that he would be able to play. Still, he lined up to receive the opening kickoff.

Dixon caught the football at the 2-yard line and eluded tacklers to midfield. Teammate Alex Hawkins blocked the final defender, and when Dixon cut to go around the block, he had an accident. He crossed the goal line to complete a 98-yard return, dropped the football, and sped to the locker room for a change of uniform.

He returned to team with Hawkins in leading a fourth-quarter comeback from a 21-7 deficit to a 27-21 victory over a Longhorn team that wound up in the Sugar Bowl.

Dixon served 22 years in the U.S. Marine Corps and was named the top service football player in the world while playing for the Quantico team. He coached several Marine teams, had a tour in Vietnam, and retired as a colonel.

He was the University of South Carolina's director of athletics for six years (1987-92). Dixon retired to his hometown of Laurens, S.C., but soon went back to work at the bank where he was employed before joining the University of South Carolina staff.

Dixon is in both the South Carolina Athletic Hall of Fame and the University of South Carolina Athletic Hall of Fame.

Hawk & the King

Alex Hawkins and King Dixon were the top two stars of South Carolina football teams from 1956 through 1958 under Coach Warren Giese. Both were recruited by Rex Enright but played on the freshman team the last year that Enright was varsity head coach.

Dixon was an honor student, a Phi Beta Kappa, active in the Fellowship of Christian Athletes, and a campus leader. He married his high school sweetheart, Augusta Mason, to form a new "Mason-Dixon Line." Augusta also was elected to Phi Beta Kappa. Dixon was elected vice president of the freshman, sophomore, and junior classes. He won the Algernon Sydney Sullivan Award as the university's most outstanding student.

Hawkins was the direct opposite. Yet, on the football field they were a winning combination and remained friends after completing their college eligibility. Hawkins and Dixon were the original odd couple.

While Dixon pursued a military career, Hawkins played ten seasons in the National Football League. Drafted by the Green Bay Packers, the first player chosen in the second round and 13th overall, he was traded to the Baltimore Colts, where he played eight seasons before going to the Atlanta Falcons in the expansion draft. After one season in Atlanta, Hawkins returned to the Colts for his final season.

He served several seasons as a CBS-TV analyst during NFL telecasts and later wrote two autobiographical books about his misadventures. The title of his first volume, covering his high school days at South Charleston, West Virginia, his years at the University of South Carolina, and his career in the NFL, was entitled *My Story and I'm Sticking to It.*

The second book, about adjusting to life after football, was titled, *Then Came Brain Damage.*

The first title was based on an incident that Hawkins said occurred between NFL seasons when he came back to Columbia to complete his degree requirements. He came home about 7 a.m., after a night on the town and was greeted at the front door by his wife, Libby, a former campus beauty queen from the little South Carolina town of Manning.

Alex Hawkins (USC Sports Information)

His excuse was that he actually came home early but had forgotten his keys and didn't want to awaken Libby, so he slept in a hammock strung between two trees in the yard.

His wife replied that the hammock had been taken down weeks earlier, to which Alex retorted, "Well, that's my story and I'm sticking to it."

Hawkins recounted his first meeting with Dixon when both enrolled as freshmen at South Carolina.

"He was short, stocky, bowlegged, and his hair was cut short in a military fashion. He was positively charming, and the minute we shook hands, I liked him."

As for himself, Hawkins said, "I was a C student because I did not consider it fair to cheat and make A's." He said he was a coach's nightmare, except on game days, when he became a coach's dream.

It was said that Hawkins never had a good practice and never had a bad game. King Dixon's assessment of Hawkins in clutch situations was: "When the Hawk got mad, the other people got sad."

After his senior season, Hawkins was named to the Paul Williamson All-America team, third-team All-America by the Associated Press, and All-Atlantic Coast Conference and Player of the Year in the ACC.

Following his NFL career, Hawkins settled in Atlanta, where he was involved in several business ventures, most with limited success. He claimed he received a $200,000 check when he and a partner sold their garbage collection business. Hawkins said he deposited the money in his checking account and spent it all within a year.

In the late 1990s, he returned to South Carolina, where he lives in the little town of Denmark.

Baltimore Colts coach Don Shula was the first in the NFL to employ three captains. Johnny Unitas was the offensive captain, Gino Marchetti the defensive captain, and Alex Hawkins the captain of the special teams. The first time the trio went to midfield for the coin toss and the referee introduced Captain Hawkins, the opposing captain asked, "Captain who?"

Alex was called "Captain Who" for the remainder of his NFL career.

Hawkins is in the South Carolina Athletic Hall of Fame and the University of South Carolina Athletic Hall of Fame.

Dixon is also in both Halls of Fame. He retired from the Marine Corps as a Lieutenant Colonel and was vice president of a bank in his hometown of Laurens before becoming alumni director at the University of South Carolina. He became athletics director in 1987 and served in that capacity for six years. He retired to Laurens but soon went back to work for the bank.

In his book *They Wore Garnet and Black*, Don Barton had this to say about the Hawk:

"If Alex Hawkins had lived in 18th century America, he would have been host at the Boston Tea Party. As an ancient Greek he would have remained with Leonidis at Thermopylae. In the War for Texas Independence he would have volunteered for Alamo duty.

"His motivation wouldn't necessarily be patriotism. It's just that Alex Hawkins loves a confrontation about as much as Dale Carnegie liked making friends."

Memoirs from the Pitts

Ed Pitts was a two-way tackle for the University of South Carolina from 1957 to 1959, and as a senior, was named to some All-America teams and All-Atlantic Coast Conference teams. He was a cocaptain in 1959 with fullback John Saunders.

When Alex Hawkins was drafted by the Green Bay Packers after the 1958 season, Pitts recalled, Hawkins took his bonus check to a bank and asked for all the money in one-dollar bills, which he placed in the trunk of an old Plymouth that he co-owned with teammate Jake Bodkin.

Pitts said Alex stopped at a service station, told the attendant, "Fill 'er up," opened the trunk, and said, "Just reach in and grab yourself a handful."

South Carolina opened the 1958 season with an 8-0 home win over Duke, but had to travel to West Point, N.Y., the following week, where Col. Earl Blaik, the Army coach, introduced the lonesome end. South Carolina was not prepared for this unheard- of formation that kept an end split wide on every play—an end who never joined the huddle.

The lonesome end kept catching passes and the score kept mounting until Army had piled up a 45-8 victory.

Late in the game, someone said in the huddle, "Let John run it," but Saunders replied, "John don't want the ball." Then someone said, "Give the ball to Hawk," and Hawkins replied, "Hawk don't want the ball, either," Pitts remembered.

As Army kept scoring touchdowns, Coach Warren Giese asked assistant Marvin Bass, "What are they doing?"

"They're beating the hell out of us," Bass answered.

Pitts also recalled that Jack Lindsey was an ACC referee who was an insurance executive in Greenville.

In one game, said Pitts, Lindsey remarked to the Gamecock offense, "Okay, guys, its fourth-and-1. Let's go."

Uncovering a pileup after a fumble in a game against Virginia, Lindsey once indicated South Carolina had recovered and said, according to Ed Pitts, "Our ball."

Lindsey later became insurance commissioner for the state of South Carolina.

Boo

George Rogers's nickname was "Boo," and he became the No. 1 hero in the football history of the University of South Carolina. His charismatic smile and friendly nature, coupled with tremendous ability, endeared him to all Gamecock fans.

Heavily recruited out of Georgia's Duluth High School near Atlanta, Rogers almost signed with the University of Tennessee before casting his lot with Coach Jim Carlen at the University of South Carolina.

In 46 games (1977-80), including two bowl games (1979 Hall of Fame Bowl, 1980 Gator Bowl), Rogers rushed for 100 or more yards 27 times, including the final 22 games of his career.

Prior to George Rogers, only two South Carolina backs had rushed for more than 1,000 yards in a season, and both accomplished the feat during the 1975 season. Kevin Long compiled 1,133 yards and Clarence Williams had 1,073. Rogers topped the 1,000-yard plateau three times.

After gaining "only" 623 yards his freshman season, Rogers finished with 1,006 yards in 1978, 1,681 in 1979, and 1,894 in 1980. His 5,204 total yards far exceed the 3,055 yards compiled by runner-up Brandon Bennett (1991-94) and the 3,005 by third- place Harold Green (1986-89).

Rogers's 1979 yardage was second to Heisman Trophy winner Charles White of Southern California, and Rogers was named to five All-America teams, including first team by The Associated Press and second team by four other organizations. Despite these numbers, he placed seventh in the Heisman voting and was considered a long shot for the award going into his senior season.

The next year, Rogers led the nation in rushing yardage, was a unanimous first-team choice on every All-America team announced, and won the Heisman Trophy in a landslide. He was the first player selected (by the New Orleans Saints) in the 1981 NFL draft.

His No. 38 was retired in a ceremony before his final home game, a 39-38 win over Wake Forest, making Rogers the first University of South Carolina athlete to have his number retired before he ended his playing career. He played on the road at Clemson and in the Gator Bowl against Pittsburgh after the retirement ceremony.

George Rogers (USC Sports Information)

Rogers led the NFL in rushing with 1,674 yards and was named Rookie of the Year in 1981. He played four years with the Saints and three seasons with the Washington Redskins, including a Super Bowl championship season in 1987. He rushed for more than 1,000 yards in four of his seven NFL seasons.

Involvement with drugs shortened Rogers's professional football career, but he beat the problem and became a goodwill ambassador for his alma mater. He has been involved in numerous charitable efforts, including "the George Rogers Foundation," and sponsors an annual charity golf tournament that is attended by many of his NFL acquaintances.

Rogers, a charter member of the New Orleans Saints Hall of Fame, was inducted into the University of South Carolina Athletic Hall of Fame in 1987 and is a member of the State of South Carolina Hall of Fame.

Rogers celebrated his 39th birthday December 8, 1997. Four days later, several hundred friends and admirers—including fellow Heisman Trophy winners Johnny Rodgers of Nebraska and Billy Sims of Oklahoma—gathered in The Zone at Williams-Brice Stadium for the George Rogers Roast, a fund-raiser for the George

Rogers Foundation, which awards scholarships to deserving students based on academics and essays on challenges in their lives.

The following day, Rodgers was inducted into the National Football Foundation's College Hall of Fame at the Waldorf-Astoria in New York City.

In introducing the new Hall of Fame members ACC commissioner Gene Corrigan made one error. Corrigan said Rogers rushed for more than 100 yards 22 times in his Gamecock career. Actually, George gained more than 100 yards 27 times, including 22 consecutive games over the century mark.

The street between the north end of Williams-Brice Stadium and the South Carolina State Fairgrounds was renamed George Rogers Boulevard.

As a goodwill ambassador—and since 1997 a Hall of Fame member—he has accompanied the University of South Carolina official party to the National Football Foundation Hall of Fame ceremony each December. Traditionally, the group dines the night before at Smith and Wollensky, a well-known Manhattan steak house.

Since George's first visit, the maitre d' at Smith and Wollensky has remembered George and greets him on his once- a-year visit with: "George, how 'ya been? Haven't seen you since last year."

On one occasion a waiter brought a cell phone to the table and told George to answer it when it rang. The call was from a group of Cincinnati businessmen at a table across the room. They wanted to talk to a Heisman Trophy winner. The way to get a table at Smith and Wollensky without a long wait is to make the reservation in the name of George Rogers.

If you accompany George Rogers to the Downtown Athletic Club—sponsor of the Heisman Trophy—you will receive a royal welcome.

The first time Rogers accompanied the University of South Carolina group to New York for the National Football Foundation Hall of Fame banquet, we were at Columbia Metropolitan Airport, when Harold White remembered he had forgotten to pack his tuxedo.

"I didn't know we needed a tuxedo," George said.

Harold called home and I called a Columbia formal wear rental store and gave the store George's measurements. Early the next morning, two Federal Express packages containing two tuxedos, were delivered to the Waldorf-Astoria Hotel.

When Herschel Nissenson was AP sports editor, he met George Rogers on a 1980 preseason ABC-TV promotional tour of prominent college football players. Later in the season, Nissenson was in Columbia to cover the future Heisman Trophy winner and a South Carolina game.

Coach Jim Carlen, by way of introduction, asked Rogers, "You remember Herschel?"

"Sure," Rogers replied. "Aren't you that Herschel Walker guy?"

Herschel Walker was the University of Georgia freshman back who would win the Heisman two years later.

George was a laid-back superstar. He never showed any nervousness going into a tough game, and his humbleness stood out after every outstanding performance. Radio broadcaster Bob Fulton recalled two prime examples.

Fulton said he glanced over to the seat occupied by Rogers on a hotel to stadium bus trip and noticed that George was sound asleep; just catching a little nap before game time. After rushing for 152 yards at Georgia in 1979, Rogers asked Fulton, "Do you think I played all right today?"

Before George began his senior season in 1980 his mother obtained an automobile and had a friend follow her from the Rogers home in Duluth, Georgia, to meet George at Greenville. George and his roommate, Robert Perlotte, were tied up with practice, meetings, etc., until late in the evening.

Without clearing the trip with Coach Jim Carlen, they slipped out of the dorm at midnight, planning to be back in Columbia in time for morning classes.

They met George's mom halfway between Duluth and Columbia to pick up the car. About 6 a.m., near the Newberry exit on I-26, George fell asleep and the car was totaled as it rolled over several times.

The All-America tailback wasn't injured and enjoyed a Heisman Trophy senior year.

Oyster Caper

Mort Persky was my shadow on the staff of *The Gamecock*, the student newspaper at the University of South Carolina. He insists he was my protégé. His given name was Mordecai, but he quickly shortened it to Mort.

When I was sports editor, Mort was my reporter. When I was managing editor, Mort was sports editor. When I was editor in chief, Mort was managing editor. When I was editor emeritus and columnist, Mort was editor in chief.

In 1950, Mort accompanied me to Charleston for the South Carolina football game against The Citadel. The Citadel hadn't defeated the Gamecocks since 1926. The rivals had played 16 times during the 25-year period, and the closest the Bulldogs had come was a scoreless tie in 1928.

We planned a postgame oyster roast at my parents' home, Hart's Bluff Plantation on Wadmalaw Island, 20 miles from Charleston, to celebrate another Gamecock victory.

A Citadel linebacker named Sam Rubino blocked two punts, and his teammate Paul Drews, brother of my former roommate, Rupie Drews, caught a touchdown pass on the old sleeper play as The Citadel claimed a 19-7 upset.

There wasn't much joy at the postgame party, but Mort Persky was introduced to roasted oysters.

Forty years passed before The Citadel defeated South Carolina again in football, a 38-35 upset at Williams-Brice Stadium in Columbia in 1990.

After graduation, Persky enjoyed a long journalistic career. He started as sportswriter in Augusta, Georgia, and Atlanta. Then came editorial jobs at the *Miami Herald* and the *New York Herald -Tribune.* He was assistant managing editor of the *Detroit Free Press;* assistant executive editor of the *Philadelphia Inquirer;* editor in chief at *Family Weekly;* editorial director for new publications at *Playboy,* and for 11 years, until retirement, an editor with *Newsday* in New York City.

A few days after The Citadel win in 1990, I received a greeting card from Persky with a note that said, "It's my turn to buy the oysters."

A wholesale seafood distributor in Columbia called and said two 40-pound boxes of oysters ready for pickup.

I cleaned out everything else from the refrigerator, and my family ate oysters on the half shell and oven-roasted oysters every day for the next two weeks.

Mort Persky was from Aiken, where his father, who had immigrated from Byelorussia (now called Belarus), owned a dry-goods store and was a civic leader. As a college freshman, Mort didn't look to be a day older than 15.

Fifty years later, as a retired journalist, he lives in Manhattan. We get together for breakfast every time I visit the Big Apple.

Mort's daughter, Lisa Jane Persky, made her screen debut as the teenaged daughter in *The Great Santini*, a movie based on the autobiographical novel by Pat Conroy, an alumnus of The Citadel. The movie was filmed at Beaufort, S. C.

Lisa Jane has since appeared in many films and television series.

The Old Nipper

Weems Baskin, Jr., was a national champion hurdler at Auburn in 1927 and coached track and field at Mississippi and Georgia before becoming the head track coach at the University of South Carolina in 1948.

As an athlete, Weemie competed in a number of venues, including Madison Square Garden in New York City, and picked up spending money by writing a track column that was syndicated in several newspapers.

An injury prevented Baskin from qualifying for the 1928 Olympic games in Amsterdam, but he traveled to Holland and delighted in telling the story of how he gained admission to the track and field venue without a ticket.

He said he fell in with the entourage of the king and queen of Holland and marched unchallenged into the venue.

As a coach, Weemie was a stickler for punctuality. His slogan was, "Be late, be left."

In the early 1960s, the sports information operation at the University of South Carolina was a one-man shop, and it was seldom that I was able to accompany teams other than the football or basketball squad on the road. There was one occasion, however, when I was able to get away for a bus trip with the track team for a dual meet at the University of North Carolina.

We were scheduled to depart from the Russell House student union at 8 a.m. Three athletes were not there at the appointed time. Weemie gave them two minutes, and at 8:02 told bus driver Marty "Peanut" Hooper, "Let's go."

About 10 miles north of Columbia on U.S. Highway 1, a small imported car, its horn sounding, overtook the bus. One of the athletes said, "That's Billy Nies' girlfriend's car."

"Peanut. Stop the bus and pick him up," Weemie said.

As a sheepish Billy Nies—the track team's discus and shot-put entrant and a football tight end—boarded the bus, Weemie's only comment was, "Good morning."

The team was scheduled to stop at the restaurant at Ingram's Motel in Cheraw about 10 a.m. for a prearranged premeet meal. As we filed into the restaurant, an automobile bearing sprinters Dean Fowble and Dick Melton arrived. Weemie's only comment was, "Good morning."

Since they had driven about 80 miles of the 200-mile trip to Chapel Hill, the two sprinters asked if they could continue in the automobile. Weemie's reply was, "That car will be here when we come back tonight."

Nies won the discus and placed third in the shot put that afternoon. The competition then moved to the final event, the mile relay, the result of which would decide the winner of the meet.

The two tardy sprinters comprised half of the four-man relay team that won the event, and the Gamecock track team came home a winner.

When Weems Baskin was an assistant football coach and track coach at the University of Georgia, he was left to supervise a bus trip that took the Bulldog football team to Atlanta for a game with Georgia Tech, while head coach Harry Mehre traveled in advance to make it in time for a speaking engagement.

According to the story, Georgia's star back was late and was left by the punctual Baskin. The athlete hitchhiked to Atlanta and played in the game.

Weems Baskin served as assistant football coach under head coaches Rex Enright, Warren Giese, and Marvin Bass, in addition to coaching South Carolina's track team, and was perhaps the best recruiter of talent on the staff. The State of Georgia was his recruiting territory, and a few of the athletes he had a hand in recruiting from that state included Billy Gambrell, Dan Reeves, and Bobby Bryant.

Gambrell, after his collegiate career, played seven years in the NFL with the St. Louis Cardinals and the Detroit Lions and also saw action in the Canadian Football League. Reeves played seven years with the Dallas Cowboys and was head coach of the Denver Broncos, New York Giants, and Atlanta Falcons. Bryant played 14 seasons with the Minnesota Vikings and was a member of four Super Bowl teams.

Once, when the Gamecock track team was scheduled to compete in the ACC indoor meet, Baskin's long jumper was shelved by an injury. Baskin asked Billy Gambrell to accompany the team to

Weems Baskin,
The Old Nipper
(USC Sports
Information)

North Carolina and compete in the event, even though the little halfback hadn't worked out with the track team all season. Billy went along and won the event.

When Baskin recruited Bobby Bryant for the South Carolina football squad, he hoped Bryant would join the track team in the spring as a sprinter or a hurdler. Bryant, however, opted for baseball as a left-handed pitcher and was the first Gamecock to strike out 100 batters in a season. Bryant was twice selected in the baseball draft, by the Boston Red Sox and the New York Yankees, but opted for the Vikings and the NFL.

Weems Baskin III, son of the old track coach, played football at South Carolina (1956-58), earning three letters as an end under head coach Warren Giese.

When Paul Dietzel became director of athletics at the University of South Carolina in 1966, one of his first acts was to name the track and field facility the Weems Baskin Track.

South Carolina once had a law requiring liquor stores to close at sunset. Each store displayed a red ball—imitating the sun—and was commonly referred to as a "red dot" store.

Weems Baskin was fond of a little libation each evening. Retired groundskeeper Sarge Frye said that while running track and field practice, "Weemie spent a lot of time watching the sun so he could get to that red dot store before it closed."

Members of the track team nicknamed their coach "The Old Nipper."

Baskin dabbled in several outside businesses to supplement his coaching salary. Pig farming was one of his sidelines. Sarge said Weemie once asked him to inspect his herd of pigs.

"He had this big old Chrysler, about a block long," Sarge recalled. "He said, 'Come with me' and lit this big, long cigar. It was about a $2 cigar, but he pulled up to this gas station and told the attendant 'give me a dollar's worth.'" Gasoline was about 20 cents a gallon in those days.

According to Sarge, Weemie was recruiting a high school football player named W. L. Strickland whom a number of other schools were after.

"He got Strickland in that big old Chrysler and drove him around all night" to keep him away from the competition. Strickland played linebacker at South Carolina (1957-59) under Warren Giese and later served as an assistant coach under Marvin Bass.

A Knight to Remember

Coach Bob Knight brought his Indiana University basketball team to Columbia in December of 1972 to do battle with Coach Frank McGuire and the University of South Carolina Gamecocks.

Indiana sported a 5-0 record and was ranked ninth nationally. The Hoosiers had a two-sport superstar freshman in Quinn Buckner. He had been a starting safety on the Indiana football team and was averaging 11.6 points per game for the basketball team.

South Carolina's record was 4-2, and the Gamecocks had a budding superstar of their own in 6-8 Alex English, who had averaged 13.5 points and 9.5 rebounds through his first six collegiate games. The Gamecocks also had Kevin Joyce, a 6-3 guard just back from Munich, where he had competed for the U.S. Olympic team. Joyce was averaging 17 points a game and had 27 assists in six games.

Brian Winters was a future NBA star who was averaging 11.5 points for the Gamecocks despite being weakened by a bout with mononucleosis. South Carolina also had Mike Dunleavy, a guard who would move on to the NBA and eventually serve as head coach of the Los Angeles Lakers, Milwaukee Bucks, and Portland Trailblazers.

Joyce scored 14 of South Carolina's final 16 first-half points to keep the Gamecocks within striking distance, but Knight's Hoosiers led McGuire's Gamecocks 40-30 at halftime.

Indiana's lead expanded to 16 points with 16 minutes remaining in the game; that's when Joyce took charge of the situation. He made seven consecutive outside jump shots, and for the night made 18 of 32 field-goal attempts. He made 12 of 19 from the floor in the second half and played the entire 40 minutes.

Joyce scored 41 points, 26 of them in the second half. He also controlled a jump ball in the closing seconds to lead South Carolina to an 88-85 victory. Frank McGuire walked into the media interview room after the game and asked: "What would we do without Kevin Joyce?"

Bob Knight, traveling in an Indiana University-owned airplane, flew back to Bloomington and, according to reports from Indiana, kicked in a glass door at the airport terminal.

Flick

Frank McGuire recruited most of his star basketball talent from his native New York, but he found a superstar in the University of South Carolina's backyard. Alex English was born and reared in Columbia and graduated from Dreher High School.

Possibly the most graceful player ever at South Carolina, English was as smooth as a ballet dancer on the basketball court. His nickname was "Flick."

The two finalists in the recruiting battle for his basketball talents were South Carolina and Duke. The winner was South Carolina. English would start 111 consecutive games for the Gamecocks and finish his career with 1,972 points, a school record at the time. He also grabbed 1,064 rebounds.

As a freshman, English accompanied the Gamecocks to New York City in December 1972 to compete in the Holiday Festival at Madison Square Garden. In his eighth collegiate game, he scored 27 points and pulled down 13 rebounds to lead the Gamecocks to an 80-64 win over Villanova.

In a postgame interview, the New York media asked English if he were awed by Madison Square Garden.

"Carolina Coliseum is a nicer place to play," English replied. "It's much nicer than this."

The next question asked why a black youth would choose to remain in the south, rather than leave the area, since he was a heavily recruited prospect.

"Because Columbia is my home, and it's a nice place with nice people," English answered calmly.

Nearly 25 years later, September 27, 1997, Alex English stood before 200 fans, friends, relatives, and admirers and echoed those words. The occasion was the Alex English Basketball Hall of Fame Dinner and Roast to honor the Columbian nine days before he was inducted into the National Basketball Hall of Fame in Springfield, Massachusetts.

"I have been all over the world—to Africa, Europe, and Japan," the former NBA scoring champion, poet, actor, businessman, philanthropist, and all-around good person said.

"But I always come back to Columbia, because Columbia is my home."

Frank McGuire died October 11, 1994, at the age of 80. When South Carolina played Georgia January 28, 1995, many of McGuire's former players gathered in Carolina Coliseum for a memorial tribute to the National Basketball Hall of Fame coach. Alex English, South Carolina's second African American basketball player, an accomplished poet, penned and recited the following poem during the memorial ceremony:

> *He was a big-city coach;*
> *I was a skinny country kid.*
> *He asked me to play;*
> *That's what I did.*
> *He said, "Come trail blaze a path*
> *For others of your race."*
> *We were civil rights comrades*
> *In a non-civil rights place.*
> *Your compassionate side*
> *Was most impressive to me.*
> *It turned out to be*
> *The most impressive lesson you'd teach.*
> *For when you believed*
> *You were standing for the right and truth,*
> *Your Irish stubbornness*
> *Would not let anything else through.*
> *I consider myself lucky*
> *To have played for the man.*
> *And like hundreds of your other players,*
> *I will always be your fan.*
> *He was a big-city coach*
> *Who showed that he was just a man.*

English left South Carolina for a 15-year career in the NBA with the Milwaukee Bucks, Indiana Pacers, Denver Nuggets, and Dallas Mavericks. He led the NBA in scoring with a 28.4 average in 1983 and scored 25,343 points in 1,193 NBA—a career average of 21.2 points per game.

English scored more points during the decade of the 1980s than any other NBA player and scored more than 2,000 points in eight consecutive seasons from 1982 to 1989.

He also starred as a basketball player in a feature-length film entitled *Amazing Grace and Chuck.*

English was elected to the National Basketball Hall of Fame in 1997 and previously had been inducted into the South Carolina Athletic Hall of Fame and the University of South Carolina Hall of Fame. The Denver Nuggets retired his No. 2 jersey, and the University of South Carolina retired his No. 22 jersey.

English lives in the suburban town of Blythewood near Columbia and is a member of the University of South Carolina Board of Trustees. He started the Alex English Endowment Fund for Disadvantaged Athletes, and he and his wife, Vanessa, co-founded an African-American cultural event entitled, "Let's Share."

Alex and Vanessa have four children. Their eldest, Alex, Jr., played basketball at the College of William & Mary during his freshman year (1999-2000) until sustaining a season-ending injury. In 2001 he transferred to Winthrop University in Rock Hill, S.C.

What's to Drink

In 1977 both South Carolina and Clemson won regional baseball tournaments and advanced to the College World Series in Omaha.

Clemson did not offer radio broadcasts of its baseball games at that time while Bob Fulton did the play-by-play, and I was the color analyst for South Carolina games. Clemson was contacted for permission to broadcast its World Series games. AD Bill McLellan agreed, on condition that Clemson's play-by-play announcer, Jim Phillips, be a part of the operation.

A network of 29 South Carolina radio stations was organized, and Fulton and Phillips shared the play-by-play. When South Carolina played, Fulton announced the first three and final three innings, with Phillips doing the middle three. When Clemson played the play by play, innings were switched.

I was the color announcer for the South Carolina games while Clemson sports information director Bob Bradley handled color when the Tigers played. Bradley was a tobacco chewer at the time and used a soft drink cup as a spittoon.

Fulton returned to the booth for his three-inning stint and picked up what he thought was his soft drink and took a big swig. He had picked up Bradley's spit cup. After a few minutes of gagging while Phillips pinch-hit at the microphone, Bob was able to continue the broadcast.

Broadcast Quality

Bob Fulton set the standard, but South Carolina baseball has been blessed with two other play-by-play announcers who went from the Gamecock booth to a major league baseball booth.

Jim Powell filled in during parts of two seasons with the Minnesota Twins before landing a full-time job as Bob Uecker's partner broadcasting Milwaukee Brewers games. Steve Stewart has worked some Baltimore Orioles games since moving from WVOC Radio in Columbia to WBAL in Baltimore. Both were the voices of Gamecock baseball for several years.

Jim Forest broadcast Gamecock baseball one season before moving to Detroit to become sports director at WJR, where he was involved in Detroit Pistons basketball broadcasts. Forest returned to Columbia and is now the public-address announcer for Gamecock football, men's basketball, soccer, softball, and some baseball games.

Mick Mixon left the Gamecock Network to return to his hometown of Chapel Hill, N.C., and join announcer Woody Durham in broadcasting University of North Carolina games.

Len Hathaway was the baseball play-by-play announcer one season while news director at WIS Radio in Columbia. Len had prior experience with Washington Redskins football games, but had never broadcast baseball.

South Carolina opened the 1986 season in Charleston against Baptist College on a cold February day. The plate umpire came out in short sleeves, and I remarked that he was a pretty tough guy. Between innings, the umpire turned to face the press box as he brushed off home plate. When we returned from the commercial break, Hathaway said on the air, "You said that umpire is a tough guy, but I see he's wearing a sweater under his shirt.

"Len," I said. "That's his chest protector."

Hathaway's response, "Well, it looks like a sweater."

When it came to football and basketball, Bob Fulton was the star of the Gamecock broadcast booth for more than 40 years. When he retired after the 1994 season, he was replaced by another award-winning veteran broadcaster. For more than 20 years, Charlie McAlexander had broadcast Mississippi, Vanderbilt, and Kentucky games. He has been named Sportscaster of the Year in four different states.

For nearly 30 years, former star quarterback Tommy Suggs (1968-70) has shared the booth with Fulton and McAlexander as analyst and color commentator. Former star quarterback Todd Ellis (1986-89) has been the football sideline announcer since 1993.

Casey Manning, the first African-American basketball player at the University of South Carolina, is a circuit court judge, but he moonlights during basketball season as an analyst with McAlexander on the Gamecock Radio Network. Charlie Mac doesn't broadcast baseball on radio, but he was the play-by-play announcer for several Gamecock games that were televised during the 2000 season.

Obeying the Rules

Raynard Brown believed in obeying the rules no matter what the circumstances.

The South Carolina halfback (1983-86) was returning to The Roost, South Carolina's dormitory for scholarship athletes, when he encountered a long stationary freight train blocking his way. Brown abandoned his car, climbed over the couplings between two box-cars, and made it to his room just in time for bed check.

A couple of hours later, two Columbia police officers knocked on his door to say they had located his automobile parked in the street.

"There was no way that I was going to break curfew," Brown explained.

In 1984, Raynard Brown turned in one of the most spectacular and controversial plays in South Carolina football history. The Gamecocks were undefeated (8-0), while Florida State's record was 6-1-1. South Carolina was ranked fifth in the wire-service polls. Florida State was tenth in the Associated Press and eleventh in the United Press International rankings.

The Gamecocks lined up to receive the second-half kickoff, holding a 17-7 lead. Brown caught the football at his 1-yard line as his right knee dipped close to the turf. He came up the middle, bounced off a tackler, did a 360-degree spin, cut to the left sideline, and raced 99 yards for a touchdown that increased South Carolina's lead to 24-7.

Frank Broyles, analyst for the ABC-TV telecast, was adamant that Brown's knee had touched the ground, and the ball should have been downed at the South Carolina 1-yard line. Low-level footage shot by Columbia station WIS-TV seemed to indicate that Brown's knee did not touch the ground.

After the game, which South Carolina won 38-26, Brown said, "My knee didn't touch. It almost did, but it didn't. Anyway, the official didn't call it. I was afraid he might have."

I'm Wide Open

Johnny Gregory is still mad at quarterback Tommy Suggs more than 30 years after Suggs threw a touchdown pass to the wrong receiver.

Gregory set a school record with three touchdown receptions in a 34-21 win over Wake Forest at Winston-Salem in 1968.

"I should have had four," Gregory said. "I was wide open in the end zone. Tommy looked at me, faked the throw, and threw to [tight end] Doug Hamrick. He scored one touchdown that should have been my fourth."

When asked for his recollection of the play in question, Suggs replied, "We had four receivers, and all of them were wide open. I threw to the one who was the most open."

Gregory's record has been tied six times over the years, but never surpassed.

The Little QB

Tommy Suggs remembers his two varsity trips to Clemson in 1968 and 1970.

According to Suggs, prior to the 1968 game, "the bus was moving slowly through traffic near the stadium, when we passed a group of tailgaters. There were some nice-looking women in the group. They threw chicken bones at our bus."

Suggs never lost to Clemson. His freshman team defeated the Tiger Cubs in 1967; and in three varsity seasons, Suggs quarterbacked the following Gamecock victories, 7-3 at Clemson: 27-13 at Columbia, and 38-32 at Clemson.

In the 1970 game at Clemson, South Carolina led 17-10 at halftime, despite three Tiger interceptions.

"As we entered the locker room at halftime," Suggs remembered, "Coach Dietzel said to me, 'Thomas, you're eight for eight; five to us and three to them.'"

In the second half, Suggs kept the football out of reach of the Tiger defenders and ended the day with 19 completions in 29 attempts for 316 yards and four touchdowns—three of them in the second half—as the Gamecocks held on for a 38-32 win.

Since graduating, Suggs has enjoyed a long career in banking and the insurance industry. During the football season, he has been the color analyst for South Carolina football radio broadcasts since 1973.

Hootie

The University of South Carolina has been fielding football teams for more than a century. The Augusta National Golf Club has existed for nearly three-quarters of a century.

What's the link between Gamecock football and the famed site of the Masters?

The chairman of Augusta National was a three-year University of South Carolina football letterman.

A backup right halfback to Bishop Strickland in 1950 and a starting fullback in 1951 and 1952, W. W. "Hootie" Johnson rushed for a modest career total of 582 yards. For most of his career, he labored in the shadow of Strickland and Steve Wadiak, two of the greatest running backs in Gamecock history.

As a blocker, however, Johnson excelled. He won the Jacobs Blocking Trophy as the best collegiate blocker in the State of South Carolina as a senior.

At age 34, Johnson became the youngest bank president ever in South Carolina. By the time he reached retirement age, he was one of the top executives at Bank of America, the nation's largest banking firm.

Fox

On July 17, 1997, Fox Beyer threw out the first pitch before a Yankees-Indians game at Yankee Stadium and was photographed with comedian-actor and super baseball fan Billy Crystal.

The following spring, Fox Beyer was a student manager handing out baseball equipment as an 18-year-old freshman at the University of South Carolina.

As a senior at Chatham High School in New Jersey, Fox pitched 47 innings, struck out 23 batters, walked only five, recorded a 1.98 earned run average, and compiled a 4-2 record.

Fox has cerebral palsy. He was born three months premature, weighed three pounds, six ounces, his lungs collapsed; and he was placed on a respirator and was given a 25 percent chance of survival.

He did survive, although he underwent four major surgeries. His parents named him Fox because they said he had outfoxed the doctors.

The photograph with Billy Crystal appeared on the cover of *Exceptional Parent* magazine, a publication for parents who have children with disabilities. The Madison Square Garden cable television network broadcast a feature on Fox, and he has been the subject of several newspaper and magazine features including a story in *Reader's Digest.*

After Fox spent two seasons as team manager, South Carolina baseball coach Ray Tanner promoted Fox to student coach before his junior season in 2000. A history major, he plans to become a high school teacher and a baseball coach.

Triple Digits

The NCAA recognizes 100 yards as the maximum distance on any football play, but at least five plays turned in by University of South Carolina players have started in the end zone or at the goal line and reached or exceeded the maximum.

The longest recorded play in Gamecock history occurred in 1985, when Sterling Sharpe returned a kickoff 104 yards for a touchdown against Duke.

Mel Baxley intercepted a Georgia Tech pass in the end zone and returned it 102 yards in 1973.

In 1982, the University of the Pacific was at the Gamecock 1-yard line and about to score, when a ball carrier was hit, and the football popped into the air. Harry Skipper caught the airborne fumble a yard behind the goal line and raced 101 yards for a touchdown.

South Carolina's first 100-yard-plus play occurred in 1949. Ed Pasky intercepted a Wake Forest pass a yard behind his goal line and raced the length of the field to score.

Boo Williams caught a kickoff on his goal line against Vanderbilt in 1997 and returned it an even 100 yards.

Anchors Aweigh

South Carolina won its first nine football games in 1984, but was upset by Navy the week before ending the regular season at Clemson. The loss denied the Gamecocks an opportunity to move up to No. 1 in the national polls and knocked them out of contention for the Orange Bowl.

The Clemson band taunted the Gamecocks during pregame warm-ups by playing *Anchors Aweigh* and threw oranges mixed with lemons onto the field.

After falling behind 21-3 in the second quarter, South Carolina rallied and scored with 50 seconds remaining in the game to win 22-21. The Gamecocks accepted a bid to the Gator Bowl.

Mobile Fans

At home football games in Williams-Brice Stadium, up to 200 motor homes displaying Gamecock colors create a fair-sized village. Fifty or more of them follow the South Carolina football team on the road.

A couple of fans and their wives take it a bit further. Their recreational vehicles show up at Gamecock baseball games—at home and on the road.

Neither Dixie Howell nor Bill Golding is a South Carolina alumnus. Neither of their wives attended the University either, but all four of them are dyed-in-the-wool fans of the garnet and black.

Howell and his wife, Carol, live in Greenville and they make the 100-mile trek to Columbia for the weekend baseball series and park their motor home at the soccer stadium across the street from Sarge Frye Field. Bill and Gloria Golding live in Elgin. That's about 40 miles north of Columbia; but on baseball weekends at Sarge Frye, the Golding RV is parked next to the Howell motor home.

The two RVs have been spotted at Charleston, Clemson, Auburn, Birmingham, Tuscaloosa, Columbus and Athens, Baton Rouge, Nashville, Knoxville, and other cities where the Gamecock baseball team plays.

Bill and Gloria Golding (Tom Price)

Howell is a former Furman University baseball coach and football assistant and is a native of Alabama. He grew up in Washington, D.C., and first attended the University of Alabama to play football and baseball, but ended up in the navy during World War II.

When he returned to Alabama, he said he was on the 14th team in spring practice, so he transferred to George Washington University, where he played guard and defensive end on the football team.

Golding is from Amonate, Virginia. He was stationed at Fort Jackson, and when he retired from the Army, South Carolina became his home. The Goldings became Gamecock fans in the 1960s and follow 100 percent everything connected with the Gamecocks.

"Football, basketball, baseball, soccer—we see it all," he declared. He did miss four football games in 1985 when he had open-heart surgery, but noted, "I haven't missed a football game since."

You can't miss the Goldings at baseball games. He's the guy with a gray beard wearing the batting helmet plastered with Gamecock decals. He wears a garnet sweatshirt with an inscription over

Carol and Dixie Howell (Tom Price)

the left breast that reads, "Bill. Gamecocks #1 Fan." The inscription on his wife's shirt reads, "Gloria, Gamecocks #2 Fan."

Bill is also the guy who makes the sound, sort of like a barking dog, "Ooh, Ooh," when the Gamecocks do something exciting. He and Gloria have been married for more than 35 years.

The Howells are not quite as conspicuous. They have been married for more than 55 years, and Carol said that following the South Carolina teams is a nice hobby.

"We enjoy the travel and seeing the teams play," she said.

Freak Injury

Bill Landrum came to the University of South Carolina after two years in junior college and compiled an 18-4 pitching record over two seasons, but they weren't consecutive years.

Landrum went 8-2 in 1978, but missed the entire 1979 season. In a preseason accident, he fell off the stage while dancing at a Columbia disco and tore knee ligaments. He came back in 1980 to pitch 96 innings and go 10-2.

Bill's father, Joe, was the first Clemson baseball player to be named to an All-America team. He made it to the big leagues, appearing in seven games (with no record) with the Brooklyn Dodgers in 1950 and in nine games (with a 1-3 record) with the Dodgers in 1952.

Bill Landrum didn't make All-America at the University of South Carolina, but he surpassed his dad at the major league level. In eight seasons as a relief pitcher with the Reds, Cubs, Pirates, and Expos, Bill appeared in 268 games. He won 18 games, lost 15, and saved 58. He led the Pirates in saves in 1989.

Landrum's dance-floor injury was one of many freak injuries sustained by Gamecock athletes over the years. All-ACC defensive back Wally Orrel tore knee ligaments while getting off a bus when the football team was in Tallahassee to play Florida State in 1967. Center Don Somma missed several football games in 1967 when he stepped on an upright toothpick imbedded in a carpet at The Roost athletics dormitory while barefooted.

Duck Walk

The Peabody Hotel in Memphis is famous for its ducks, which are kept in a pen on the hotel roof and are herded down to the lobby several times a day and put on display, much to the delight of hotel guests and visitors.

The ducks parade around and swim in a lobby fountain.

The University of South Carolina basketball team stayed at the Peabody during the 1984 Metro Conference Basketball Tournament, and Cocky, the Gamecock mascot, made the trip. Approval was obtained from the Peabody management for Cocky to parade through the lobby at the head of the column of ducks.

When the ducks spied the monster garnet-colored bird with its huge yellow bill, they panicked. Although their wings were clipped to keep them from flying, the ducks tried anyway, flopping around the lobby and quacking loudly. Several of them defecated on the lobby floor. The bell captain in charge of the duck parade was running around, shouting, and attempting to restore order.

189

Cinematographer Randy Herald had planned to tape the duck walk for use in the team's season highlight video but he was laughing so hard, and there was so much chaos, he didn't get much useful footage.

Bourbon Street Fight Song

The South Carolina basketball team played in the Sugar Bowl Classic at New Orleans in December 1986. Due to budget constraints, the pep band did not make the trip.

A group of Gamecock fans went down to Bourbon Street and hired a Dixieland band that provided music to back the Gamecock team. The Gamecocks defeated Vanderbilt in two overtimes in the first round, but lost to Villanova in the championship game.

Bus Breakdown

Ty Coppenger was administrative assistant to University of South Carolina head football coach Joe Morrison during the 1984 season.

In preparing for the first of Morrison's weekly television programs, the producer asked Coppenger to assess each opponent on the schedule. He pointed out things the Gamecocks had to do to defeat the first nine opponents, but when he reached the 10th, Coppenger said, "The only way we can lose to Navy is if the bus breaks down."

South Carolina defeated its first nine opponents to rise to No. 2 in the national polls. But the Gamecocks were upset by Navy 38-21, before defeating Clemson to finish the regular season at 10-1.

Zambolist

Zam Fredrick was a home-grown product. He was from the little Calhoun County, South Carolina town of St. Matthews, about 35 miles from where he played his college basketball at the University of South Carolina.

His given name was Zambolist, but it was quickly shortened to Zam.

The first three years of Fredrick's career at South Carolina were the final three seasons for Coach Frank McGuire. Zam averaged just 1.9 points per game in limited playing time as a freshman, jumped into double figures at 13.9 as a sophomore, but dropped to a 7.0 average as a junior.

Although he was a gifted outside shooter, there was nothing to indicate that the 6-2 guard would zoom to the top among the nation's elite scorers in his final season, but that's what he did.

When he got off to an 0-3 start in the 1980-81 season as McGuire's successor, new coach Bill Foster realized he had to find a scorer to hitch his star to if the Gamecocks were to have a successful season. Zam was his man. The Gamecocks won 17 of their remaining 24 games to finish 17-10.

Fredrick scored 781 points to lead all NCAA Division I scorers with a 28.9 average, and that was before the advent of the three-point goal. He made more than half of his field-goal attempts, recording 300 two-pointers on accurate outside shooting and

Zam Fredrick (USC Sports Information)

191

quick moves to the basket that frequently drew fouls. He converted more than 81 percent of his free-throw opportunities, making 181 of 223.

He scored 19 field goals in a game against Hofstra in Carolina Coliseum.

Fredrick was the second South Carolina NCAA Division I scoring champion in basketball. Grady Wallace led the nation in 1957 with a 31.3 average.

Zam never quite caught on in the NBA, but he had a successful professional basketball career in Europe before returning to his roots in St. Matthews where he has developed state championship teams as basketball coach at Calhoun County High School.

Below the Blimp

The 1980 South Carolina football team, led by Heisman Trophy winner George Rogers, played the University of Pittsburgh in the Gator Bowl at Jacksonville, Florida, on December 29, while Florida State was set to play Oklahoma in the Orange Bowl at Miami on New Year's night.

Meanwhile, the South Carolina basketball team was scheduled to play Florida State in Tallahassee on December 31. The Florida capital city was a ghost town, with the vast majority of its fans in Miami for the bowl game. With the encouragement of the South Carolina administration, sponsors of the Gator Bowl made a pitch to have the basketball game transferred to Jacksonville.

Florida State, however, wasn't about to move a basketball game to Jacksonville, where an estimated 50,000 Gamecock fans were eagerly awaiting the Gator Bowl. Florida State made a counterproposal, offering to move the game to Miami and play it in the Miami Dade South Junior College arena.

South Carolina coach Bill Foster agreed to the switch if Florida State would provide his basketball team with tickets to the New Year's Day bowl game. With the University of South Carolina shut down for the holidays, Foster planned to stay over in Miami a couple of days before traveling to a game at East Tennessee State.

The Gamecock tickets were in the end zone at the top row of the upper deck of the Orange Bowl, prompting Foster to remark, "We're just two rows below the blimp," as the Goodyear airship hovered over the stadium.

South Carolina lost the Gator Bowl to Pittsburgh, and Florida State lost the Orange Bowl to Oklahoma, but the Gamecocks prevailed in the basketball game, defeating the Seminoles in a thriller, 80-78.

Bypass

Coach Gene Keady brought his Purdue Boilermakers to Columbia to meet Bill Foster's South Carolina basketball Gamecocks December 11, 1982 in Carolina Coliseum. South Carolina's record was 3-2, while Purdue's was 5-0.

Forward Brad Jergenson had a perfect night. He was 5-for-5 from both the floor and the charity stripe, and he and guard Harold Martin each scored 15 points in a 59-53 South Carolina win.

When I went to the coaches' locker room to escort Coach Foster to the postgame media interview room, I found Foster stretched out on the floor, with Dr. Emmett Lunceford, an orthopedic surgeon, bending over him.

"He's having a heart attack," Lunceford said. Foster had begun experiencing a tightness in his chest and chest pains during halftime. By the end of the game, he was perspiring profusely.

Assistant coach Steve Steinwedel filled in at the press conference while Foster was transported to a hospital. Foster underwent quadruple coronary bypass surgery two days later.

Keady and his wife came to the hospital and waited with Foster's family until Foster's condition stabilized. The Purdue team had a 5 a.m. wake-up call for an early-morning flight back to Indiana, but the Keadys remained until about 4 a.m.

Eleven months earlier, I had undergone a similar experience, and for several weeks following Foster's episode, I was often called on by the news media to explain the procedure for bypassing blocked arteries around the heart.

Steinwedel ran the team as interim coach for 17 games while Foster recovered. The head coach returned to the bench and directed the team to two victories in the National Invitation Tournament and a final record of 22-9.

Foster coached three more seasons at South Carolina before he was fired by AD Bob Marcum. He became head coach at Northwestern University in the Big Ten and then became associate commissioner of the Southwest Conference. When the Big Twelve Conference was formed, he worked for that league.

A native of Pennsylvania, Foster was given a testimonial dinner in Lancaster, Pennsylvania, in 1994, which also included a reunion of many of his former players and assistant coaches. Foster missed the affair due to illness, and several months later underwent bypass surgery for the second time.

Achtung!

Stefan Eggers was from West Germany. Six feet, eight inches tall, he averaged two points a game in three basketball seasons at the University of South Carolina (1990-92). In 64 career games, Eggers tallied 130 points.

When his father came over from Germany to see him play against Clemson on February 2, 1991; however, Stefan had his moment of glory.

Playing up front against two future NBA stars—Dale Davis and Elden Campbell—Eggers scored 18 points and pulled down 12 rebounds in a 59-53 South Carolina victory.

Prevoz

Dave Prevoznik played in only 23 basketball games during his career at South Carolina and scored 58 points to average 2.5 points per game. A third of his career total came in one game.

Coach Frank McGuire, who three years later would become South Carolina's head basketball coach, brought his heavily favored

North Carolina Tar Heels to Columbia to play the Gamecocks, coached by Bob Stevens, on February 8, 1961.

Prevoznik, a 6-6, 235-pound center from Cleveland, Ohio, wore thick horn-rimmed glasses, wasn't very quick of foot, and didn't jump well.

He was pressed into service when Art Whisnant, South Carolina's top star, was sidelined by injury and foul trouble. Prevoznik took nine turnaround shots from about 15 feet, making eight of them. He also sank three free throws to tally 19 points, as South Carolina upset McGuire's Tar Heels 89-82.

Numbers Game

South Carolina and Maryland were scheduled to tip off the Atlantic Coast Conference Basketball Tournament in Greensboro, N. C., on March 11, 1971. Both teams retired to the locker rooms after their pregame warm-ups.

When Maryland returned to the floor, the Terp players had swapped uniform jerseys. Every player was wearing a different number than listed in the tournament program. The name on the back of each player's uniform was that of a teammate. Fans were confused, but the news media—especially the radio and television announcers—were even more confused.

Maryland coach Lefty Driesell had pulled the switch in an effort to upset South Carolina's defensive alignment. It didn't work. South Carolina won the game, 71-63, and the ACC quickly adopted a rule requiring players in the annual tournament to wear the numbers that are listed on the rosters furnished for the program.

Inside the Park

Inside-the-park home runs are rare in baseball. An inside-the-park home run that decides an extra-inning game is even rarer. That's what Chuck McLean accomplished in the first game of the 1977 College World Series in Omaha.

McLean was a senior left fielder from Rockingham, N.C. He was hitting only about .260, but he was the ultimate competitor on the Gamecock squad—the kind of player that Coach June Raines liked to have at the plate when the game was on the line.

After popping up or striking out, McLean would grimace and scream at the opposing pitcher, "You've got nothing! I'm going to rip you next time!"

South Carolina All-America Randy Martz—the national Player of the Year—and Baylor's Panamanian right-hander, Jaime Cocanower, were locked in a pitcher's duel. After nine innings, the score was 1-1. With two out in the top of the 10th, Baylor scored a run on three ground-ball singles to take a 2-1 lead.

In the bottom of the 10th, South Carolina second baseman Mark Van Bever led off with a double down the left-field line. Van Bever advanced to third base when Mookie Wilson grounded out to deep shortstop. Chuck McLean stepped to the plate. Coach Raines was hoping for a sacrifice fly to tie the game.

McLean hit a line drive over the head of Baylor's center fielder and rounded second, trying for a triple, as Van Bever scored the tying run. Assistant coach Johnny Hunton—who had relieved Raines as third-base coach after nine innings—waved McLean home, and the little outfielder beat the throw for an inside-the-park homer and a 3-2 South Carolina win.

Raines said he would have held McLean at third if he had still been in the coaching box.

Bo

Senior quarterback Harold "Bo" Hagan of Savannah, Georgia, had two bad knees and was not scheduled to play against Clemson in the Big Thursday football game in October 1949. He was replaced by John Boyle, a 6-4, 220-pound sophomore from Brooklyn, N.Y.

Boyle had a reputation as a great passer, but he threw two interceptions in the first 16 minutes of the game, and Clemson converted both into touchdowns for a 13-0 lead. Out of desperation, South Carolina coach Rex Enright called on Hagan. The World War

II army veteran, who saw combat in France, from Savannah, Georgia, limped into the game.

By halftime, the score was tied. South Carolina dominated the second half under Hagan's leadership to win 27-13.

Hagan later became head football coach at Rice University before returning to the University of South Carolina as assistant athletics director. He left athletics to serve as director of the Alumni Association, a position he held until he retired.

Boyle quit the football team after being yanked from the Clemson game and returned to Brooklyn.

Clutch Performance

Jim Rogers didn't get a lot of playing time as backup quarterback to Dan Reeves in 1963 and 1964 but when called upon in the clutch, the junior from Charlotte, N.C., came through in the 1964 Clemson game.

Reeves was playing with a badly injured foot and was ineffective as the Gamecocks trailed Clemson 3-0 late in the fourth quarter at Clemson Memorial Stadium, which the Tigers like to call Death Valley. Clemson had kicked a field goal on its first possession, but the game had since settled into a defensive struggle.

Rogers relieved the limping Reeves and South Carolina began a drive. Rogers passed to J. R. Wilburn for a 45-yard gain as South Carolina moved to the Clemson 15-yard line. On third down, Rogers rolled out to pass, couldn't find an open receiver, and scrambled into the end zone.

South Carolina coach Marvin Bass said Death Valley was actually Bird Paradise.

The 7-3 win was South Carolina's first at Clemson's home stadium. The rivalry had been played in Columbia on Big Thursday of State Fair Week until 1960.

Sweet E

Evelyn Johnson was from East Lansing, Michigan. She played basketball for the University of South Carolina from 1979 through 1983. She averaged 14.3 points per game. Her career total of 1,620 points ranked seventh on South Carolina's all-time list through 2000.

Evelyn "Sweet E" Johnson (USC Sports Information)

Evelyn's nickname was "Sweet E." While other team members wore their family names on their backs, Evelyn had her nickname emblazoned on her jersey. Sweet E has a brother whom you might have heard of. His name is Ervin "Magic" Johnson.

Another famous name played basketball for the Lady Gamecocks in 1978. Sue Shue is the daughter of Gene Shue. Her father was head coach at the University of Maryland and the Baltimore Bullets of the NBA.

Sue Shue played two seasons at South Carolina (1977-78) and then transferred to the College of Charleston.

Legends

Webster's New World Dictionary defines *esprit de corps* as "group spirit, sense of pride, honor, etc., shared by those in the same group or undertaking."

That definition certainly applies to a group of about 25 aging ex-jocks who performed at the University of South Carolina on the basketball court under coaches Bob Stevens and Chuck Noe over a five-year period spanning 1959-64.

They operate under the self-proclaimed title "USC Legends in Their Own Minds."

The Legends get together once or twice a year at the home of Ronnie Collins in Winnsboro, about 35 miles from Columbia, to cook steaks, have a few cold ones, and swap memories.

Two aging witnesses to the on-court exploits of the Legends— a broadcaster and a sports information director—were invited to participate. Bob Fulton and Tom Price are the permanent honorary captains of the 1963 Gamecocks. We have wall plaques to prove it.

Ronnie Collins's wife is a Clemson fan, and a couple of years before the turn of the 21st century, Clemson players from the same era were invited to join the Legends. That made for a lot of good-natured needling and a fierce free-throw-shooting contest.

The Legends were an undersized bunch who fought and clawed against bigger and deeper opponents and always battled until the final moments.

Ronnie Collins played forward at 6-3 and 170 pounds, but still averaged 17 points per game for his career. Center Art Whisnant was only 6-4. He averaged 19.1 points per game and was a tough rebounder. Scotti Ward would be referred to as a point guard today, but he scored more than 1,000 points during his collegiate career. Scotti, from Valparaiso, Indiana, was nearly blind in one eye—the result of a boyhood snowball accident.

Jimmy Collins, no relation to Ronnie, averaged 10 points a game and stood about 6-1. Bobby Robinson, also a fine outfielder with the baseball team, was also 6-1.

One of the tallest—and perhaps the fiercest—of the Legends was 6-6 John Schroeder. Teammates nicknamed him "Ice Man," because he didn't have much of a shooting touch, averaging fewer than five points per game over three varsity seasons.

As a rule, Ice Man never took a shot from more than three feet from the basket, but in one road game he heaved one up from mid-court as the clock was about to expire, and it went through the basket. At practice after returning home, Schroeder was asked to demonstrate his 45-foot shot. It hit the bottom of the basket again.

One of the Legends who doesn't make many of the reunions is 6-3 Bill Yarborough. He went to medical school, and his practice is in Hawaii. Terry Lucansky, an undersized guard, only occasionally makes the reunions. He earned a Ph.D. and heads the botany department at the University of Florida.

Bud Cronin, one of the "bigger" forwards, at 6-2, followed Coach Bob Stevens to Oklahoma as an assistant before returning to South Carolina. Bob Haney was a 6-4 center with a bad back who served as a graduate assistant coach after his playing days were over.

Joe Laird, Rich Grich, and Butch Jordan also played with the Legends. Grich was also a pitcher on the baseball team.

Jordan, about 5-8, was a walk-on paying his own way through school. He claimed all the uneaten sandwiches in the box lunches players received on bus trips back from road games. Butch "refrigerated" his scavenged food on the windowsill of his dorm room during the winter months of the basketball season.

Each road trip was good for about three or four extra meals for the little guard, who appeared in 13 career games and scored four points.

John Gorsage (6-7) and Lyn Burkholder (6-10) were the tallest Legends. Burkholder and 6-8 Skip Kickey never actually played with the Legends, but they are members of the group, anyway. Burkholder was on Chuck Noe's last freshman team and played his varsity years under Frank McGuire. So did Kickey, who was in McGuire's first recruiting class.

The Legends hail from diverse backgrounds and places: Whisnant is from North Carolina, Cronin from West Virginia, Haney and Lucansky from Ohio, Schroeder from Maryland, Ward from Indiana, Grich from Connecticut, Gorsage from Michigan, Burkholder from Virginia, and Jimmy Collins and Kickey from New Jersey.

Bob Rebhan recently moved to Beaufort, S.C., after retiring from a job in Detroit. He played with the Legends in 1961-62 and showed up for the 2000 reunion.

Ronnie Collins, Robinson, Laird, Yarborough, and Jordan are from South Carolina. All now live in South Carolina, except for Yarborough, Lucansky, and Schroeder. Schroeder lives in Atlanta.

Kickey owns a trophy company. Haney owns a business that makes signs. Whisnant is an entrepreneur involved in real estate and several other enterprises. Ward, Cronin, and Laird are in the insurance business. Jimmy Collins, until recently, managed a group of radio stations and now is in the novelty advertising business. Burkholder is an engineer. Yarborough is a urologist. Lucansky is a university professor. Schroeder is an executive with IBM. Gorsage is retired from the Columbia newspaper *The State.*

Ronnie Collins retired from an energy company in North Carolina, moved back to Winnsboro, and teaches ninth-grade English at Fairfield Central High School. Grich is a retired high school coach and athletics director.

Whiz

Art Whisnant was a fierce competitor who more than held his own in battles under the basket—in spite of giving up four to six inches to most of the other centers he competed against on the basketball court.

Whisnant was from the little North Carolina town of Icard and came to the University of South Carolina from Hildebran High School. Although only 6-4, he was the ultimate low-post player and was South Carolina's leading scorer for three consecutive seasons. He averaged 17 points a game in 1960, 19.1 in 1961, and 21 in 1962 under Coach Bob Stevens.

He scored 1,505 points in 79 games for a career average of 19.1 per game and also grabbed 723 rebounds, an average of 9.2 per game. Whisnant was fouled a lot and attempted 880 free throws in his career, an average of more than 11 attempts per game. He scored 567 points, more than one-third of his career total, from the foul line.

Nearly 40 years later, Whisnant still wears several scars from head butting that occurred during battles over rebounds or position on the court. In one game, he sustained a large gash to the side of his head. Trainer Jim Price wrapped a huge bandage around the wound, and Whisnant played the second half wearing what resembled a turban.

A doctor sewed him up after the game.

Whisnant was also the basketball team's No. 1 prankster and bad boy.

On one occasion he stole a mule and wagon belonging to an old man who lived in a slum area near the campus. He drove around Davis Field, a baseball diamond and football practice area across the street from Preston Hall, and offered wagon rides to other students.

"We took up a collection and raised about $50 and gave it to the old guy who owned the mule," Whisnant remembered. "That mule wasn't worth half that."

Student-athletes used to earn extra spending money by selling programs at football games for a commission of 10 cents for each 50-cent program they sold. Before the final Big Thursday game with Clemson in 1959, the price of the commemorative program was increased to a dollar, and the commission doubled to 20 cents.

However, football coach and AD Warren Giese decided that only freshman football players and other football players who weren't on the dress-out squad for the game could take advantage of the increased commissions.

"I went to Coach Giese and complained," Whisnant said, "and he said okay, I could be the only non-football player allowed to sell programs."

Whisnant checked out a large quantity of programs and sub-contracted them to other members of the basketball team.

"Of the 20 cents, they kept a dime and gave me a dime," he said.

As for those he sold himself, he said, "I worked over in the Clemson section, and every time those fans would jump up to cheer, I would grab the programs they left on their seats and sell them again."

Whisnant remembers the team staying at the DuPont Plaza Hotel in Washington, D.C., on a road trip. He and teammate Joe Laird were standing on a balcony, dropping water-filled balloons onto the street several floors below. One balloon landed on a car and another splashed a pedestrian.

"We were having a good time, but then Jim Price (athletics trainer and team disciplinarian) came by, and he took my balloons away," Whisnant said.

Whisnant recalled a snowball fight outside the dorm in which he hit campus police chief Coley Bundrick with a snowball. Bundrick was a no-nonsense former military policeman, and Art had to run fast to avoid being apprehended for that stunt.

"I had accumulated about 60 or 70 parking tickets, and the police came knocking at my door," Whisnant recalled. "They said I owed them several hundred dollars. I told them I didn't have but 20 or 30 dollars. They took my 20 or 30 dollars and let me go."

At the beginning of each semester, students were supposed to fill out their requested class schedules and take them to the dean for approval. Whisnant swiped the dean's rubber approval stamp, and students began stopping by Whisnant's room in Preston Hall to have their proposed schedules stamped "approved."

Panty raids on women's dormitories were the rage, and Whisnant said he and Joe Laird pulled off the most successful panty raids in history.

"I went through a dorm window, and the housemother threw a bucket of hot water on me," he recalled. "A cop grabbed me, but I pointed to a guy holding a laundry bag who was watching and told the cop the guy had a bag full of panties. He turned me loose and grabbed that guy. The bag was full of his dirty laundry."

Whisnant said there was a dormitory counselor who was giving him a particularly hard time. The counselor and his wife lived in an apartment in the dormitory. Whisnant found two filthy, mangy stray dogs and put them in the dorm counselor's living quarters.

The janitors who cleaned up the dorms wore green uniforms and were called "Green Beetles" by the students.

"I got a key from one of the Green Beetles," Whisnant said. "Those dogs sure messed up that guy's apartment."

Whisnant acquired a quiver of arrows and a long bow and endangered the safety of Preston Hall residents by conducting archery practice in the hallway. However, it wasn't Whisnant, but another student athlete, who rolled a bowling ball down the hall in Preston. The ball ruptured the radiator pipe and flooded the hall.

Track coach Weems Baskin taught classes in physical education, and Whisnant said Baskin was the only teacher he was afraid of.

"He grabbed me one day on campus and told me he would beat my ass if I didn't show up for his class," Whisnant said.

"I told him, 'Coach, I'll be there,' and I always was."

Grant's Bomb

One of the biggest comebacks in University of South Carolina basketball history occurred February 1, 1998, in Carolina Coliseum.

Coach Eddie Fogler's Gamecocks trailed Cincinnati by 20 points at halftime, 39-19. The game was televised nationally by CBS, and the announcers were yawning. Things got worse before they got better, as the Cincinnati lead widened to 23 points at 42-19.

South Carolina slowly cut into the Bearcat lead, but the deficit was still 10 points with seven minutes remaining when Melvin Watson cut it to seven with a three-pointer. D'Juan Baker hit a trey for Cincinnati, restoring the lead to double digits. B.J. McKie (pronounced Mackey) quickly hit a three for the Gamecocks, and Cincinnati never led by more than seven again.

Cincinnati led by six, 65-59, with 2:43 remaining but never scored again. Three free throws and a jump shot by Melvin Watson brought the Gamecocks within a point with 44 seconds to play. A steal by Cincinnati's Melvin Levett with 12 seconds remaining seemed to seal the Gamecocks' fate, but Cincy's Bobby Brannon knocked Antonio Grant down and was called for a charge.

South Carolina had possession in the backcourt with 5.2 seconds showing on the clock, then moved the ball into the frontcourt and called time out with 4.1 seconds to play. The ball was inbounded to McKie, South Carolina's best scorer, and he was immediately double-teamed. McKie appeared to be falling down and punched the ball toward mid-court.

Freshman Grant grabbed the loose ball and launched a 25-foot shot just a 10th of a second before the final horn sounded.

The basketball hit the bottom of the net for three points. Final score: South Carolina 67, Cincinnati 65.

Deja Vu

Nearly three years after Antonio Grant's last-second three-point bomb that produced a basketball win over Cincinnati in Carolina

Coliseum, it happened again. This time, Grant, a senior, was not the perpetrator. But he witnessed it.

Travis Kraft came from a small town in North Dakota called Mayville, to play basketball for the University of South Carolina. His high school coach and father, Tim Kraft, retired, and both parents moved to South Carolina after Travis's freshman year—partially to escape the cold North Dakota weather, but mainly to see their son play.

Travis, at 6-7 and 205 pounds, came to South Carolina with a reputation as an outstanding three-point shooter. He broke his high school's record for three-pointers in a game with nine, and in a season with 86. He averaged 28.6 points per game as a senior.

A stress fracture hobbled him much of his freshman season, but he did play in 25 of 32 games, averaging 10 minutes per contest. Of his 31 field goals, 27 were from three-point range and he ended the season with 96 points for a modest average of 3.8 points per game.

Another leg injury kept Kraft out of eight of the first 11 games of the 2000-01 season, and when fifth-ranked Florida came to Carolina Coliseum January 7, 2001, for the first Southeastern Conference game of the season, Kraft had seen only 32 minutes of playing time. He had two three-point goals in nine attempts and had scored only seven points.

He sat on the bench for 39 minutes and 40 seconds of the Florida game but had been told by Coach Eddie Fogler at halftime, "Be ready, we may need you."

Florida, which entered the game with a 10-1 record, compared to South Carolina's 8-3, held a 10-point lead, 63-53, with less than five minutes remaining. The Gators scored five more points, but turned the basketball over five times in their final 11 possessions against South Carolina's pressing defense.

South Carolina cut the margin to one point, but Matt Bonner made one of two free throws with 11.5 seconds to play. Kraft entered the game for the first time with 19 seconds left, but played only two and a fraction seconds before going out. He returned when Bonner went to the free-throw line. The ball was twice knocked out of bounds, and South Carolina had an in-bound play with two-and-a-half seconds left.

Knowing that teams frequently don't closely guard the inbound player, Fogler had Kraft throw the ball in to Calvin Clemmons, who was closely guarded. He threw it back to Kraft, who launched a 25-foot shot. It swished through the net as time expired.

The final score was South Carolina 69, Florida 68. The final score was almost the same as the score of the last-second win over Cincinnati three years earlier.

Antonio Grant, the hero of the Cincinnati win, played 29 minutes in the Florida game and contributed five points and six rebounds. Kraft actually played 13.7 seconds, but the computer doesn't deal in partial minutes, so he was credited with one minute of playing time.

Kraft was mobbed and pummeled to the floor by teammates and a few fans who rushed onto the court despite the efforts of security guards.

Kraft's reaction when he was finally extricated from the bottom of the pile: "It was kind of shocking. It's an unbelievable feeling. I was open and I shot it."

Webster's New World Dictionary defines *déjà vu* as "a feeling that one has been in a place or had a specific experience before."

Kraft's foot injury flared up again, and he didn't see a second of action in 2001 after his miracle shot. He left school and his family returned to North Dakota.

Ted Remembers Ueck

Bob Uecker appeared in 297 major league baseball games during a six-year period (1962-67) with the Milwaukee Braves, St. Louis Cardinals, Philadelphia Phillies, and Atlanta Braves.

His career batting average was an even .200, and for many years as the Milwaukee Brewers' play-by-play broadcaster and an actor in television commercials, Uecker has become famous for demeaning his athletic ability and making fun of himself.

Early in his broadcasting career, Uecker worked with the Marquette University basketball broadcasts and came to Columbia in 1972 for a Marquette-South Carolina game.

I invited the Marquette sports information director and media representatives, including the radio crew, to dinner the night before the game.

We went to a Chinese restaurant, and there was a large party of about 15 seated in the rear of the restaurant. Ted Williams, the Hall of Fame Boston Red Sox outfielder, appeared to be in charge of the group. I learned later that Williams was the sporting goods consultant with Sears-Roebuck and was in town briefing the sales staff of the local Sears store on its new line of fishing equipment. Ted had invited the staff out to eat.

As he was walking to the front of the restaurant to pay the check, the Splendid Splinter stopped by our table and asked, "What the hell is this group?"

I was explaining just who we were when Williams recognized Uecker.

"Hey, Uecker," Ted said. "I know you. You were one horse-manure baseball player."

Hi, Jack

Jack Thompson was probably the best passing guard ever to play basketball at the University of South Carolina. He was also never at a loss for words, and his mouth was as quick as his passing touch.

A member of Frank McGuire's first recruiting class in 1964, Thompson was one of the first of many New Yorkers who rode McGuire's mythical underground railroad to South Carolina. He dazzled spectators who came early to watch the freshman games until he suffered a season-ending ankle injury at mid-season.

Thompson made his varsity debut in December of 1965, along with fellow Brooklynite Frank Standard and two players from New Jersey—Skip Kickey and Skip Harlicka.

With point guard Thompson running the show, South Carolina won its first two games, against Erskine and Furman, but then faced third-ranked Duke in the old Carolina Field House. The building had been constructed in 1927 and seated 3,200. Several hundred more than that crammed into the facility.

Duke, under Coach Vic Bubas, had gone to the NCAA championship game the previous season before bowing to UCLA. At the time, the media were paying more attention to Duke's upcoming rematch with UCLA at Durham a few days later than to the Blue Devils' trip to Columbia.

Duke had a six-point lead midway through the second half, but South Carolina pulled within three points with just over four minutes remaining. With less than three minutes left, the Duke margin was one point. The Blue Devils spread the floor and went into a stall.

Jack Marin took a shot with a minute and a half left, missed, and Al Salvadori claimed the rebound for South Carolina and quickly put the basketball in the hands of Jack Thompson. His thread-the-needle pass found Salvadori breaking from the left corner to the basket. Salvadori scored and was fouled. The 6-10 West Virginian converted, and the upstart Gamecocks had a two-point lead with less than a minute remaining on the clock.

Steve Vacendak scored for Duke with 34 seconds left, and again Thompson controlled the South Carolina attack. He spotted Frank Standard breaking from right to left along the baseline and whipped him a pass for a layup. South Carolina led 73-71, but 20 seconds still remained.

A Duke shot and two tips missed, and Standard tipped the loose ball out to Skip Harlicka as time expired. The crowd surged onto the floor and lifted McGuire and Thompson on their shoulders.

Five days later, the South Carolina team was in Philadelphia to play the University of Pennsylvania at the Palestra. Both teams were undefeated, and both coaches decided to play a slow, deliberate game. South Carolina controlled the basketball and dominated the game in a 42-39 Gamecock victory.

A Philadelphia station was televising the game, and former Philadelphia Phillies and New York Mets outfielder Richie Ashburn was one of the announcers. I was asked to bring Jack Thompson over for an interview as Player of the Game. Jack had never been on television before.

As I pushed him onto the set, the red light came on signifying "on the air," and Ashburn said, "Hi, Jack, I'm Richie Ashburn."

Thompson looked at him in disbelief and blurted in his Brooklyn accent for all the television viewers to hear, "Richie Ashburn! Geez! I seen youse play for the Mets."

Thompson signed with the Indiana Pacers of the American Basketball Association, but his professional career was cut short by recurring injuries. He became a stockbroker and lived in New Orleans for a number of years before moving back to South Carolina. He's now a stockbroker in Columbia.

Thompson was working in a New York City candy store when he was convinced by basketball guru and Frank McGuire friend Harry Gotkin to give college basketball a try. Jack almost didn't finish high school. According to the story, he was enrolled in summer school to make up some work, but left after 15 minutes. One of the brothers at the Catholic school chased him to the subway, grabbed him by the collar, and brought him back.

Thompson, whose specialty was behind-the-back passes, was a sleepwalker, according to Skip Harlicka. Once, he jumped out of bed, grabbed a pillow, and made a perfect pass behind his back to his wife, Chrissie.

Shooter

Skip Harlicka was a great shooter, but Bobby Cremins once said if he ever passed the basketball to Skip, he would never get it back.

"I'd fake a pass to him, and he would shoot," Cremins claimed.

Harlicka blamed his preference for shooting over passing on an incident during a game at Assumption College during his sophomore season.

"I threw a pass to Skip Kickey, and he took a shot that missed everything," Harlicka said. "Coach McGuire called a timeout, punched Kickey in the chest, and asked him why he took that shot. Then he punched me in the chest and asked me why I threw to ball to Kickey.

"And they wonder why I didn't pass."

Cremins blamed Harlicka and Thompson for his slow academic start in college. He was a freshman when they were juniors.

"I went to their room and there were no books," Bobby claimed. "They never went to class. They got A's and B's, and I got F's."

A Higher Standard

Frank Standard was a sneaky basketball player. He was 6-4, although he insisted he was 6-5. He would roam the baseline, get position on much taller forwards and centers, and outrebound them.

Standard had a craggy face that sportswriter Jeff Denberg said resembled "a young Abe Lincoln."

Off the basketball court, he was the team card shark. His ambition was to become a dealer in Las Vegas.

Standard was in the first recruiting class that rode Frank McGuire's underground railroad from New York to South Carolina. He played on the 1964-65 freshman team, and for the next three seasons was one of the mainstays of the varsity as McGuire built the Gamecocks from laughingstock to national contender.

Standard's witty retorts rivaled his quick moves on the basketball court and his sleight of hand at the card table.

In December, 1967, the Gamecocks were in Lexington, Kentucky, to compete in the Kentucky Invitational Tournament. The Gamecocks defeated Cincinnati 64-61 in the first round and were scheduled to meet the host team, Coach Adolph Rupp's Kentucky Wildcats, for the tournament championship.

Coach McGuire called a team meeting to go over game strategy, but Standard was missing when the meeting began. McGuire sent the team manager to find the missing forward, and when Standard entered the room, McGuire asked, "So where were you, Frank?"

"I was down in the lobby arguing with a guy that you were a greater coach than Rupp," Standard replied.

The Irishman burst into laughter.

As a general rule, McGuire never told his players what defense they would employ in a game until just before they took the court. At a team meeting on one occasion, to see if Standard was paying attention, McGuire asked him, "What defense would you use tonight, Frank?"

"I'm sorry," Standard replied, "but I never reveal my defense until just before game time."

In 67 varsity games (1966-68) Frank Standard collected 720 rebounds, an average of 10.7 per game. He scored 923 points to average 13.8 per game for his career.

Standard never did become a dealer in Vegas. Instead, he went overseas for a time to play with the Spanish National Team and then became a sky marshal. In the early 1970s, in an effort to thwart the hijacking of airliners, U.S. marshals were stationed on overseas flights, and Standard spent some time flying to Europe and back.

When the sky marshal program was eliminated, Standard transferred to the customs service. When South Carolina traveled to East Lansing to play basketball against Michigan State in 1973 and to Ann Arbor to play Michigan in 1975, Standard came to the games. He was a customs agent stationed in Detroit at the Canadian border.

The Gamecock community was saddened to learn during the summer of 2000 that Frank Standard had passed away. He was only about 53 years old.

Play Forever

Frank McGuire ended his collegiate coaching career February 23, 1980, in Carolina Coliseum. The opponent was Western Kentucky University.

The score was 54-54 at the end of 40 minutes, and the game went into overtime. Neither team scored in the first OT, and a second overtime was in order. A writer on press row commented, "He doesn't want to retire. He's going to keep playing this game forever."

South Carolina outscored Western Kentucky 18-11 in the second overtime to win 73-65. It was the 550th victory for McGuire in 30 collegiate seasons, the final 16 of them at South Carolina. His record with the Gamecocks was 263-142.

The Coach's Ladies

Pat McGuire was a queen. As the wife of the University of South Carolina head basketball coach, she was regal in her bearing and always in charge of the situation.

Born in New York City, she was a child actress who was featured in early episodes of the *Our Gang* films that were in later years rereleased as *The Little Rascals*.

Patricia Johnson and Frank McGuire were married in 1940. They had two daughters—Patsy Jean and Carol Ann—and a son, Frank, Jr. Frankie was born with cerebral palsy and was a lifelong invalid. He was confined to a wheelchair and learned to speak only a few words.

Pat had a knack for putting people in their place. Once at a social gathering, a very talkative woman was sounding off about all the celebrities she knew. Pat looked at her and said, "You're a name-dropper." The embarrassed woman shut up.

One thing Pat never got quite right was the name of the sports information director's wife. Margaret was always Marge to her.

In September of 1967, three years after the McGuire family came to Columbia, Pat died of cancer. Some time later, Frank married Jane Henderson. She was from Newberry, S.C., where her father was sheriff of Newberry County.

Frank McGuire's first wife was an Irish girl from New York City. His second was a country girl from a rural South Carolina town.

Buck

Frank McGuire called Buck Freeman "one of the greatest basketball coaches of all time."

James A. "Buck" Freeman graduated from St. John's University in 1927 at the age of 27 and immediately became the school's head basketball coach. One of the many players he developed was Frank McGuire.

212

Buck became famous as coach of St. John's "Wonder Five," who compiled an 88-8 record during Buck's first four years as coach. Four of the eight losses came in the first year that Matty Begovitch, Mac Kinsbruner, Max Posnack, Rip Gerson, and Allie Schuckman were together.

Author Al Hirshberg, in his book *Basketball's Greatest Teams,* wrote that Buck Freeman introduced many basketball techniques to the college game that modern fans take for granted. His innovations included switching on defense, the use of screens in offensive patterns, and the give-and-go style of offense.

In 10 seasons at St. John's, Freeman won 179 games and lost only 32.

Buck was an alcoholic, which cost him his job at St. John's, as well as at the University of Scranton. He joined Alcoholics Anonymous and became a teetotaler. Frank McGuire brought him to North Carolina as his assistant and advisor, and Buck later followed McGuire to South Carolina

A lifelong bachelor, distinguished looking, with a mane of white hair, Buck was a father figure to countless intramural student-athletes as well as varsity stars. Before Carolina Coliseum was built, he would often keep the old Carolina Field House open to 2 or 3 a.m., because there were students there who wanted to play. Retired groundskeeper Sarge Frye remembered Buck Freeman as a man "who had so much interest in everything."

Boiled peanuts are a southern delicacy that Buck had never encoun-

Buck Freeman (USC Sports Information)

213

tered. One day he bought a bag, probably thinking they were roasted. "They sold me wet peanuts," Buck complained.

Buck lived in the Heart of Columbia Hotel a couple of blocks off campus and maybe five blocks from the Capitol News Stand on Main Street. He would walk to Main Street, buy *The New York Times* and other newspapers and start back to his room, stopping under each streetlight to read his newspapers.

Buck once took the South Carolina freshman basketball team to play a game at Georgia Southern. Varsity teams were using the main locker rooms, so the South Carolina frosh were relegated to dressing and meeting in a men's restroom. At halftime, Buck had his team in the restroom, some of them seated on a row of toilets, as he mapped out his strategy.

A Georgia Southern student entered, said excuse me and began using one of the toilets.

"How can I talk to my team with all these toilets flushing around me?" Buck complained.

On another occasion, he took the freshman team to Charleston for a game at The Citadel. South Carolina teams under Frank McGuire, including the freshmen, did everything first class. A pregame meal featuring prime rib was set up at a Charleston restaurant, which also featured she crab soup, a South Carolina low-country delicacy.

Since Charleston is my hometown, I went along on this trip and asked Buck if he would like to sample the she crab soup. He declined when told the soup was laced with sherry.

"I shouldn't touch anything with alcohol in it," he said.

On another occasion, a group of staff members and families were at dinner together during a road tournament, when McGuire went to the kitchen and found that the steaks he had ordered were marinated in wine. Buck's meal was switched to something else.

Carolina Coliseum was under construction for the 1968-69 season, and the last game in the Carolina Field House, which was completed in 1927—the year that Buck Freeman became basketball coach at St. John's—was played March 2, 1968. It was a one point, 55-54, loss to N.C. State.

Three weeks later, the field house was gutted by fire. The site was roped off and secured but caught fire again a short time later and was totally destroyed.

There was no truth to the rumor that Buck Freeman had set the field house on fire to hasten completion of the new coliseum.

Due to declining health, Buck Freeman retired in 1973, but remained a special consultant and advisor to Frank McGuire. Eight months later, February 14, 1974, Buck passed away. McGuire said one of the secrets to Buck's success was that he never overlooked the smallest detail.

"He had a fantastic knowledge of basketball," McGuire said. "He won games because he actually knew more about the game than the other coach."

In more than 40 years as a basketball coach, Buck Freeman was assessed only one technical foul. That came in a December 1965 game against Duke, a game won by South Carolina 73-71 in a major upset.

Buck said after the game that he was embarrassed, and he apologized for receiving the "T."

Lawn Service

Coach Mark Berson took his 1987 South Carolina soccer team on the road to play at the University of Akron. One of the rented vans conked out on the way from the team hotel to the game site. A pickup truck belonging to a lawn service stopped at a nearby traffic light and Berson asked the driver, "Can you help a soccer team in distress?"

"Sure," the landscaper replied. And half the soccer team piled into the back of the pickup among the mowers and edgers. The soccer match ended in a scoreless overtime tie.

The student manager was left behind to wait for a tow truck.

Huddle Up

South Carolina opened its 2000 soccer season in the Soccer Showcase at Fort Wayne, Indiana. Its first-round opponent was Notre Dame.

For pregame introductions, players were instructed to trot to midfield when their names were announced, be recognized by the crowd, and then return to their team's huddle. It was a first- time experience for freshman forward Ryan Daley of Modesto, Calif.

He waved to the crowd and then jogged to the huddle–the Notre Dame huddle.

South Carolina won the soccer match 2-0.

Record Setters

The sports information office is the keeper of records, but sometimes the SID can have a hand in setting new marks.

In 1968 at Charlottesville, Virginia, South Carolina wide receiver Fred Zeigler had 11 pass receptions, tying the school record, when he was taken out with South Carolina holding a substantial lead. Coach Paul Dietzel was informed, and he sent Zeigler back into the game with instructions to catch a screen pass. He did and established a new record.

In 1971, John Roche had 52 points against Furman when Coach Frank McGuire benched his starters. McGuire was told the school record was 54 points set by Grady Wallace against Georgia in 1957. Roche returned to the game and scored two quick baskets to total 56 for the game.

South Carolina played Elon in the Charlotte Coliseum in December of 1966, and Gary Gregor had 32 rebounds when Coach McGuire relieved his starters. When advised that the school single-game rebounding record was 33 set by Lee Collins against The Citadel in 1956, McGuire called Gregor to his side and said, "Go back in and get two more rebounds."

Gregor rebounded three missed shots before the next dead ball to finish the game with 35.

Woody

Gary Gregor was from South Charleston, West Virginia. He was 6-7, weighed 235 pounds, and had the physique of Charles Atlas. His nickname was Woody.

Recruited by Chuck Noe, Gregor played his varsity career in spurts at the University of South Carolina under Coach Frank McGuire. Academic problems limited him to nine games as a sophomore in 1965 and kept him out of the lineup altogether in 1966, so his varsity career was limited to less than two-and-a half seasons.

Gregor scored 843 points for a career average of 15.6 points per game and averaged 12.6 rebounds per game, totaling 678 in 54

Gary Gregor (USC Sports Information)

games. He led the ACC in rebounding in 1967 and was a second-team All-ACC choice in both 1967 and 1968.

After his junior year, Gregor was drafted as a future by the New York Knicks of the NBA and Minnesota of the ABA. After his senior season, he was selected in the first round of the NBA draft by the Phoenix Suns and was named to the NBA All-Rookie team in 1969.

Since the Dallas Cowboys were having success with former basketball players such as Cornell Green, Gil Brant, the super scout of the Cowboys, made a pitch for Gregor, too. He had been an all-state tight end at South Charleston High School in addition to starring in basketball.

His heart was in basketball, however, and he had a six-year pro career with Phoenix, Atlanta, Portland, and Milwaukee of the NBA and the New York Nets of the ABA.

In 361 NBA/ABA games, he scored 3,227 points and pulled down 2,286 rebounds.

Gregor eventually settled in Cincinnati, where he now owns a Lincoln-Mercury automobile dealership. One of his sons was a basketball letterman at the University of Cincinnati.

Skip Two

Skip Kickey and Skip Harlicka were both from New Jersey — Union City and Trenton, respectively—and were among Frank McGuire's first class of basketball recruits in 1964.

Kickey's given name was Alfred, and Harlicka's was Jules. Both were nicknamed "Skip" at an early age. Kickey was described in the 1965-66 basketball media guide as a fun-loving, "loose" type, who excelled with his imitation of Harlem Globetrotter Goose Tatum.

Kickey was six-feet-eight-inches tall and battled injuries and a weight problem throughout his career. Harlicka was six-feet- one and a deadly outside shooter. His father, Jules, Sr., was an editor with the Trenton newspaper and often sent the sports information office suggestions for feature stories.

After playing in all 24 games as a sophomore, injuries limited Kickey to two games in 1967 and 17 in 1968. Harlicka, on the other hand, scored 1,209 points in a much longer career. He averaged 21.8 points per game as a senior and was the first-round draft choice of the Atlanta Hawks in 1968.

Harlicka played one season in the NBA and then went into business. He lived in South Carolina for a while before moving to Raleigh, N.C. His son played basketball under Bobby Cremins at Georgia Tech.

Kickey owns a trophy company in Columbia.

Hold the Presses

The Florida State football team came to Columbia in 1972 with a bowl bid in the offing.

The Seminoles needed only to defeat South Carolina in a night game November 18 to sew up a trip to the Peach Bowl. South Carolina's record was 3-6, with a game remaining at Clemson, and the Gamecocks weren't going anywhere in the postseason.

The *Atlanta Constitution* was interested in the game, since the Peach Bowl is played in Atlanta, but the paper had a deadline problem because the game was to be played at night. The writer assigned to cover the game was instructed to prepare a sidebar beforehand, assuming in the article that Florida State had won, and file it before the game was actually played.

The writer obtained quotes from several Seminole officials, and the sidebar was dispatched to Atlanta.

But Bobby Marino kicked a field goal in the waning minutes, and South Carolina upset Florida State 24-21. Someone on the sports desk in Atlanta neglected to kill the sidebar until after the early edition was printed. Quite a few thousand newspapers went out with Florida State quotes on how nice it was to be going to the Peach Bowl.

The Seminoles never made it to the Peach Bowl.

March of Dimes

During halftime of a 1963 basketball game between Duke and South Carolina at the old Carolina Field House, spectators were encouraged to throw coins onto the court to raise money for the March of Dimes.

Cheerleaders, aided by a number of children from the stands, recovered the coins. The three youngsters from the sports information director's household—Tommy, 11, Melissa, 8, and Richard, 7—participated. The only problem was, Richard thought charity began at home.

When the cheerleaders asked for his collections, his reaction was, "No Way." His older brother grabbed him, kicking and screaming, turned him upside down, and coins tumbled from his bulging pockets.

The overflow crowd in the field house thought it was hilarious. Richard's mother was mortified.

I'll Have Gamecock

The Price family went to the South Carolina State Fair when Melissa was three years old. Dinnertime found the family in an establishment sponsored by a Columbia church. Melissa was asked what she would like for dinner.

"I'll have gamecock," she replied. She got a hamburger.

Melissa grew up to earn four degrees at the University of South Carolina and is on the faculty as professor and senior lecturer at Staffordshire University in Stoke on Trent, England.

Adolph

Legendary Kentucky basketball coach Adolph Rupp never missed an opportunity to needle an opponent. When South Carolina traveled to Lexington in December 1967 to participate in the

Kentucky Invitational Tournament, Rupp noticed a typographical error in the opponent's section of the Kentucky basketball media guide.

The University of South Carolina enrollment was listed as 63,000, when actually it was 13,000.

"I believe you ought to be able to find five kids who can play basketball in a crowd like that," Rupp said.

The cagey old Wildcat coach delighted in mispronouncing the names of opposing players. While handing out watches during the tournament awards banquet, Rupp pronounced Gary Gregor's name "Gree-gore." Skip Harlicka was "Hard-likker."

He got one name right. Corky Carnevale was the son of former U.S. Naval Academy coach and New York University AD Ben Carnevale.

"You must be old Ben's boy," Rupp said as he handed Carnevale his tournament watch. "I know your daddy well."

South Carolina was in Lexington on December 10, 1979, to play Kentucky. That was the day of Adolph Rupp's funeral, and a special tribute to the legendary coach preceded the game. Rupp had always enjoyed poetry, especially the verse of Robert Burns.

Just before the game tipped off, the lights in Rupp Arena were dimmed, and a spotlight shone on the mid-court chair that had been reserved for Rupp after he retired from coaching. A tape recording of Rupp reading a Robert Burns poem echoed throughout the arena.

South Carolina never had a chance in the game. The Gamecocks lost 126-81.

Burning Broom

The South Carolina basketball team was in New Orleans for the Sugar Bowl Basketball Tournament in December 1969.

The fourth race at the New Orleans Fairgrounds track the day the Gamecocks met Notre Dame for the tournament championship was named "South Carolina Gamecocks." The race was won by a horse named Burning Broom, and the jockey's silks were garnet and white, the colors of South Carolina's basketball uniforms.

A $2 win ticket on Burning Broom paid $8. South Carolina defeated Notre Dame 84-83 in overtime.

Brad

Brad Jergenson was 6-8, handsome, and the object of a spirited recruiting war between Marquette University and the University of South Carolina.

Jergenson was from Manitowac, Wisconsin but decided to leave his home state to play basketball for Coach Bill Foster and the Gamecocks. He was the prize signee of Foster's first recruiting class after Foster replaced retired coach, Frank McGuire.

Jergenson was a freshman when South Carolina traveled to Milwaukee in February of 1981 to play Coach Hank Raymond's Marquette Warriors. Raymond had succeeded Coach Al McGuire. Two busloads of Jergenson's friends and relatives made the trip from Manitowac to Milwaukee to see Brad play.

The Manitowac newspaper sent a writer to cover the game.

Jergenson was so excited when he came off the bench, the first shot he attempted sailed completely over the backboard and into the crowd. He recovered his composure and contributed eight points to a 91-89 South Carolina win.

After graduation Jergenson became the administrative assistant to Columbia's mayor for several years and eventually moved away from South Carolina. He now lives in Tampa, Florida.

Leprechaun

The University of South Carolina held a memorial service for Frank McGuire on January 28, 1995, in Carolina Coliseum the day the Gamecock basketball team played Southeastern Conference opponent Georgia.

A reunion of McGuire's greatest team was held the same day. The 1970 Gamecocks compiled a 25-3 record, and the 1971 squad won the Atlantic Coast Conference championship. In 1995, however, the second season of Coach Eddie Fogler's rebuilding program, the Gamecocks had struggled to a 4-11 mark.

Georgia had won 12 of 16 games.

The pep band played *When Irish Eyes are Smiling* as a tribute to McGuire, and perhaps buoyed by the presence of the great players from 25 years earlier, Fogler's Gamecocks battled the favored Bulldogs down to the wire.

With three seconds remaining, Malik Russell's tip-in of a missed shot gave South Carolina a 60-59 victory. Writers covering the game called it the luck of the Irish, and one of them hinted that a leprechaun actually tipped in the winning basket.

That may have been true. Malik Russell transferred to South Carolina after playing two seasons at Notre Dame. After graduating from South Carolina, Russell attended Georgetown University Law School and now practices law in New York City.

Frank, Al, and Dick

Contrary to reports in several newspapers during Frank McGuire's tenure as basketball coach at the University of South Carolina, Al and Dick McGuire were not Frank's younger brothers, although they were close enough to be brothers.

Frank coached Al and Dick at St. John's University but was not related to them. Al and Dick were brothers. Frank grew up in the Greenwich Village section of Manhattan, and Al and Dick were from Rockaway Beach on Long Island.

After college, both Al and Dick played in the NBA. Dick was the better player, and he wound up as head coach of the New York Knicks and later as a talent scout for the Knicks. He often visited Carolina Coliseum and his old coach at St. John's in search of talent for the NBA.

Al had a brief fling as an assistant coach at Dartmouth before going home to Rockaway Beach and working as a bartender in a saloon owned by his mother. When Belmont Abbey, a small Jesuit college in North Carolina, called on Frank McGuire in its search for a basketball coach, Frank recommended Al, and that's how he became a head coach.

From Belmont Abbey, Al graduated to Marquette University in Milwaukee, again thanks to a recommendation by Frank. Al had an outstanding career at Marquette, including one NCAA championship. His son, Allie, played point guard for him, and whenever Marquette lined up to defense an opponent's free-throw try, Al's instructions to his son could be heard throughout the arena, "Take da shooter, Allie!"

Frank and Al had some classic battles when they played each other. One of the most exciting occurred in Milwaukee on December 16, 1966. The occasion was the opening round of the Milwaukee Classic, a four-team tournament.

Frank Standard, South Carolina's 6-4 sophomore forward, and 6-2 Marquette guard George Thompson were former teammates. They had led Brooklyn's Erasmus Hall High School to an undefeated season and a New York City championship.

The game was a physical struggle that went down to the wire. Four technical fouls were called on South Carolina, two on Frank Standard and two on the Gamecock bench. Media reports said both were on Frank McGuire, but the second actually was on trainer Jim Price.

Al McGuire was on his knees in front of the Marquette bench when the fourth technical was called. Without rising to his feet, he waddled onto the court and pleaded with the officials to call a technical on Marquette.

"Every time you hit them with a T, then you kill us," Al pleaded. The refs were not amused and denied his request for a technical foul.

South Carolina held a two-point lead with seconds remaining. A Marquette shot bounced off the rim and high into the air. George Carbins of Marquette crammed the missed shot into the basket as the horn sounded. Overtime appeared in order, but no. One of the officials waved his arms frantically and shouted, "No basket! No basket!"

Carbins had put his hands in the imaginary cylinder to hit the basketball. That's called basket interference when the offense does it, and goaltending when done by the defense. South Carolina thus had its 63-61 victory.

Another classic battle between teams coached by Frank and Al occurred January 9, 1972, in Carolina Coliseum. Al won this one 72-71, but not until after what media reports described as an "under the basket altercation" between Bob Lackey of Marquette and South Carolina's Tom Riker.

In battling for position, the 6-9 Lackey delivered a hard elbow to Riker's face. The 6-10 Gamecock center countered with a left hook to the side of Lackey's head. The left-handed Riker broke a bone in his hand, and both players were ejected from the game.

Lackey went ballistic and kicked a chair near the Marquette bench. Al McGuire grabbed him by the shirt, shook him hard, and administered a few love taps with an open hand. The game continued.

The broken hand resulted in Riker missing a win over Manhattan, and posting average numbers in wins over St. Bonaventure and Niagara and a loss to Iowa. The big center from Hicksville, N.Y., on Long Island returned to form when the Gamecocks took a two-game trip to Madison Square Garden in New York City and the Chicago Stadium.

Riker scored 19 field goals, including his final 10 attempts in scoring 42 points in a win over Fordham in the Garden. He hit his first five attempts, running the string to 15 in a row two nights later in a 34-point performance to help defeat Northern Illinois in Chicago. He made 15 of 22 field-goal tries in that game.

Riker finished his South Carolina career with 1,343 points and 774 rebounds. He averaged 19.6 points per game his senior season and was a consensus All-American.

He was selected by the New York Knicks in the first round of the 1972 NBA draft. However, his professional basketball career was undistinguished. Over three seasons, he played in 82 games for the Knicks and scored 225 points. He had 138 rebounds, 107 of them in his final season, 1975, when he appeared in 51 games.

Riker eventually returned to Columbia and completed requirements for a degree in nursing at the University of South Carolina. In 2000 he moved to North Carolina.

J. P.

Jim Price was an athletics trainer at the University of South Carolina for more than 30 years. He was a student trainer at the University of Texas when Coach Warren Giese brought his South Carolina football team to Austin in 1957 and upset Coach Darrell Royal's Longhorns 27-21.

The following year, J. P. became a member of the Gamecock training staff. Worsening health forced him to retire in 1989.

J.P. developed rheumatic fever as a child, resulting in damage to his heart. Two mechanical valves were implanted in his heart in 1973.

While we shared the same surname, Jim and I were not re-lated, although many people assumed we were brothers. I told him this was because we both had red hair, freckles, and were ugly. Many acquaintances got us mixed up and called him Tom and me Jim. He was from Jefferson, Texas, and I was from Wadmalaw Island, South Carolina.

Retired athletics department pilot and student ticket manager Joe Baier still calls me Jim. Joe also says, "How's Martha?" every time I see him. My wife's name is Margaret.

Jim had three children by his first marriage, and his second wife, Harriett, had three children from her first marriage. Together they raised six children, and the stepchildren were as close to Jim and received as much love as his biological offspring.

The Gamecock basketball team was in Tokyo during a 1982 goodwill trip to Asia, and Jim called home to wish his stepdaughter Elizabeth a happy 12th birthday. He and I were roommates on the trip, and I wanted to know the results of the NCAA baseball regional tournament the Gamecocks were hosting. South Carolina had been scheduled to play West Virginia in the championship game.

At my urging, Jim asked Elizabeth, "Who won the baseball game?"

Her reaction was: "Who played?"

I urged Jim to get Harriett on the phone. Her reaction was: "Who did Carolina play?"

After much prompting, Harriett consulted the newspaper and reported the Gamecocks had won 2-1. Jim and I had a trip to Omaha and the College World Series the day after we returned to South Carolina from Japan.

In the spring of 1996, Jim's heart gave out.

The University of South Carolina partially financed the installation of chair seats at Sarge Frye Field, the Gamecock baseball stadium, by selling personalized seats. Next to the seats bearing the name of the retired sports information director are two seats labeled, "In Memory of Jim Price."

We weren't blood relatives, but he was my brother.

J.P. still ministers to the health needs of South Carolina basketball players. The current trainer for the Gamecock basketball program, Jeff Parsons, proudly noted in a January 2001 speech to the Columbia Tipoff Club that he had "the same initials as Jim Price."

Parsons said when he became the basketball trainer, Jim Price gave him a list of all the Gamecock players he had treated over the years and said, "If any of these guys ever asks you for anything, you take care of them."

The Natural

Brian Williams was from the little South Carolina town of Fort Lawn. His nickname was "The Natural."

As a freshman on the University of South Carolina baseball team, Williams played seven positions—everywhere except second base and catcher. He saw action in 21 games at shortstop, 17 at first base, nine as a designated hitter, five at third base, two in left field and center field and eight games as a pitcher.

His batting average was .332 with eight home runs and 18 stolen bases. In regular-season games, his pitching record as a freshman was 1-1; but in the Metro Conference Tournament, he struck out 12 Southern Mississippi batters in a complete-game 6-2 victory.

That performance earned Williams a start against Georgia Tech in the NCAA regional tournament at Coral Gables, Florida. He allowed an infield single in the first inning and a clean single in the second. He struck out 15 Yellow Jackets and walked two in a two-hit 5-0 shutout.

There was something about Georgia Tech that brought out the best in Brian Williams. Two years after the Coral Gables outing, he met the Yellow Jackets again on April 17, 1990, at Sarge Frye Field. He almost missed the assignment. His mother was hospitalized in Lancaster, and Williams returned to Columbia from her bedside just in time to pitch.

After eight innings, he had a no-hitter and a 1-0 lead. Georgia Tech's leadoff batter hit a high chopper off the plate to lead off the ninth. Realizing he couldn't throw the speedy runner out, Gamecock shortstop Burke Cromer deliberately bobbled the ball in hopes of preserving the no-hitter by drawing an error.

I was the official scorer and ruled it a hit, drawing the ire of the 2,117 fans in attendance. The boos grew louder when Williams picked the runner off first base and retired the next batter. After a base on balls, a clean single got the official scorer off the hook and put the 1-0 lead in jeopardy. A weak infield ground ball ended the game. It was the first time Georgia Tech had been shut out in 106 games, but the second career shutout of the Yellow Jackets by Brian Williams.

There were 20 major league scouts at the game, and Coach June Raines said, "That's why [Williams] is one of the best pitchers in the country."

Williams was drafted in the third round as a high school senior by the Pittsburgh Pirates, but spurned professional baseball for a collegiate career. After his junior season, he was a supplemental first-round pick by the Houston Astros.

Between 1991 and 2000, he pitched in more than 230 major league games with the Astros, San Diego Padres, Detroit Tigers, Baltimore Orioles, Houston again, Chicago Cubs, and Cleveland Indians.

Where's Lewie?

In the summer of 1976, Hall of Fame pitcher Robin Roberts recommended four recent Pennsylvania high school graduates to his friend, University of South Carolina baseball coach Bobby Richardson. One of them was the son of another outstanding former Philadelphia Phillies pitcher, Curt Simmons, and another was Tim

Lewis, a six-foot-four-inch left-handed pitcher.

"I took Timmy because I liked the way he threw the ball and he was the best student of the four," Richardson explained. "I advised the other three to go to junior college and they did."

Four years later, when he completed his collegiate eligibility, Tim Lewis had won 36 games for the Gamecocks, a school record at the time. Perhaps his greatest win was in an elimination game against Arizona State in the 1975 College World Series.

Lewis was a junior and hadn't pitched in 19 days when he was called upon to face Arizona State. The winner would advance to the national championship game against the University of Texas.

The game was scoreless for seven and a half innings, but Arizona State scored in the bottom of the eighth on a pop-fly triple that landed just inside the right-field foul line.

In the top of the ninth, South Carolina second baseman Mark Van Bever doubled to put the potential tying run on base. A sacrifice moved him to third. Right fielder Garry Hancock tied the game with an RBI single. The Gamecocks scored three more runs to take a 4-1 lead.

Lewis was missing when the team took the field for the bottom of the ninth. Thinking the fluke triple had cost him the game, he had retreated into the tunnel from the dugout to the locker room and was throwing a temper tantrum.

Located and sent back to the mound, he retired the Sun Devils on a pop foul, a strikeout, and a weak ground ball to end the game.

Lewis compiled a 36-6 record during his collegiate career (1973-76) and was signed by the New York Yankees. He reached the AAA level but never pitched in the major leagues. Hancock, on the other hand, appeared in 273 major league games between 1978 and 1984 with the Boston Red Sox and the Oakland Athletics.

Shortstop U.

Since Ray Tanner became head coach at the University of South Carolina before the 1997 season, the Gamecock baseball program has become Shortstop University.

229

Adam Everett played as a freshman under Tanner at North Carolina State University and transferred to South Carolina when Tanner moved to the Gamecocks. In two seasons at South Carolina, Everett had a career batting average of .366, was outstanding defensively, was named to All-America teams, and was drafted in the first round by the Boston Red Sox.

Traded to the Houston Astros before the 2000 season, Everett played at the AAA level in New Orleans and won a gold medal in the Sydney, Australia, Olympics when the U.S. team defeated Cuba 4-0.

Brian Roberts played two seasons at the University of North Carolina but transferred to South Carolina after his father was fired as the Tar Heel coach. Roberts led the NCAA in stolen bases with 63 at North Carolina in 1998 and repeated as national stolen-base leader with 67 as a Gamecock in 1999. He also batted .353 with 12 home runs.

An All-America selection for the third time, Roberts was a supplemental first-round draft pick by the Baltimore Orioles after one season at South Carolina.

Drew Meyer attended Bishop England High School in Charleston. The Los Angeles Dodgers drafted him in the second round in 1999, but he chose to play collegiate baseball at South Carolina under Ray Tanner.

Meyer batted .320, hit 11 home runs, drove in 49 runs, stole 13 bases, and was chosen second-team All-Southeastern Conference and named to the freshman All-America team. He helped South Carolina compile a 56-10 record, the most wins by any NCAA Division I team in 2000.

While Everett, Roberts, and Meyer were outstanding shortstops, South Carolina has had some other stellar performers at the position.

Eddie Ford, son of Hall of Fame Yankee pitcher Whitey Ford, played for Bobby Richardson (1972-74) and was drafted in the first round by the Boston Red Sox. He advanced to the AAA level before quitting professional baseball for law school.

Tripp Cromer played shortstop under Coach June Raines (1987-89) and also played nearly 200 major league games with the St. Louis Cardinals, Los Angeles Dodgers, and Houston Astros. He

Ray Tanner (USC Sports Information)

retired after the 2000 season, and in 2001 helped coach a private high school team in Columbia.

Kent Anderson played under Raines (1982-84) and enjoyed two major league seasons with the California Angels, appearing in 135 games.

Jeff Grantz, a second-team All-America quarterback in football, set fielding records at both shortstop and second base with the Gamecock baseball squad from 1973 to 1976.

The Lambeau Leap

Robert Brooks gained fame in the National Football League by perfecting the Lambeau Leap. He would leap into the end zone stands to be congratulated by adoring Green Bay Packer fans after scoring a touchdown at Lambeau Field.

Brooks, from Greenwood, was just as spectacular during his collegiate career at the University of South Carolina. Between 1988 and 1991, he caught 156 passes, third-most in Gamecock history. His career receptions covered 2,211 yards.

He scored 19 touchdowns on pass receptions and had a 98-yard kickoff return for a touchdown against Virginia Tech. Brooks holds the school record for longest gain on a pass receptions—97 yards for a touchdown from quarterback Todd Ellis against East Carolina in 1988.

Heisman Hogs

More than 35 members of the 1980 South Carolina football team gathered on the weekend of the game with Arkansas in October 2000 for the 20th anniversary of George Rogers' Heisman Trophy season and trip to the Gator Bowl.

The offensive linemen from that team dubbed themselves the "Heisman Hogs" and claimed much of the credit for Rogers being recognized as the best football player in the nation. Two of the hogs— Kenny Gil and Steve Gettel—had some memories of life in the Roost.

They remembered rolling a bottle rocket under the door of a foreign member of the track team. The exploding rocket set the track man's mattress afire, and he ran out of the room carrying the burning mattress and threw it out a second-story window.

"We got into a lot of trouble for that," Gettel recalled.

Gil remembered rooming with huge middle guard Emanuel Weaver, who was from New Orleans and had never seen snow. When Columbia was blanketed with a rare snowfall, Weaver looked out the window and then ran up and down the hall knocking on doors, waking up Roost residents, and shouting, "It's snowing! It's snowing!"

Gil also recalled a stern lecture from Jim Carlen, the head football coach. Carlen warned the players against inviting women to their rooms.

"Remember, women are smarter than you," Carlen was quoted.

"I never got caught," Gil said. He is now a special investigator with the office of the solicitor [prosecutor] of South Carolina's Fifth Judicial Circuit.

Gettel remembered one player had a female visitor in his first-floor room, and she placed her purse on the sill of an open window.

"We swiped her purse and ordered a pizza. When she came out, we were eating pizza," Gettel said. He is now a manufacturer's representative living in Aurora, Colorado.

Mark Austin remembered what he thinks was a ghost story from his time living in the Roost.

"Something grabbed me and pulled me through the door. I don't know what it was." There's a good chance it was one of his teammates.

Joy Thomas, who is now Mrs. Chuck Slaughter, was a student at the College of Charleston when the 1980 Gamecocks upset Rose Bowl-bound Michigan at Ann Arbor.

"Several of us were so excited, we drove up to Columbia from Charleston to meet the team at the airport," she recalled. "I knew girls weren't supposed to be in the Roost, but there were about 20 of us there. We were dancing on tables and having a great time."

Chuck Slaughter was one of the Heisman Hogs. An offensive tackle, he played in the NFL with the New Orleans Saints. He, Joy, and their children now live in Rock Hill.

Slaughter remembered when he and fellow tackle Chuck Allen jumped the fence to sneak into the state fair. Allen is a former member of the South Carolina legislature.

Joe Doyle was a Heisman Hog who came to South Carolina as a running back. When introducing himself at a function for freshman players, he said, "Joe Doyle, Wilmington, North Carolina, running back," and hearing Coach Jim Carlen saying in an aside, "Linebacker."

He wound up as an excellent offensive guard. Two other high school running backs were freshmen with Doyle. George Rogers rushed for 5,204 yards during his career, while Johnnie Wright rushed for 2,589 yards.

Mrs. K

Sue Kurpiewski was the dietitian in charge of feeding South Carolina athletes in the Roost cafeteria. The athletes called her "Mrs. K."

She was hired by Paul Dietzel, athletics director and head football coach when the Roost was built in 1967. Several years after leaving South Carolina, Dietzel became athletics director at Louisiana State University and attempted to hire Mrs. K as dietitian for the LSU athletes.

Jim Carlen, Dietzel's successor, was in Columbia for the 20th reunion of the 1980 Gamecock football team in October of 2000 and recalled what it took to keep Mrs. K at South Carolina.

"She said if I would buy her a soft ice cream machine so she could make ice cream for the boys, she would stay," Carlen said. Business manager John Moore received a memo the next day, and soft ice cream became a daily feature at the Roost.

Moore allegedly remarked to Carlen, "Mrs. K is the only person I know who could overspend an unlimited budget." When asked about the remark 20 years later, Moore replied, "I don't remember saying that, but it sounds like me. Anyway, it's true."

Mrs. K often prepared special dishes to cater to the desires of the athletes.

She remembered that football and baseball player Jeff Grantz (quarterback and infielder, 1972-76) "loved macaroni and cheese, but he wanted Velveeta instead of the usual sharp cheddar cheese that we used."

Jeff got his macaroni with Velveeta.

When George Rogers first came to South Carolina, he wasn't used to eating steak and preferred fried bologna for pregame meals. George also preferred meatloaf to steak.

Kenny Reynolds, a basketball player from Brooklyn, N.Y., also didn't like steak and asked instead for hamburger. Reynolds, who was black, palled around with teammate and fellow New Yorker Mike Doyle, who was white. Mrs. K called them "Salt and Pepper."

Freddie Chalmers, a football letterman (1981-82) asked Mrs. K one day why she never had neck bones on the menu.

"I went out and bought some neck bones," she said. "After that, we had them about twice a year."

When Willie Scott (1977-1980) lived in the Roost, "There wasn't a day that went by that Willie didn't come by my office to talk," Mrs. K remembered. A tight end, Scott was a first-round NFL draft choice and played professional football for nine years with the Kansas City Chiefs and the New England Patriots. In 2000, he became an assistant coach at Savannah State University.

Mrs. K remembered that Jimmy Nash (football 1969-71) and his roommate would come to the cafeteria and "fill up a gallon jar with cereal and milk and eat it in my office."

Cheeseburgers were a Wednesday tradition for lunch at the Roost. A new sandwich called steakums became popular, and for variety, Mrs. K offered steakums once as a substitute for cheeseburgers.

Kevin Long (football 1974-76) told Mrs. K the steakum was good, and he didn't like to complain, but, "it's not a cheeseburger."

"I served steakums again, but never on Wednesday," she said. "Wednesday was always cheeseburger day."

Student trainer Sid Kenyon received a sack of homegrown tomatoes from his father. Kenyon knocked on Mrs. K's door, and she produced a loaf of bread, mayonnaise, and other condiments and "we had some great tomato sandwiches."

Daredevil

Chris Hildreth is a daredevil. He's also an outstanding photographer who will risk life and limb for a good picture.

Hildreth was a University of South Carolina staff photographer in 1988 when the Gamecock football team played North Carolina at Williams Brice Stadium. Hildreth climbed to the top of one of the stadium light towers to get the shot he wanted.

The light poles at Sarge Frye Field, South Carolina's baseball stadium, are 95 feet high. Hildreth climbed the pole in left- center field and shot pictures that resembled aerial photos of a game against Clemson.

Authorities stationed a security person at the base of the light pole to prevent the possibility of baseball fans joining Hildreth on his lofty perch.

Hildreth left the South Carolina staff to work at Cornell University and is now a staff photographer at Duke University.

Streakers

Streaking was a fad that swept college campuses in the early 1970s, and the University of South Carolina was not exempt.

South Carolina's baseball stadium is adjacent to the Roost. During one baseball game, two nude figures wearing ski masks to hide their faces ran out a side exit at the Roost, hurdled over the low fence paralleling the left-field foul line, dashed into the outfield, reversed course, hurdled the fence again, and reentered the dormitory.

The perpetrators were never apprehended or publicly identified, but one of them had the physique and the hurdling technique of Mike Haggard, a football wide receiver and member of the track team.

Cheerleaders

Buzz Prescott was one of four University of South Carolina cheerleaders who drove to New York City in January of 1974 to see the Gamecock basketball team play Seton Hall in Madison Square Garden.

The two males and two females spent the night before the game in Red Bank, N.J., at the home of cheerleader Steve Schiavone.

When the four arrived at the South Carolina team hotel in Manhattan, they encountered Coach Frank McGuire in the lobby. When he asked who had financed their trip, they told him they paid their own way.

McGuire told business manager Ralph Floyd to give the cheerleaders $200 apiece to cover their meals and to get them rooms in the hotel.

"That was the beginning," Prescott said. "After that, Coach McGuire saw to it that cheerleaders were taken on basketball road trips."

Go 'Cocks

South Carolina State Sen. John Martin of Winnsboro was a rabid Gamecock fan. Martin was once in Phoenix and went to an NBA game between the Phoenix Suns and the Denver Nuggets.

Former South Carolina All-American Alex English was a member of the Denver team, and Martin was yelling, "Go 'Cocks!" to English, when a security guard admonished him, "You can't say that here."

The security guard thought Martin was yelling something obscene.

Shots in the Dark

Kenneth "Red" Martin was a University of South Carolina student in the early 1960s. He was a gym rat who never missed an opportunity to shoot a few baskets. Martin was from Winnsboro, which also happened to be the hometown of basketball star Ronnie Collins.

Ronnie swiped a key to the gym from the coach's office, and he and Red would sneak into the darkened building at night and shoot baskets by the light of a clock on the wall.

"We weren't supposed to be there after hours," Martin remembered. One night, Ronnie took a chance and turned the lights on.

The campus policeman on patrol checked on the lighted gymnasium, and when he discovered the culprit was the star of the basketball team, he said, "Oh, it's you, Ronnie. Just turn out the lights when you leave."

Red Martin was recruited by the sports information office to keep statistics at basketball games. Nearly 40 years later, he's still a member of the statistics crew. He also works with the football statistics crew, but Red's passion for hunting sometimes takes precedence over football.

He missed the Tennessee game in 2000 because he was hunting pheasants in North Dakota. He also keeps the retired sports information director's home freezer stocked with venison.

It Ain't Swaying

Bumper stickers appeared on automobiles throughout South Carolina in the mid-1980s proclaiming, "If it ain't swaying, we ain't playing."

The reference was to "harmonic vibrations" that caused the recently constructed upper deck on the east side of Williams-Brice Stadium to sway when Gamecock fans became excited during football games.

The swaying first became noticeable in 1983 during South Carolina's 38-14 upset of Southern California. It became alarmingly noticeable in 1986 when heavily favored Nebraska was forced to come from behind to claim a 27-24 victory over the Gamecocks.

Newspapers and radio talk shows were flooded with calls from fans claiming to have witnessed the swaying. Eyewitness accounts

Williams-Brice Stadium—It Ain't Swaying (USC Sports Information)

ranged from movement of an inch or two to more than a foot. Some fans claimed to have feared for their lives.

The phenomenon was blamed on the band for playing *Louie, Louie*, a song aimed at inciting excitement among the student body and other fans to the foot-stomping enthusiasm of the students themselves.

University officials took steps to relieve the situation by banning the song from the band's repertoire. When the band director defied that edict and played the song anyway, he was censured by the university's president, and the band was moved to another section of the stadium. Student seating sections were also relocated.

Architects and engineers were called in to study the situation that they blamed on "harmonic vibrations" or "harmonic resonance," which one expert likened to vibrations from an opera singer's voice causing a water glass to shatter.

A Purdue University civil engineering professor noted that every structure has a natural frequency, the speed at which vibrations move through it. A structure's natural frequency remains constant, the professor said, and when an outside force hits it at a similar rate, there is movement. He said football stadiums can experience a cumulative effect when fans get excited, if they're all moving together to cheers or fight songs.

While the architects insisted the movement was natural for a cantilevered stadium deck, and there was no danger involved, enough fans expressed concern that additional construction was undertaken to shore up the deck and eliminate noticeable movement before the 1987 season.

Nowadays, nobody is saying it's swaying, but Williams-Brice Stadium is still jumping with crowds in excess of 80,000 on football Saturdays.

Flying Low

Sandra Williams is a Gamecock fan who regularly follows the South Carolina football team on road trips by chartered bus or airplane. She was returning from Mississippi in 1998, when the trip was delayed because a bus collided with the airplane.

Sandra traveled on a charter flight, along with the South Carolina cheerleaders and some members of the pep band, to Memphis, at which point the group was transported by bus to Oxford. After the game, the bus returned to Memphis for the flight home, but the group was told the flight had been canceled because a bus had collided with the airplane.

The plane, chartered by the South Carolina group, had transported the Texas A&M team home to College Station, Texas, from a road game and was scheduled to continue on to Memphis to pick up the South Carolina group. A bus scheduled to pick up part of the Texas A&M team, attempting to maneuver close to the aircraft, had backed into one of the plane's wings, causing some damage.

A substitute plane could not be found until the next day, so the South Carolina group was transported to a hotel. Since it had been planned as a day trip, none of the passengers had any luggage.

"There were some rough-looking women on that flight the next day when we finally left Memphis," Sandra Williams recalled.

"Even those beautiful cheerleaders didn't look so beautiful the next morning."

Williams said that on one charter trip to Mississippi, the wife of South Carolina head coach Brad Scott fell and broke her ankle, and a horde of yellow jackets invaded the bus, causing Gamecock fans to scurry for cover.

Smarter than Me

Mike Doyle was a 6-4—he liked to be listed as 6-5—swingman from the Bronx who played four seasons of basketball (1977-80) under Coach Frank McGuire.

In 107 games as a Gamecock, Doyle scored 1,360 points. His highest average came during his junior season, when he tallied 15.3 points per game. Doyle was one of the team captains for both his junior and senior seasons. He was a very good basketball player who might have been great if he had had a little more foot speed.

Mike Doyle left the University of South Carolina with a B.S. degree in business administration and a wife from Hampton, S.C. named LaVonda. She earned a Ph.D. and works for a New York City firm as its marketing director. Mike is a Wall Street bond broker.

"My wife works 10 hours a day at her job, and I work about four hours a day at mine," Doyle said while attending the Frank McGuire Foundation awards banquet in November of 2000. "But she's a lot smarter than me."

The Doyles maintain their South Carolina connection with a vacation home on Ladies Island in Beaufort County. LaVonda likes to shrimp, crab, and fish and spends a lot of time on the dock. Mike said he would rather watch television, so he had cable TV installed on the dock so he could be with his wife without missing his favorite programs.

Hot Pants

South Carolina met Indiana December 28, 1988, in the Liberty Bowl at Memphis. It was a bitter cold night, and the teams used propane gas heaters for warmth on the sidelines.

South Carolina assistant coach Al Groh backed up to one of the heaters but got too close, and his pant leg caught fire. His son, Mike, a student-athlete at Columbia's Spring Valley High School, was on the sideline with his dad and managed to extinguish the fire before Al received serious burns.

Al Groh left South Carolina for other coaching jobs and was the head coach of the New York Jets in the NFL in 2000 before returning to his alma mater to succeed the retired George Welsh as head coach at the University of Virginia. Mike Groh became a star quarterback at the University of Virginia.

United Nations

Pity the poor public-address and radio play-by-play announcers at games played by the University of South Carolina women's basketball team during the 2000-01 season. Lady Gamecock coach Susan Walvius scouted the European continent for talent. Nine of her 15 players hailed from seven European countries.

Names the announcers had to cope with included Petra (PET-rah) Ujhelyi (oo-HEY-ee), Ildiko (eel-dee-go) Szakacs (SO-kotch), and Viki Hollosy (HOL-oh-see) from Hungary; Nihan (KNEE-hawn) Anaz (AH-nahz) from Turkey; Ines (ee-nehz) Ajanovic (ah-YAHN-o-vitch) from Yugoslavia; Christina Ciocan (cho-KAHN) from Romania; Tatyana (tot-e-ah-nah) Troina (troy-nah) from Belarus; Daniela Strohm (strom) from Germany; and Linda Hoagland (hoag-lund) from Sweden.

To make matters tougher on the announcers, the women opened play with an exhibition game against a team from Russia. Names on that roster included Rebstovskaya, Stelmaakh, Jurgalina, Hazova, Cherni, Gustilina, Shouneikina, Shnilukova, and Deviatkina.

The 2000-01 Lady Gamecocks led the NCAA by a large margin in international players with nine. Duquesne and Florida International were distant seconds with six foreign players each. The Lady Gamecocks played Duquesne at Pittsburgh in December, with the Duquesne foreigners claiming a two-point victory, 67-65, over the Carolina foreigners.

Coach Eddie Fogler's men's roster for 2000-2001 included only one international player—6-10 center Marius Petravicius (peh-TRAH-vicious) from Lithuania.

Decoupage

Decoupage is the art of cutting out designs or illustrations from paper, foil, etc., mounting them decoratively on a surface, and applying several coats of varnish or lacquer.

One of Margaret Price's hobbies was making decoupage purses for women. She would purchase wooden boxes and decoupage them with figures of songbirds, flowers, and animals or gamecocks.

Margaret, with her own gamecock decoupage purse, was shopping in a Columbia supermarket one day, when she was approached by Dolly Wells, a University of South Carolina graduate who was married to a former Clemson basketball player.

"Where did you get that purse?" Dolly asked.

Margaret, who had never before met Dolly Wells, answered, "I made it."

"Would you make me one?" Dolly asked.

Margaret agreed to make the purse. Dolly took it to a Clemson football game and sat in the VIP section of the stadium near the wife of then-Clemson football coach Hootie Ingram.

Dolly called Margaret and said the Gamecock purse had caused quite a stir in the Clemson stadium. She asked if Margaret if she would decoupage a purse with tiger paws, the Clemson athletics symbol.

"We're a Gamecock family," Margaret replied. "We don't do tiger paws."

Choreographed

Del Wilkes was a consensus All-America offensive guard on the University of South Carolina football team his senior season in 1984.

He had a brief tenure with the Tampa Bay Buccaneers of the NFL before turning his attention to a career as a professional wrestler. Wilkes learned the tricks of the trade under Lillian Ellison, a Columbia resident who was a world-champion wrestler in the 1950s who was billed as the "Fabulous Moolah." She operated a training school for aspiring young wrestlers.

Wilkes fought in the World Wrestling Federation under the title "The Trooper" for several years, during which time he wore a highway patrolman's hat into the ring. After pinning an opponent, he would write out a ticket for the fallen foe. Then Wilkes became "The Patriot," a red, white and blue clad gladiator who was always the good guy in the ring.

Much of Wilkes's wrestling career was spent in Japan, where Sumo wrestlers are national heroes; but according to Wilkes, American wrestlers are also very popular. Wilkes says professional wrestling is "entertainment," but he denies that the bouts are fakes. Instead, he says, they are "choreographed."

An arm injury ended his wrestling career after 12 years, and Wilkes returned to the Columbia area, where he is a salesman for an automobile dealership in Lexington, S.C.

The USC

Peggy Binette was seven months' pregnant and needed some back support for the 2000 South Carolina-Clemson football game.

Wal-Mart had advertised that a new shipment of USC stadium seats had just been received, so a stop was made there on the way from Columbia to Clemson. There was a large display of stadium seats bearing the letters USC—in University of Southern California colors.

The University of South Carolina colors are garnet and black. Southern California's colors are cardinal and gold. Peggy bought the seat anyway.

The stadium-seat blunder was not the first time the two USC's have been confused. When South Carolina made its first trip to the College World Series in 1975, the Gamecock baseball coach was introduced to a media luncheon as Coach Bobby Richardson of Southern California. Two years later the Gamecocks returned to the World Series under first-year coach June Raines. He was introduced at the media luncheon as being from Southern California.

When Southern California's football team came to Columbia in 1983 to play the Gamecocks, the scoreboard operator had some fun with the two USC's. Southern California was at first identified on the scoreboard as "USC," with South Carolina labeled "The USC."

That setup appeared to be a little unbalanced, so the designations were changed to "USC West" and "USC East." For the record, USC East won the game 38-14.

The University of Southern California was founded in 1880. The University of South Carolina is 79 years older. Chartered in 1801, South Carolina celebrated its bicentennial in 2001.

The Dog Ate It

Fans seeking replacement of lost or destroyed tickets to athletic events have been known to use the excuse that their dog ate the tickets. That actually happened to a media credential to a football game between South Carolina and Clemson.

Lou Brierley was a professor who taught graphics in the South Carolina College of Journalism. He also moonlighted as a writer for *Spurs & Feathers,* the weekly tabloid devoted to University of South Carolina athletics.

Brierley contacted the South Carolina sports information office to plead his case. He said he had left his media credential to the Clemson game on the coffee table in the living room at his home.

His Pekingese puppy, named Spike, had found the ticket and chewed it to pieces.

The SID took him at his word and the credential was replaced.

Hold Onto Your Hat

Gary Hassen was the long snapper for punts and field goals on South Carolina football teams of 1977-79. His final game was against Missouri in the Hall of Fame Bowl at Birmingham, Alabama.

Word got back to assistant equipment manager Mac Credille that Hassen planned to take his football helmet home as a keepsake. Credille was a jealous guardian of university property, and when Coach Jim Carlen replaced Hassen with Randy Teston late in the game, Credille confiscated Hassen's headgear and sent it to the equipment truck.

Later, when Teston made a bad snap over the head of punter Jay Feltz, Carlen ordered Hassen back onto the field for the last punt of game. Gary couldn't find his helmet but finally located one from a teammate that fit.

Hassen was from Pennsylvania, but he remained in Columbia to work for his alma mater after receiving a business administration degree in 1979. He is now director of development at the University of South Carolina.

The Shoe

Tony Ciuffo (pronounced SHOE-foe) dearly loved baseball, especially University of South Carolina baseball and Cincinnati Reds baseball. If he had to pick one over the other, the feeling is he would probably go with the Reds, but not by much.

"The Shoe" was from Charleston and pitched two seasons for Anderson Junior College in upstate South Carolina before transferring to the University of South Carolina to complete his degree requirements. Soon after enrolling at the Columbia campus, the Shoe volunteered his services to the sports information office.

There were a couple of baseball road trips that the sports information director couldn't make due to other commitments, and the Shoe eagerly volunteered to fill in. The only problem was that the Gamecock team, which usually won two-thirds of all its games, couldn't win when Tony traveled.

On a spring-break trip in March 1989, South Carolina lost at Southern Mississippi 16-6, South Alabama 9-4 and 7-6 in 12 innings, and Alabama 12-5. A year later, in March 1990, the Shoe accompanied Coach June Raines and his team to Tampa, where the Gamecocks lost 6-4 to Alabama, 5-4 to South Florida and 9-4 to Western Michigan.

In the same season, South Carolina defeated North Carolina-Charlotte 16-4 at home, but the Shoe made the trip when the Gamecocks traveled to North Carolina, and Charlotte claimed a 7-5 victory. When the Shoe completed his postgame work, he went to the parking lot and found that the team bus had left for Columbia. The student manager had forgotten to include him in the head count and had told Coach Raines that everyone was on the bus.

Fortunately for the Shoe, radio broadcasters Bob Fulton and Jim Powell had traveled to the game by automobile and were just leaving when the Shoe ran them down and hitched a 100-mile ride home.

Ciuffo did manage to witness one road win, but he had to weather a snowstorm and a final-inning rally. Knowing the Shoe's love for the Reds, Raines agreed to take him along on a three-game trip to Cincinnati in 1989, even though the sports information director was also on the trip.

The team bus plowed through an early-April snowstorm between Lexington, Kemtucky, and Cincinnati and arrived about midnight before the Friday game. The game was snowed out, but the Reds and Giants played that night despite the cold, and a shivering Shoe was in attendance at Riverfront Stadium to witness a 16-inning marathon that his beloved Reds won 4-3.

South Carolina's Saturday game at Cincinnati was rained out, but the Shoe was again at Riverfront Stadium for the night game between the Reds and Giants. After a three-hour rain delay, that game was called off.

South Carolina and Cincinnati settled for a Sunday double-header, two seven-inning games. Cincinnati won the first game 6-5, but the Shoe was spared a complete shutout when the Gamecocks rallied to win the second game 12-5.

Tony Ciuffo graduated from the University of South Carolina and landed a job as sports information director at the College of Charleston, where he quickly earned a promotion to assistant director of athletics for media relations. In addition, he has been the radio play-by-play voice of College of Charleston basketball since 1996.

Ciuffo has had a lot more success with College of Charleston basketball than he had traveling with the University of South Carolina baseball team. The Cougars have consistently had outstanding teams under Coach John Kresse.

Shortly after Ciuffo became sports information director, he learned that the daughter of former major league pitcher Jack Billingham was enrolled at the College of Charleston. Six of her dad's 13 major league seasons were spent with the Cincinnati Reds. She quickly became a student assistant in the College of Charleston sports information office.

That relationship paid off when Ciuffo and the South Carolina sports information director slipped away from the College Sports Information Directors of America convention in Lexington, Kentucky, for a Braves-Reds three-game series at Riverfront Stadium in Cincinnati. A telephone call to the Reds' ticket office by Billingham, then a pitching coach in the Houston Astros organization, produced seats in the eighth row, directly behind home plate.

Where's Will

Will Lewis was 6-3, handsome, an honor student, and left-handed. He was also a pretty good pitcher for the South Carolina Gamecocks during four baseball seasons (1988-91).

Will also suffered from that malady that often afflicts left-handers: He was sometimes a little weird. He even had four names. His parents christened him Willman Bee Ravenel Lewis when he was born February 10, 1969, in Charleston.

In 1988, when Will was a freshman, the South Carolina baseball team made a long road trip to Cincinnati and Louisville. The Gamecocks split two games with the University of Cincinnati with one rainout and swept three at Louisville for a successful 4-1 road trip.

On the long bus trip home from Louisville, the team stopped about 3 a.m. at a 24-hour convenience store off Interstate Highway 26, about 60 miles from Columbia. After a brief rest stop, the Gamecocks clambered aboard the bus. They had traveled a few miles when someone asked, "Where's Will?"

There was a quick head recount, and the tall left-handed freshman was not on the bus. The driver had to travel several more miles to the next exit and head back to the rest stop. Will was patiently standing in front of the convenience store.

"If you hadn't come back to get me," he told Coach Raines, "I would have called a taxi from Spartanburg to take me to Columbia."

Spartanburg was 30 miles from the rest stop.

Lewis pitched in 70 games as both a middle reliever and a spot starter during his four-year career at South Carolina. In 152 2/3 innings, he won 13 games, lost eight, and registered one save.

After graduation, Will went to Egypt, where he became a schoolteacher and taught American baseball to youngsters. He later returned to South Carolina and graduated from law school. He now practices law in Charleston and lives on Sullivan's Island.

Dynamite Dom

Dominic Benito Fusci (pronounced FEW-see) was born in New York City, grew up in Greenwich Village and played football at Manual Training High School in Brooklyn. He rode the subway to school and planned to ride the subway to Fordham University, but Fordham discontinued its football program for the duration after the United States entered World War II.

At Manual Training High School, he was All-New York, All-Metro, and was named to the Schoolboy Hall of Fame. A boyhood neighbor in Greenwich Village was Frank McGuire who would become a Hall of Fame basketball coach at St. John's North Carolina and South Carolina. Fusci said he and McGuire were friends because, "I'm half-Italian and half-Irish. My grandfather was named Patrick J. Maloney."

Fusci enrolled at the University of South Carolina because he said he liked head coach Rex Enright and Ted Twomey, one of Enright's assistants.

His nickname was "Dynamite Dom," and Fusci spent the next half century perfecting the image of a colorful character. He also answered to the nicknames of "Rowdy Roman" and "Frolicking Fusci."

He was also an outstanding football player, earning letters in 1942 and '43, taking time out for service in the navy aboard PT Boats in the Pacific, and returning to school to earn a final football letter in 1946.

Fusci was named an All-Southern Conference tackle in 1943, and when the University of South Carolina selected an all-time team in 1969, Dom Fusci was one of the tackles. He was inducted into the South Carolina Athletic Hall of Fame in 1991, and the University of South Carolina Athletic Hall of Fame in 1993.

As a high school senior, Fusci received recruiting letters from South Carolina's Enright and also Herman Hickman, then an assistant coach at North Carolina State. The U.S. Naval Academy and the U.S. Military Academy also recruited him, but Fusci said he didn't want a military career. He had an appointment to meet a Navy coach at the Hotel New Yorker in Manhattan and met Enright in the hotel lobby on the way up to the Navy coach's room.

He agreed to visit South Carolina, but stopped off in Raleigh to take a look at N.C. State. He also considered Columbia University, but was tired of subway. He enrolled at South Carolina in the fall of 1942 and soon wound up in the Naval ROTC. After washing out of the navy's preflight program, he wound up as a seaman aboard a torpedo patrol boat in the South Pacific. So much for not wanting a military career.

Fusci was in Okinawa shortly after World War II ended, when he received a letter from the Washington Redskins advising him that he had been selected in the third round of the NFL draft.

"I went to my commanding officer and told him I had a letter saying I was needed in Washington and asked him to issue orders,"

Fusci said. "He said the navy should have notified him first, and when I showed him the letter, he said, 'Get your ass back on the boat.'"

After his discharge, Fusci checked out the Redskins. But the pay for rookie interior linemen in 1946 was $175 a game, so he decided to resume his college career.

Fusci said that when he was a freshman at South Carolina, "all those tough southern boys" on the team chewed tobacco and offered him some.

"I took a big plug of Brown Mule just before kickoff, and the first time I was hit, I swallowed half of it. I was gagging and heaving, and Lou Sossamon (All-America center) told me to get out of the huddle before I made them all sick. I went up to the line, and Sossamon told me what the play was. We had a lonesome tackle long before Army came out with the lonesome end."

An opposing lineman saw Fusci gagging, heaving, and slobbering tobacco juice and asked. "What's the matter with him?"

"He's like that when he's mad," Sossamon answered.

At the height of World War II, many college teams were manned by trainees in the navy V5 and V12 programs, and rosters fluctuated with additions and subtractions from game to game. During the 1943 Big Thursday game with Clemson, a new face reported into the game without saying who he was replacing.

"What position do you play?" Fusci asked the newcomer, who replied, "Right tackle."

"Well, I play right tackle, too, so why didn't you tell me you're supposed to replace me?" Fusci asked.

"I thought you might get mad," the replacement tackle replied, and Fusci rushed toward the sideline to avoid a penalty for too many players on the field. He exited on the Clemson side, almost at the feet of Tiger head coach Frank Howard. Some of the Clemson defenders reacted to Fusci's motion by shifting to that side of the field. South Carolina halfback Phil Cantore took a pitchout the opposite way for a 70-yard touchdown run.

Howard demanded to know what Fusci was doing, and Dom advised Howard to take his team back to Clemson before some of them were hurt. Fusci started the long trek around to the South Carolina sideline, but stopped at an end zone concession stand and ordered a hot dog and a soft drink. The concessionaire demanded 35 cents, but Fusci pointed to his pocketless football uniform and said, "Just chalk it up to oversubsidization of athletes," as he stuffed the hot dog into his mouth.

South Carolina won that game 33-6, and Fusci went home on a navy leave and was scheduled to return in time for a game against a military team, the Charleston Coast Guard Base, at the Orangeburg County Fair. The train from New York was late arriving in Columbia, and the team left without him. Fusci set out to hitchhike the 40 miles to Orangeburg.

He was picked up by Kit Fitzsimmons, a team trainer, and arrived in time for the game, but his uniform had been left in Columbia.

"They found me a pair of halfback's pants that were so small, I had to take out all the pads," Fusci recalled. "I put on a jersey with no shoulder pads and played the entire game." South Carolina won that game 20-0.

At one point, an official dropped a flag at the line of scrimmage to nullify a sizeable South Carolina gain. Fusci picked up the marker and followed the official downfield to where the play ended, dropping the penalty flag about halfway. The penalty was stepped off from the final spot of the penalty flag, resulting in a Gamecock gain.

Fusci played before the days of mandatory uniform numbers for interior linemen. He wore No. 43 in 1942. In one game, South Carolina back Earl Dunham was trapped and attempted to throw an incomplete pass to avoid a substantial loss. Fusci made a diving catch for a completion. An official reached for his penalty flag and said, "Aren't you an interior lineman?"

"Hell, no, I'm an end," Fusci replied. He whispered to right end Red Wilson to line up at tackle on the next play with Fusci on the end of the line smiling at the official.

"See, there? I told you I was an end," Dynamite Dom said.

After graduation, Fusci settled in Columbia, where he had a long and successful career in sales and retired as district sales manager for Southern Radio Corp., a distributor of RCA radios and televisions and other appliances. He also officiated football and basketball games, umpired baseball games, and refereed boxing matches at the high school, college, and military levels.

Fusci remembers umpiring baseball games at Fort Jackson when many major league players were in the service, including Willie Mays, Wilmer "Vinegar Bend" Mizell, Faye Throneberry, and Haywood Sullivan.

Mizell was pitching and Sullivan catching for Fort McPherson, with Fusci the plate umpire. McPherson led 1-0 in the eighth inning when Mizell threw a two-strike fastball "right down the middle" past Throneberry, the batter, and Fusci called it a ball.

"What?" asked Sullivan, and Fusci replied, "I really blew that one."

Throneberry hit the next pitch for a double to drive in two runs, and the next batter complained to Fusci that Mizell was throwing a spitball.

"I went out to warn him about the spitball but he wanted to talk about the pitch I had missed," Fusci recalled. "He started ranting and raving and asked me what I was getting paid for. I said, 'Look, there's Haywood Sullivan. He's worth $75,000. There's Throneberry. He's worth $35,000. And look at you. You're worth $100,000. What do you expect out of a lousy $25 umpire?"

Fusci said Mizell started laughing, and when he returned behind the plate, the commanding generals of Fort Jackson and Fort McPherson, who were sitting together in the stands, sent an aide down to ask what was so funny. When the aide delivered Fusci's explanation, both generals joined in the laughter.

Fusci once traveled with an officiating crew to a football game in North Carolina, and the group had a case of beer cooling in the car for after the game. A pass that skipped off the turf was caught by a receiver and ruled a completion by the nearest official, whose view was obstructed by several players. When the defensive team protested, and all of the other officials claimed they weren't in position to see the play, Fusci was asked for a ruling.

"That beer should really be cold by now," Fusci declared in all seriousness. He let the exasperated looks on the faces of his fellow officials sink in before breaking into a grin and ruling the pass incomplete.

In 1961, the Columbia Touchdown Club staged a "This Is Your Life, Dom Fusci" program. Although the skit was a total surprise, Fusci rose to the occasion, and his 45-minute speech dwarfed the remarks made by the roasters—except for one coach who claimed that Fusci was the only football referee who had been carried off the field on the shoulders of the winning team.

Fusci proudly recalled that he was game captain for South Carolina's 200th football victory, a 14-7 decision over Furman at Greenville in 1946. He was also captain of the 1958 alumni team that played the South Carolina varsity to climax spring practice. At midfield for the coin toss, South Carolina captain Alex Hawkins handed Fusci a pair of dice and suggested they shoot high dice rather than toss a coin.

"I shot a nine, and Hawk said, 'I can beat that,' and he shot an 11," Fusci recalled. "The referee looked at me, and I said, 'Toss the coin and I call heads.'"

Fusci once refereed a boxing match at Columbia's Township Auditorium, when an out-of-shape fighter went down without absorbing a punch. Suspecting the fighter was taking a dive, Fusci told him, "Get up. You're not hurt. The man didn't hit you. If you don't get up, I'm going to kick you in the ribs."

The fighter got up but began to take a pounding, so Fusci stopped the fight and ruled a TKO.

Admirers claim Fusci was one of few debaters to get the best of Clemson's Frank Howard. They once went at it nose to nose, swapping insults for 20 minutes at an athletic function, when Howard fell back and sat down.

Colorful basketball official Lou Bello was once the speaker at a meeting of the Columbia Tipoff Club, and Fusci introduced him with these words: "This is the first time that two Italians have stood before a microphone without saying, 'I refuse to answer that question on grounds that it might tend to incriminate me'."

Larry

Larry Price was one of the most intense athletes ever to play baseball for the University of South Carolina. He was also, without doubt, the biggest eater.

Larry was a right-handed pitcher from Cherry Hill, N.J. He was also a good hitter, and Coach June Raines often used him as a pinch hitter or as the designated hitter. He was seldom called on to

DH when he was pitching, however. Larry blamed his voracious appetite on a metabolism problem.

Price once rode with me in my car on a trip to play the University of North Carolina at Wilmington. As we arrived on the outskirts of Wilmington, Larry spotted a delicatessen displaying a sign that advertised Philadelphia cheese steaks. Being from the Philadelphia area, Larry loved Philly cheese steaks and insisted that we stop for lunch.

While I perused the menu, Larry ordered two Philly cheese steak sandwiches with french fries. The waitress started to walk away when Larry pointed to me and said, "You haven't taken his order."

She said, "I thought you were ordering for both of you. These cheese steaks are huge. There's no way you can eat two of them."

Larry polished off both cheese steak sandwiches and ordered a large slice of lemon meringue pie for dessert. Despite his appetite, Larry never seemed to gain weight and was always in great shape at 6-1 and about 195 pounds.

Larry pitched against the University of North Carolina—a team that included future major league stars Scott Bankhead, Walt Weiss, and B. J. Surhoff—in the 1984 NCAA Regional Tournament at Starkville, Mississippi. The Tar Heel battery included Bankhead on the mound and Surhoff behind the plate, both of whom would be selected for the U.S. Olympic team that summer. Bankhead was undefeated over the previous two seasons and had won 20 decisions in a row.

Weiss was the Tar Heel shortstop.

Bankhead held a 3-1 lead in the sixth inning, when North Carolina coach Mike Roberts relieved him with a left-handed pitcher to face a battery of South Carolina left-handed batters. The strategy worked until the eighth inning, with the Tar Heel lead increased to 4-1. Gamecock outfielder Rob Rinehart—a left-handed hitter who had one home run during the regular season—hit a three-run homer over the scoreboard in right-center field to tie the game.

In the ninth, a South Carolina runner was on second base with two outs and the Gamecock designated hitter due up. Coach Raines called on Larry Price to pinch-hit, and he lined a double off the fence to give the Gamecocks a 5-4 lead. The bullpen was ready, but Larry insisted he could get the Tar Heels out in the bottom of the ninth.

He was so hyper, he was jumping around on the mound. He promptly hit the first North Carolina batter to put the tying run on base. Raines called on the bullpen. With one out, the North Carolina batter hit a screaming line drive that South Carolina third baseman John Sullivan speared. He quickly doubled the runner off first base to end the game.

On another occasion, Larry rode with me to a game at Clemson. On the return trip to Columbia after dark, Larry opened the glove compartment of the car and placed a textbook under its light so he could study for an exam. He was an honor student.

Larry Price's father was a public relations man who worked in Philadelphia, but he spent a lot of time on the road following the South Carolina baseball team. A navy reserve pilot, he showed up at several games wearing the three-stripe uniform of a commander. There just happened to be a training flight to the areas where the Gamecocks were playing.

When South Carolina played a series at the University of Miami in 1983, the elder Price attended and brought Larry's 11-year-old brother, a tall, skinny, red-headed kid. The Price family was eating breakfast in the Coral Gables Holiday Inn when the little brother upset a plate of ham and sunny-side-up eggs into his lap. The kid burst into tears.

A few years after Larry graduated from South Carolina, his father showed up when South Carolina played a game at the University of North Carolina at Charlotte. This time he wasn't rooting for the Gamecocks. That red-headed kid who had dumped the eggs in his lap was playing first base for UNC-Charlotte.

Larry Price earned a business administration degree in 1985. He works for ADC Telecom, Inc., in Richardson, Texas. He lives in Plano, Texas.

Nation's Best

In 2000, South Carolina was the only NCAA school to have three performers named National Athlete of the Year in the year 2000. In addition, the American Baseball Coaches Association voted Ray Tanner National Coach of the Year after his Gamecocks won

*South Carolina had three National
Athletes of the Year and a Coach of the
Year in 2000. Left to right: Baseball
Coach Ray Tanner, Male Track Athlete of
the Year Terrence Trammell, Female Track
Athlete of the Year Miki Barber, and
Baseball Player of the Year Kip Bouknight.
(USC Sports Information/John Ayer)*

the Southeastern Conference Championship and led the nation in
wins with a 56-10 record.

NCAA champion and Olympic 400-meter hurdles silver medalist Terrence Trammell was both indoor and outdoor Male Track
Athlete of the Year. NCAA champion and U.S. Olympic team member Miki Barber was voted National Women's Outdoor Track Athlete of the Year. Pitcher Kip Bouknight, whose record for the Game-

cocks in 2000 was 17-1, was named Baseball Player of the Year by four different organizations.

A year earlier, in 1999, South Carolina track coach Curtis Frye was named both indoor and outdoor National Coach of the Year for Track and Field.

Hot Meal

In addition to his duties as athletic trainer for the South Carolina men's basketball team, Jeff Parsons handles travel arrangements, hotel accommodations, and team meals on the road.

In November of 1997, the Gamecocks played Maryland in the Black Coaches Association Classic in Minneapolis. Parsons arranged for a buffet to be set up in a private dining room at the team hotel. While waiting outside the room for the team to arrive, Parsons noticed smoke seeping from under the closed door.

He opened the door to find the buffet table ablaze. An alcohol burner under a food warmer had ignited the tablecloth.

"We had to make other arrangements," Parsons said in a January 2001 speech to the Columbia Tipoff Club.

In the basketball game, South Carolina defeated Maryland 76-72 in overtime.

Olympics

Seventeen athletes with ties to the University of South Carolina traveled to Sydney, Australia, in 2000 for the Games of the XXVII Olympiad. Five of them came home with medals.

Two Gamecock coaches were also Down Under—Ray Tanner, as an auxiliary coach on the staff of the gold-medal baseball team, and Curtis Frye, as personal coach of the South Carolina track-and-field athletes.

Adam Everett, an All-America shortstop (1997-98) and current player in the Houston Astros' minor league system, won a gold medal when the U.S. team defeated Cuba 4-0 in the championship game. Terrence Trammell, was the silver medalist in the 110-meter high hurdles. Charmaine Howell, running for her native Jamaica, won a silver medal in the 800 meters.

Monique Hennagan attended the University of North Carolina at Chapel Hill, but she lives in Columbia, trains on the USC track, and serves as a volunteer assistant coach under Frye. She won a gold medal in the 4 x 400 relay. Melissa Morrison graduated from Appalachian State, but she also trains under Frye and helps out as a South Carolina volunteer coach. She won a bronze medal in the 100-meter hurdles.

Allen Johnson, a University of North Carolina graduate and 1996 gold medalist, trains under Frye in Columbia and is a volunteer coach. He competed in the 110 hurdles in Sydney but did not win a medal.

Miki Barber went to Sydney as an alternate in the 4 x 400 relay but did not get to run. Michelle Davison competed in diving. Josh Wolff, now playing professionally with the Chicago Fire, was a member of the U.S. soccer team. Dawn Ellerbe, a 1997 South Carolina graduate, represented the U.S. in the hammer throw.

Tonique Williams represented the Bahamas in Sydney, while Michelle Fournier represented Canada in the hammer throw. Brad Snyder threw the shot for the Canadian team. Lisa Misipeka, a 1999 South Carolina graduate, competed for American Samoa in the hammer throw. Marvin Watts competed for Jamaica in the 800 meters. Zsolt Gaspar swam for the Hungarian team. Istvan Bathazi also swam for Hungary, competing in both the 200- and 400-meter individual medleys.

Early Checkout

George Wells of Columbia took his family to a time-share near Kissimmee, Florida, during the 2000 Christmas holiday. They stayed until January 7.

George and his wife planned to baby-sit their grandchild and watch the Outback Bowl between South Carolina and Ohio State on New Year's Day while their daughter and her husband attended the game in Tampa. George was distressed to learn that the *Tampa*

Tribune wasn't available in the area of his time-share, because he wanted to keep up with South Carolina's preparations for the bowl game.

Each morning, he would travel on I-4 to exit 23, where the Tampa newspaper was available. It was a round trip of more than 20 miles. George was even more distressed to learn that ESPN, the network televising the Outback Bowl, was not available on the cable system servicing his time-share. But George solved the problem.

"We packed a picnic lunch and checked into a motel at 10:30 a.m. [only half an hour before kickoff] and we checked out at 2:30 p.m.," he related. The game ended about 2:15.

Wells, a retired textile-mill worker attends South Carolina baseball games with a group that varies from six to 12 fans, all of them retired textile-mill workers.

"We call ourselves the lint-head group," he said.

Drop Kick

When was the last time that South Carolina—or any other college football team, for that matter—used a drop kick to put points on the scoreboard? The drop kick, in lieu of the kick from placement, to score a field goal or a PAT is still a legal play, but most fans, coaches, and players have never seen one.

The drop kick has become extinct because of the difficulty in executing it. The timing has to be perfect, as the football is dropped and kicked the instant it hits the ground while it is standing on end. Kicking from placement with a holder is much more practical.

Cursory research indicates that the last successful drop kick —and probably the only successful drop kick in Gamecock history— provided the only points in a 3-0 win over Clemson in the Big Thursday game of 1920.

Tatum Gressette was a 20-year-old halfback from St. Matthews who had attended Furman for two years before transferring to the University of South Carolina. He was known more for his running, passing, and punting skills than for his drop-kick ability.

Early in the contest, South Carolina surprised Clemson with a 15-yard gain, followed by a 40-yard pass from Gressette to Dave

Robinson, but the Tigers held on for the next three plays. On fourth down, Gressette drop-kicked a 25-yard field goal, and South Carolina led 3-0 after only 2:24 of the first quarter. Nobody scored after that.

Tales of athletic feats tend to grow taller with each telling, and, in later years, some old-timers swore the kick was at least 45 yards. Printed accounts of the feat, however, place it at a modest 25 yards.

Gressette was elected captain of the 1921 Gamecock team. While he didn't score on Big Thursday, he did lead South Carolina to its second consecutive shutout of the Tigers, 21-0, behind two touchdowns by Rusty Waite. The win marked the first time that South Carolina had defeated Clemson in consecutive seasons.

South Carolina compiled a 10-5-2 record in Gressette's two seasons. He also played one season of baseball as a first baseman. His brother Marion Gressette was a three-year letterman as a center fielder for the Gamecocks and later became a powerful force in South Carolina politics as a leader in the state senate. A younger brother, Bob Gressette, was a South Carolina football letterman (1928-30).

Tatum Gressette became head football coach at The Citadel and later became the first director of the BAM (Buck a Month) Club, the forerunner of today's Gamecock Club—South Carolina's athletic fund-raising organization. He was also a prominent amateur golfer.

Gressette retired as head of the South Carolina State Employees Retirement System, and until his death in 1997 at the age of 97, he was the oldest living Gamecock football captain.

He is a member of the University of South Carolina Athletics Hall of Fame, the State of South Carolina Hall of Fame, The Citadel Hall of Fame, and the South Carolina Golf Hall of Fame.

Dry Rock

Steven Whetstone is an accomplished artist and right-handed pitcher on the University of South Carolina baseball squad whose diamond career has been hampered by injuries. He was limited to one inning in 1998, and injuries kept him out all of 1999. In 2000,

Pitcher Steven "Dry Rock" Whetstone

he appeared in eight games and pitched 18 2/3 innings.

An art studio major from West Columbia, Whetstone has been busy since he entered the university in the fall of 1997. While his ambition is to become a serious artist, Whetstone's talent at drawing caricatures brightened the pages of the annual baseball media guides in 2000 and 2001.

Coach Ray Tanner (Steven Whetstone)

On the serious side, his landscape entitled "Storms of Life" won first prize in the amateur division's printmaking category at the South Carolina State Fair in October 2000. The first-place ribbon was accompanied by a check for $125.

While Whetstone uses his drawings to put the needle to his teammates and coaches, he hasn't spared himself in his satirical creations. Teammates nicknamed him "Dry Rock," a play on his surname. Whetstone pictures himself, pencil behind his left ear, working with a sketch pad while sitting high and dry on a rock surrounded by a puddle of water. He emphasizes his prominent Adam's apple.

His interpretation of head baseball coach Ray Tanner features oversized forearms. Home-run slugger Tripp Kelly brandishes an uprooted tree, and pitcher Lee Gronkiewicz sports a gap-toothed grin. Pitching coach Jerry Meyers is depicted at a blackboard teaching a class in velocity and rotation. Assistant coach Jim Toman has a rotund face and wears oversized glasses. The caricature of catcher Tim Whittaker depicts a head atop a brick wall.

Pitching Coach Jerry Meyers (Steven Whetstone)

Whetstone was an all-state pitcher at Brookland-Cayce High School who put up a 10-2 record his senior season. He was 9-3 his junior year. He also earned letters in basketball and cross-country. Whet-

Relief Pitcher Lee Gronkiewicz (Steve Whetstone)

stone, who stands 6-5, won his high school's most improved basketball player award. In addition to drawing, his hobbies include playing the guitar.

Goofy

Colie Livingston Dyson III was the resident clown on University of South Carolina baseball teams as the 20th century moved into the 21st. He was also the team's top scholar in the classroom and Coach Ray Tanner's best clutch hitter.

Just about every young man who is the third generation to bear a name is nicknamed either "Trey" or "Tripp". Dyson is known as Trey, but his comic activities have brought on the additional moniker of "Goofy."

Teammate Otis Thomas Kelly the Third bears the nickname Tripp as did shortstop Roy Bunyan Cromer the Third who played for the Gamecocks, 1987-89, and parts of seven seasons (193 games) in the National League with the Cardinals, Dodgers and Astros.

One of Dyson's comic activities could be called the first baseman/outfielder/designated hitter toss, since Dyson plays all three positions. Just before the South Carolina team takes the field to begin home games, the public-address system plays the theme from *2001: A Space Odyssey*, as teammates toss the 6-4, 220-pound left-hander high into the air several times. That gets Dyson and his teammates motivated.

In 2000, Dyson averaged one run batted in for every three at-bats. He hit home runs in five consecutive games to establish a school record. His ninth-inning homer tied the score against Clemson and sent the game into extra innings. After Clemson scored in the top of the 11th, Dyson doubled in the bottom of the inning, again driving in the tying run. South Carolina won the game in 12 innings.

In another game, South Carolina trailed Vanderbilt 1-0 through eight innings, but Dyson tied it with a clutch RBI double, and the Gamecocks went on to win 2-1.

Later that season, South Carolina trailed 9-4 at Duke, but battled back to win 10-9, as Dyson hit for the cycle. His three-run, seventh-inning home run cut the deficit to 9-7, and his two-run, ninth-inning triple tied the score. Dyson scored the winning run on a single by Brennan Dees.

Dyson compiled a 3.8 grade-point average in the 2000 spring semester as a finance/management major in the College of Business Administration and has been an honor student throughout his academic career.

Academics and baseball aren't Trey Dyson's only talents. After the game at Duke, the team was invited to the Mike Roberts home in Chapel Hill for ice cream and cake. Son Brian Roberts had been an All-America Gamecock shortstop and NCAA base-stealing champion in 1999.

Outfielder Marcus McBeth sat down at Mrs. Roberts's piano and began playing. Dyson opened a hymnal and told McBeth, "Play this." Dyson accompanied with a fine baritone rendition of *Amazing Grace*.

West Virginia Long Rifle

Basketball player Jamal Bradley came from Beckley, West Virginia, with a reputation as a terrific three-point shooter. He enrolled as a freshman at the University of South Carolina in the fall of 1999, and in three seasons he has lived up to his reputation as a long-range bomber.

Gamecock radio play-by-play broadcaster Charlie McAlexander nicknamed Bradley "The West Virginia Long Rifle." In his three varsity seasons, approximately 75 percent of the 6-2 Bradley's field goals have been scored from outside the arc. He has hit about 36 percent of his three-point attempts.

During his junior season, Bradley made seven three-point goals in ten attempts in a road win at Louisiana State. He hit five of his first six in that game. He made four three-pointers in a game against Wyoming, Virginia Military, Florida, Tennessee, Georgia, and Alabama.

Jamal Bradley is an outstanding ambassador for the University of South Carolina off the court. He visits and counsels handicapped children, especially those who are hearing impaired.

Jamal Bradley wears a hearing aid in each ear. He lost most of his hearing as an infant, but has not let his handicap interfere with his goal to become a star basketball player and also to earn a college degree. His major is administrative information management.

It is common for basketball games to be temporarily halted while a player recovers a contact lens dislodged in the heat of battle. Several times during his career at South Carolina, Bradley has had to recover one of his hearing aids knocked loose by an on-court collision.

And what does a hearing-impaired basketball star do for a hobby? Jamal Bradley listens to music. His favorite style is rhythm and blues.

The Gaffney Ghost

Earl Clary was recruited by a number of schools when he graduated from Gaffney High School, including national powers Michigan and Princeton, but he decided to stay in his home state and play for Coach Billy Laval at the University of South Carolina.

After Clary's first varsity game, against Duke in 1931, an opponent remarked that trying to tackle Clary was "like trying to tackle a ghost."

Clary became known as "The Gaffney Ghost." He led the Gamecocks to a 7-0 victory that day, and South Carolina would go 25 years, until 1956, before recording another win over the perennially powerful Blue Devils.

In his first Big Thursday game against Clemson, Clary rushed for 136 yards and scored one touchdown. His yardage was more than the total for the entire Clemson team. South Carolina shut out Clemson three times with Clary in the backfield: 21-0 in 1931, 14-0 and 1932, and 7-0 in 1933.

When South Carolina tied an unbeaten Auburn team 20-20 in 1932 and defeated the Plainsmen 16-14 in 1933, Earl Clary had a hand in all the Gamecock scoring in the two games. He scored four touchdowns, passed for another, and tackled an Auburn runner in the end zone for a safety.

Clary was inducted as a charter member of the University of South Carolina Athletics Hall of Fame in 1967 and is also in the State of South Carolina Hall of Fame.

Four members of the Clary family—cousins and brothers and all from Gaffney—played football for the University of South Carolina. Wilburn Clary, who lettered (1933-35); Ed Clary (1936-38); and Buford Clary (1940-41). Ed Clary also played baseball in 1937-39. Wilburn Clary became a Southern Conference and Atlantic Coast Conference football official and was inducted as an official into the National Football Hall of Fame.

Ed Clary played in the Blue-Gray All-Star Game in 1938. Chip Clary, son of Ed, was director of the Gamecock Club for a number of years.

8

Family Affairs

The Anderson Family

Katrina Anderson was the first University of South Carolina women's basketball player to win All-America honors. She was also the first of three Anderson siblings to star for Gamecock athletic teams. There was almost a fourth, too.

The Anderson family was from Timmonsville, and Katrina attended Anderson Junior College for two years before enrolling at South Carolina, where she won All-America honors in both 1978 and 1979.

Butch Anderson, her older brother, played shortstop and third base for South Carolina baseball teams from 1968 to 1971. He rose as high as AA in professional baseball.

Kent Anderson starred at shortstop for the Gamecocks, from 1982 to 1984 and spent two major league seasons, 1989-90, with the California Angels. He appeared in 135 major league games.

Mike Anderson was a star tight end at Timmonsville High School and signed a football letter of intent to attend South Carolina. However, he was a first-round selection by the Philadelphia Phillies and chose professional baseball over college. In nine major league seasons, he played in 721 games as an outfielder with the Phillies, Cardinals, and Orioles.

The Cromer Family

The Cromer family furnished three baseball stars for University of South Carolina teams and almost provided a fourth.

Tripp Cromer played shortstop from 1987 to 1989, and moved on to a professional career. Through the 2001 season, he had 193 games of major league experience with the Cardinals, Dodgers, and Astros.

Burke Cromer was an infielder and occasional pitcher at South Carolina form 1989 to 1992, and was signed as a pitcher by the Atlanta Braves. After one season of minor league baseball, he became a golf pro.

D.T. Cromer was an outfielder at South Carolina from 1990 to 1992, and has played first base and the outfield as a professional. After several outstanding minor league seasons he finally made it to the big leagues in 2000. Called up by the Cincinnati Reds and used primarily as a pinch hitter, he had 47 major league at-bats and got 16 hits for a .340 average. His hits included five doubles and two home runs.

Brandon Cromer signed a letter of intent with South Carolina but was drafted in the first round and bypassed college for professional baseball. He is a shortstop.

Roy Cromer—father of the four brothers—played about five years of minor league baseball in the Cardinals' organization before enrolling at the University of South Carolina, where he was a student-coach in the early 1960s. He coached at Lake City High School until his oldest son enrolled at South Carolina. He moved to Lexington High School just a few miles from Columbia.

Another Cromer played baseball at South Carolina, but he was from a different family. Mike Cromer of Prosperity, S.C., was a left-handed relief pitcher who earned letters in 1974 and 1975. In his final appearance as a Gamecock, Mike Cromer relieved All-America pitcher Earl Bass in the ninth inning and saved a 3-1 win over Seton Hall in the 1975 College World Series.

The Small Family

Big George Small was a senior pilot with Eastern Airlines, based in Atlanta. Three of his sons played baseball at the University of South Carolina.

Hank Small was nicknamed "The Hammer", because he hit a lot of collegiate home runs at the same time that Henry Aaron, also known as The Hammer, was on a record-setting homer pace with the Atlanta Braves. Hank Small played first base and the outfield for Coach Bobby Richardson between 1972 and 1975.

He was a second-team All-America choice as a junior in 1974 and first-team All-America in 1975, when his bat powered the Gamecocks to a 51-6-1 record and a second-place finish in the College World Series. His 47 career home runs, mostly compiled before aluminum bats came into use, were still a school record through the 2000 season. His career batting average was .360, and he didn't use an aluminum bat until his senior season.

Hank Small signed with the Atlanta Braves. He led the International League in home runs in 1978 and was league MVP, earning a September call-up to the Braves. However, his major league career was limited to one game. He lives in Sullivan's Island, S.C., and is in the insurance business.

David Small was a reserve infielder and outfielder at South Carolina (1974-77), and Martin Small was a left-handed pitcher (1979-81).

When Hank Small was a freshman, he suffered an injury to his right shoulder in a physical education class before the baseball team traveled to California to play in the Riverside Tournament. Hank could swing the bat, but he couldn't throw.

The designated-hitter rule had not yet been adopted in 1972, but Coach Bobby Richardson needed Hank's bat in the lineup. He stationed Small in right field and hoped the opponents wouldn't notice his throwing difficulties.

Small collected 14 hits in 27 at-bats in seven tournament games for a .519 average, and his throwing ability was never challenged. He was a unanimous choice for the all-tournament team.

When George Small wasn't flying he would drive from Atlanta to Columbia to watch his sons play baseball. He often flew from Atlanta to Baltimore and back, a route that took him directly over Columbia. Once, while sitting in the stands at Sarge Frye Field, George pointed to a vapor trail in the sky at about 30,000 feet and said, "There goes my airplane."

The Gamecocks often traveled to Atlanta for baseball series with Georgia Tech and Georgia State University. There was always a team barbecue in the backyard of the Small home, with George cooking ribs.

Hank Small (USC Sports Information/Billy Deal)

The Wingard Family

The Wingard family of Greenwood sent two sons to play football at the University of South Carolina during the 1960s.

Ted Wingard earned letters as a quarterback in 1965 under Coach Marvin Bass and in 1966 under Paul Dietzel. Tom Wingard lettered as a guard under Dietzel in 1966 and 1967.

Ted went to medical school and is now a cardiovascular surgeon in Jacksonville, Florida. Tom majored in pharmacy and eventually took over the family drugstore. He also was in the real estate business and was elected mayor of Greenwood.

Tom Wingard sustained several concussions on the football field, and his playing career was cut short. During one of the team's theatrical skits, teammates produced an effigy in a football uniform wearing Tom's jersey number. The effigy's head was a watermelon.

The Bennett Family

Two brothers from the Bennett family played football for the Gamecocks in the early 1990s. They were from Greenville.

Braylyn Bennett earned letters in 1990 and 1991 under Coach Sparky Woods. Brandon Bennett played one season, 1991, with his brother and three more varsity seasons. He played his senior year under Coach Brad Scott. Braylyn played mostly on special teams, but he did catch four passes and score one touchdown as a wide receiver.

Through the 2000 season, Brandon was third on South Carolina's all-time rushing list with 3,005 yards. His most memorable play was a touchdown with two seconds remaining to defeat Georgia 23-21 in 1993. Another spectacular play by Brandon was an across-the-field lateral to Reggie Richardson that resulted in a 94-yard kickoff return in a 33-7 win over Clemson in 1994.

The Provence Family

Two brothers from the Provence family of Savannah, Georgia, played football at the University of South Carolina.

Jerome Provence was an offensive lineman who was a four-year letterman (1974-77). His younger brother, Andrew, was a defensive tackle (1980-82), who was named to the *Sporting News* All-America team in 1982 and to the third-team All-America by the *Associated Press* the same season. Andrew played eight seasons in the NFL with the Atlanta Falcons (1983-87), and the Denver Broncos (1988-90).

After graduation, Jerome served as South Carolina's strength-and-conditioning coach for several years. Currently he is on the staff of the university's physical education center. Andrew is in business in the Atlanta area, where he is involved in leadership training and development.

When the 1980 Gamecock team gathered for its 20th reunion the weekend of South Carolina's homecoming game with Arkansas in October of 2000, Andrew Provence shared some memories of his recruitment by South Carolina and his years as a Gamecock player.

He was constantly confused with his brother, often being addressed as Jerome, while Jerome was being called Andrew. Andrew said the misidentification was okay with him because, he said, "There's no one who has had a greater impact on my life than my brother, Jerome."

The program for the 20th reunion of the 1980 team referred to Andrew as Jerome Provence.

During Andrew's senior high school season, South Carolina coach Jim Carlen made sure that Jerome, who had graduated from South Carolina two years earlier, was at the Provence home the entire week of Andrew's recruiting visit to the University of Georgia.

"After I arrived home from Athens, Coach Carlen was on the phone," Andrew recalled. Carlen asked if Andrew was okay about coming to South Carolina, and Andrew replied that he wasn't sure.

"Within an hour, Coach Carlen and half his staff" were at the Savannah airport, Andrew recalled.

"We talked things out, and I was a Gamecock. I knew this school wanted me and they backed it up," Andrew said.

"Looking back, I am truly humbled to have been so coveted by Carolina. With all the scandals in college athletics, everything was always aboveboard with Carolina recruiting. I'm proud of that. No new cars. I drove to Columbia (in 1979) in my '72 AMC Hornet and graduated four years later driving the same car. After being drafted by the Falcons, I bought a Toyota."

Andrew Provence said South Carolina "had the perfect defensive scheme for me, the perfect campus, the perfect wife. I even became a Christian at Carolina. I would make the same choice to be a Gamecock if I had to do it over again."

Andrew's wife is the former Angie Cornell of Cayce, S.C. They have eight children ranging in age from two to sixteen.

The Hollins Family

It was a long commute from West Seneca, N.Y., a suburb of Buffalo, to Columbia, S.C., so the Hollins family moved south for the baseball season.

Paul Hollins was a freshman outfielder for the Gamecocks in 1978. Dave was a high school freshman, and Chris was in elementary school. The family rented an apartment for the spring semester and later purchased a home on Lake Murray on the outskirts of Columbia. During home baseball games, Dave and Chris ran errands for the press box.

Paul's father operated his stock brokerage business by telephone from South Carolina during the spring, and then the family returned to Buffalo when the collegiate baseball season ended. Paul played on South Carolina teams that made the NCAA playoffs in 1980 and 1981 and advanced to the College World Series in '81. Paul batted .400 that year and was a second-team All-America selection.

Paul signed with the New York Mets after graduation and reached the AA level in the minor leagues before becoming a stockbroker in Buffalo. Actually he moonlighted as a stockbroker while attending the University of South Carolina. He obtained his broker's license at the age of 19.

Four years after Paul graduated, Dave was a third baseman with the Gamecocks and played in the College World Series in 1985, his freshman year. The Gamecocks also advanced to the NCAA playoffs in 1986. Dave signed with the San Diego Padres in 1987, after his junior collegiate season, and had a ten-year major league career between 1990 and 1999 with the Phillies, Red Sox, Mariners, Angels, and Blue Jays.

Dave was chosen for the National League All-Star Game in 1993 and played in the World Series with the Phillies that season. He played in 967 major league games and finished with a .261 career batting average. He hit 112 home runs.

Paul threw right but batted left. Dave was a switch-hitter.

Chris Hollins played two seasons at Middle Georgia Junior College and then played at Appalachian State University. He played one game at Sarge Frye Field against South Carolina. In 1989 he had four hits in five at-bats, including three doubles, to lead Appalachian State to a 15-8 win over the Gamecocks.

The Hollins brothers had a sister who also attended the University of South Carolina.

The Craig Family

Tom Craig (1932-34) and Larry Craig (1935-38) played football at the University of South Carolina. Their brother Johnson played tackle on the football team at Clemson. He played against Tom in the 1932 Big Thursday game won by Carolina 14-0 with Tom catching a pass at the one-yard line to set up a Gamecock touchdown.

Another brother, Ed, also attended the University of South Carolina, and a fourth, Wally, was a Gamecock football letterman in 1938.

The Craig brothers attended tiny Six Mile High School in upstate South Carolina, about ten miles from Clemson. The school didn't organize a football team until Tom's senior year, and he was known more for his basketball skills. Larry didn't play high school football at all, but in college he became one of South Carolina's all-time greatest blocking backs and enjoyed an 11-year National Football League career (1939-49) with the Green Bay Packers.

Larry was inducted into the University of South Carolina Athletic Hall of Fame in 1976 and is also a member of the State of South Carolina and the Green Bay Packer Halls of Fame. He was named to the first all-time Packer team chosen.

Tom Craig was also a three-year basketball letterman and was backup center to Dana Henderson on the Southern Conference championship team that had a 17-2 record in 1933 and the 1934 team that was 18-1. Those two teams had a combined 33-game winning streak, still a school record at South Carolina. In 24 basketball games, Tom Craig scored 74 points. Larry played basketball one year at Carolina and appeared in seven games.

Tom and Larry were also track stars. Tom competed in six events. In one dual meet, he won the shot put, discus, javelin, high jump, high hurdles, and low hurdles. Larry broke Tom's state records in the shot put and discus.

The Craig brothers were large by the height and weight standards of the day. Tom was 6 feet 3 and weighed 190 as a freshman. By his senior season he weighed 210 pounds. Larry was 6-1, 185 as a freshman and was up to 205 pounds by his senior season.

Tom was twice named to the South Carolina All-State team and to the second-team All Southern Conference team. Larry was first-team All-State and All-Conference.

Rex Enright became South Carolina's head football coach when Larry Craig was a senior. Enright had been a teammate of Packer head coach Curly Lambeau at Notre Dame. At Enright's urging, the Packers drafted Larry Craig, whose rookie contract paid him $175 a game. He played in an NFL championship game at a time when the payoff for each player was $800. At Green Bay, Larry Craig was a single-wing blocking back on offense and an end on defense.

Tom Craig served three years as a naval officer during World War II. After the war, he went into the commercial real estate business in Columbia, At the age of 66 he underwent open-heart surgery, and doctors discovered he had a congenital heart defect— a hole in the wall between two heart chambers—that should have prevented him from participating in athletics.

Despite the ailment, he was a three-sport collegiate star and lived until the age of 74.

After professional football, Larry Craig retired to a 722-acre farm near his boyhood home and raised beef cattle.

Twins

Twins have dotted the rosters of college athletic teams over the years, but the 2001 University of South Carolina women's track team is probably one of the first to boast two sets of twin sisters.

Juniors Me'lisa and Miki Barber are from Montclair, N.J., and Mechelle and Mikisha Lewis hail from Fort Washington, Maryland. Mechelle was a junior, while Mikisha was listed as a redshirt sophomore on the 2001 roster.

Miki Barber traveled to Sydney, Australia, as a member of the U.S. track and field team. She was voted the 2000 National Female Athlete of the Year, both indoor and outdoor, as a sophomore; was the top scorer in the Southeastern Conference; and was NCAA champion in three events—two outdoor and one indoor. She won the 400-meter race and was a member of first-place relay teams in the 4 x 100 and 4 x 400 meters. She placed fifth in the Olympic 400-meter trials and made the Olympic team as an alternate with the 4 x 400 relay team.

During her first two collegiate seasons Miki Barber was a ten time All-American, won seven Southeastern Conference titles, was a gold and silver medalist in the World University Games, and was a U.S. track and field junior All-American.

Me'lisa Barber was on the 4 x 400 relay team that won an NCAA outdoor title, ran on the runner-up 4 x 400 indoor relay, and was third in the 200-meter NCAA race won by her twin sister. In her first two collegiate seasons, she won two Southeastern Conference titles, was an eight-time All-American, and a U.S. track and field junior All-American.

Mikisha Lewis was formerly a heptathlete. She was expected to help Coach Curtis Frye's team in the 400 and 800 meters and also on relay teams. Her twin sister, Mechelle, is a multi-event athlete.

Two sets of twins played basketball for the University of South Carolina, but they played 30 years apart.

Walt and Bury (pronounced Berry) Hudson were from Dreher High School in Columbia. They were both 6-5 and earned letters in 1959 and 1960. Walt scored 442 points in 62 varsity games, while Bury played in 43 varsity basketball games and scored 208 points. Bury also threw the discus on the track team.

Terry and Perry Dozier were from Dunbar High School in Baltimore, Md. Although twins, Terry was an inch shorter than his brother at 6-9. Perry was a letterman for three seasons (1986-88), until an injury ended his career. In 66 games he scored 168 points. Perry averaged 2.5 points per game. Terry lettered four years(1986-89). In 104 varsity games he scored 1,445 points, an average of 13.9 per game.

Terry Dozier was named to the Metro Conference All-Freshman team in 1986 and to the Metro All-Tournament team in 1987. He played briefly with the Charlotte Hornets of the NBA and then went overseas. He was a star in Australian professional basketball for a number of years, and in 2001 was playing professional basketball in Cyprus with the Keravnos Keo Nicosia team.

Perry became a haberdasher. He operates a big-and-tall men's clothing store in Columbia.

Twin brothers Heyward and Howard Tunstall were mainstays on the pitching staff of South Carolina baseball teams from 1952 to 1955. Their hometown was Darlington.

While Heyward had a losing career record of 9-15, his 1.94 earned run average was tops on the team his senior season, when his record was 3-4. Heyward is still in the record book nearly half a century after he played for the Gamecocks. His 15 career losses are the most ever by a South Carolina pitcher. Howard Tunstall's career record was 7-4.

Siblings

They aren't twins, but there were three siblings from the Thompson family on golf rosters at the University of South Carolina in 2001—and the first letter of all three first names was K. Kyle Thompson was a senior All-American on the men's team; Kacy Th-

South Carolina's 2001 Women's Track Team featured two sets of twins. Left to right: Me'lisa and Miki Barber, Mechelle and Mikisha Lewis. (USC Sports Information/Mitchell West)

ompson was a sophomore; and Kory Thompson was a freshman on the women's team.

All three siblings were born in Panama City, Florida, but the family moved to Easley, S.C., and Kyle graduated from Easley High School, where he was named Jay Haas South Carolina Player of the Year in 1995-96. In collegiate competition, he was a two-time All-American and was three times named All-Southeastern Conference going into his senior season.

Kyle is a marketing major who has his sights set on the PGA tour. If he could be a character in a movie, he would be Chevy Chase in *Caddyshack*. The person he would most like to spend the day with is Ben Hogan, and if he could switch places for one day, he would switch with Tiger Woods. If he were an animal, he would be a dog so he could become man's best friend.

The Thompson family moved from Easley to Irmo, a suburb of Columbia, and Kacy and Kory graduated from Irmo High School.

Kacy played in nine of 10 tournaments as a freshman and finished in the top 10 one time and the top 20 twice. She lettered six times on the girls' golf teams at Easley and Irmo and also played on the boys' team and earned four letters there. Five times she was selected to the all-state team.

Kory also played six seasons in high school and was named all-state four times. Kacy Thompson's collegiate major is marketing, while Kory is majoring in sports entertainment and management.

9

Globe-Trotters

NCAA rules allow collegiate basketball teams to make one foreign exhibition tour every four years. In addition to the cultural advantages of these trips, the opportunity allows extra practice time, which can prove beneficial.

The University of South Carolina has taken advantage of the foreign tour opportunity four times, with trips to Asia in 1982, the Caribbean and Central America in 1989, Scandinavia in 1996, and Spain and the Canary Islands in 2000.

After the 1982 trip to Asia, Coach Bill Foster's team won 22 games and received a bid to the National Invitation Tournament. After the 1996 trip, the Gamecocks, under Coach Eddie Fogler, were surprise champions of the Southeastern Conference with a 15-1 conference record that included a two-game sweep of perennial champion Kentucky.

Asia

As sports information director, I accompanied the basketball team to Asia in 1982 and to Jamaica and Guatemala in 1989. Brian Binette was the sports information representative on the 1996 trip to Scandinavia and also on the trips to Spain and the Canary Islands in 2000.

The Asian trip included two games in Manila; a rest-and-recreation stop in Hong Kong; two games in Beijing, the capital of the People's Republic of China; two games in Seoul, South Korea; and one game in Tokyo. A game scheduled in the Japanese city of Osaka was mysteriously canceled.

South Carolina first met a team of Filipino collegiate all-stars and then took on Crispa, champion of the Philippine National Basketball Association (a professional league), in an ancient building called the Rojas Coliseum. Both games were televised by the Philippine government's national network, and I was invited to sit in with the two Filipino announcers as their guest commentator.

The play-by-play was in English, but when talking to the remote truck during timeouts, the announcers would speak in Tagalog, the native Philippine language. I was told that more than 80 percent of the people in Manila and more than 50 percent of the nation's 67 million people spoke English.

The South Carolina team struggled due to jet lag but managed a 12-point win over the Philippine college all-star team, which included a couple of imports from the United States. The lethargic play by the Gamecocks prompted one of the TV announcers to say to me, "Crispa will beat you tomorrow night."

With a day to get over the jet lag, the Gamecocks easily defeated Crispa by about 21 points. The Philippine NBA champion had two former U.S. collegiate stars on its team, one from St. Mary's in California and one from St. Bonaventure University in Olean, N.Y.

The teams attended a party at the U.S. ambassador's residence, which was located in a gated community surrounded by a high fence and guarded by uniformed police wielding machine guns. The player from St. Bonaventure told me he had played against the Gamecocks in Carolina Coliseum "the night they gave Alex English's mama the roses."

Alex English Night was celebrated February 25, 1976, three games before the South Carolina All-America ended his collegiate career. His mother was presented with a dozen roses as part of the ceremony. South Carolina won that game 77-67.

After two days of shopping and sightseeing in Hong Kong, we took a four-hour flight to Beijing and made a stop at Tinjian (only a few minutes' flying time from the Chinese capital), where we deplaned while soldiers surrounded the plane. Our passports were scrutinized, and we were fed a meal before reboarding and flying the remaining few minutes to Beijing.

Arthur Tai, a Chinese American graduate of the University of South Carolina who was assigned to accompany the team as translator, whispered to me as the Communist soldiers surrounded the plane at Tinjian, "Those guys scare the crap out of me."

A native of Taiwan but an American citizen, Arthur worked in the USC president's office and had visited mainland China several times in connection with a cultural exchange arrangement with a Chinese university. About a year later, Arthur received a Rhodes scholarship.

We were quartered in an old hotel, built in 1929, which had been used for other purposes until the country was reopened to tourism. Since we were there a number of modern hotels have been built and tourism has greatly expanded.

The first game in Beijing was against the Red Army team, featuring its 7-5, 350-pound center, "Mr. Mu." A 34-year-old Mongolian, he had been a member of the Red Army team since he was 17 years old. He was slow and couldn't jump, but the Chinese referees exempted him from the three-second rule, and so he camped in the foul lane.

Mr. Mu would back in toward the basket with the basketball, turn and knock 7-0 Mike Brittain or 6-10 Duane Kendall to the floor, and bank the basketball off the backboard and into the basket. The whistle would blow, and the foul was always on the Gamecock defender.

Mr. Mu scored seven field goals but missed six of seven free-throw attempts to total 15 points and help the Red Army team to a six-point win. South Carolina managed a one-point win over the Beijing City team, despite the officiating, which was good everywhere except China.

The team visited Tiananmen Square, the Summer Palace, the Forbidden City, the Ming Tombs, and the Great Wall of China. Staff photographer and cinematographer Randy Herald took a squad picture on the Great Wall, but one team member was missing when Randy snapped the shutter. Kenny Holmes, a 6-7 forward from Savannah, Georgia, was away seeking relief from the diarrhea he suffered from eating the Chinese food.

Everywhere on the trip, except China, the players were issued meal money and frequented Shakey's Pizza in Manila, McDonald's in Hong Kong, and Pizza Hut in Seoul. In Beijing, the meals were native Chinese food. Kenny Holmes attempted to use chopsticks by wielding one in each hand.

In Tokyo, our host and translator was Yosishoru Nakamaru, who worked for a sports marketing company. "Yosh" was the first overweight Japanese I had ever seen, excluding sumo wrestlers.

One of the Carolina players asked Yosh if he had ever been to the United States.

He asked, "You ever heard of the University of Nevada-Las Vegas?"

When the questioner nodded, Yosh declared proudly, "Class of '77."

Another player asked Yosh if he had worked with any other American athletes.

"Arnold Palmer is No.1 client," he replied.

On the way to a game against the Nippon College of Physical Education, the team stopped for a pregame meal.

"We get a Big Mac and fries," Yosh declared as the bus stopped at a McDonald's.

The Gamecocks lost a six-point decision to a lightning-fast Korean national team with deadly outside shooters, but later easily defeated a team of Korean college all-stars.

The coach of the Nippon College of Physical Education had attended the Joe B. Hall Camp at the University of Kentucky, and his team's uniforms, drills, warm-up procedures, and style of play were all copied from the Wildcat system. His players weren't very good and were undersized, and the Gamecocks won easily to complete a 5-2 record on the trip.

The Caribbean

In 1989, Coach George Felton scheduled a trip to Jamaica, Guatemala, and Colombia. The final leg of the journey was aborted when a presidential candidate in the South American country was assassinated. The South Carolina team was ordered to return home.

Instead of traveling to Colombia, the Gamecocks returned to Columbia.

U.S. citizens entering Jamaica need only a passport but citizens of some European countries are also required to obtain visas. Two members of the South Carolina team—Obrad "Pookie" Ignjatovic (pronounced Ig-nok-o-vich) and Bojan "Bo" Popovic (Bo-yahn Pop-o-vich)—were from Serbia, then part of Yugoslavia.

When we went through customs upon arrival in Kingston, our host told Coach Felton, "We have a problem with the two Yugoslavians. They have no visas."

"Why do they need visas?" Felton asked. George probably thought a visa was a credit card.

The Jamaican authorities intended at first to put the two players on the next plane back to Miami. After much negotiation, it was agreed to let them stay and to work out the visa problem the next day. The U.S. consulate helped out, and the necessary documents were obtained before the team left on a bus trip across the mountains of Jamaica to visit the tourist city of Ocho Rios on the other side of the island.

The bus stopped along the road, where Jamaicans were selling barbecued pork and goat meat called Jerk, as well as a soup made from goat's testes, called "Mannish Water." It was reputed to increase virility.

Our Jamaican host drove a little red car imported from the Soviet Union called a Lada. Pookie Ignjatovic, familiar with the Soviet vehicle from his native Serbia, pointed to the Lada and said, "Russian car. Piece of s---."

There was an ancient sports building in Kingston that was called a coliseum and had several adjacent lighted asphalt outdoor basketball courts. Coach Felton was told that all practices and games would be held in the coliseum.

When we arrived for the first practice, however, Felton was told the coliseum wasn't available for practice, but would be for the games. The coliseum never did become available, so the Gamecocks played two games on the asphalt outdoor courts, winning both. The Jamaican all-stars did have one very good player who competed for a junior college in Texas. He was about 6-6 and scored about 20 points.

The team had to fly back to Miami to make a connection to Guatemala City, and arrangements were made through the U.S. Consulate to provide the two Yugoslavians with the required visas.

The Guatemalans are mostly very short. Descendants of Mayan Indians, most of the players on the Guatemalan teams were 5-8 or shorter. One player was 6-8, but he only weighed about 160 pounds. The Gamecocks finished the aborted trip with a 4-0 record.

The team took a sight-seeing trip to a Mayan village, Chichicastenanga, about 80 miles from Guatemala City. While there, the group was approached by an American tourist who asked, "Isn't this the Carolina basketball team?"

It turned out he was a professor at Clemson in Guatemala on an teacher-exchange assignment.

Scandinavia

South Carolina won seven of eight games played during its 1996 trip to Scandinavia. There was one Gamecock fan present throughout the trip. Frantisek Formanek traveled from his home in the Czech Republic. His son, George Formanek, was a member of the South Carolina team.

The elder Formanek played professional basketball in Czechoslovakia for 12 years. The younger Formanek scored only 96 points in 71 games (a 1.4 points-per-game average) during his four-year South Carolina career, but he tallied the first points of the Scandinavian tour on a slam dunk.

Maybe he was showing off for his dad, who was seeing his son play in a Gamecock uniform for the first time. George scored 42 points during the foreign tour for a 6.0 average. After graduation

George returned to the Czech Republic and plays professional basketball for USK Erpet Praha.

The team had a tough time getting to Stockholm. Fog canceled the flight from Columbia to Atlanta, so the Gamecocks missed a connection to New York. When finally rebooked, the group was still in South Carolina air space at about 30,000 feet some eight and a half hours after leaving Columbia.

Routed through Frankfurt, Germany, and switching airlines, the 20-member party finally arrived in Stockholm 24 hours after leaving South Carolina. The luggage arrived a day later.

During the layover in Frankfurt, two players, Donnie Matthews and Larry Davis, wandered away from the secured international area and were denied readmission because their boarding passes were in the possession of trainer Jeff Parsons.

"They wouldn't let us through without the boarding passes, and when we finally got someone who could help us, he couldn't leave his post," said Matthews. "I just knew we were going to spend the day in Frankfurt."

The problem was worked out just in time for them to make the flight.

Davis and Matthews were almost late again. They, along with Ryan Stack, Parsons, and equipment manager Mac Credille, were stuck for a time in a stalled elevator in the Stockholm hotel.

A couple of days later in Helsinki, three coaches and three players were trapped in another stalled elevator, but Larry Davis and Donnie Matthews weren't involved this time. They were in the lobby early, and Davis—a media arts major—videotaped the six being extracted from the elevator.

The Gamecocks were startled by the prices in Sweden: 25 krona, or about $4 U.S., for a soft drink, and 35 krona, or $6, for a hamburger at Burger King. They were also surprised by the short summer nights, with only about five hours of darkness.

Assistant coach Jeff Lebo said he was "getting a sun tan at four in the morning."

South Carolina's four 6-10 players—George Formanek, Nate Wilbourne, Ryan Stack, and Bud Johnson—walked past a group of Swedish teenagers when one of the youngsters pointed at them and said, "Shaquille O'Neal." A few minutes later two Swedes pointed to the group and said "Dream Team Four."

Nate Wilbourne said the thing from back home he missed most on the foreign trip was mayonnaise on a sandwich. "I would kill for some Dukes or Dijonnaise," he said.

Larry Davis and Melvin Watson, from the 1996 team, returned to Europe to play professional basketball in Belgium: Davis with Athlon, Leper and Watson with Bree BBC.

Spain

The 11-day trip to Spain and the Canary Islands in 2000 resulted in five games, including four wins and a one-point overtime loss. Two games were canceled due to travel difficulties.

Forward David Ross came down with food poisoning and was taken to a hospital by trainer Jeff Parsons. Parsons didn't know any Spanish and was attempting to communicate, when the doctor, in perfect English, said, "You Americans are all alike. You never learn a second language."

The team's translator, Jose Luis "Pepe" Rodriguez, had a similar problem. Assigned by World Wide Basketball to accompany the Gamecock team, Pepe spoke very little English. The players dubbed him "Uno lingual translator."

Pepe would point to every beautiful señorita who passed by and say, "Mamacita." The South Carolina players pointed to the señoritas and said, "Fine." Pepe added one word to his English vocabulary.

Some of the players complained about the length of the overseas flight, but 6-10 sophomore center Tony Kitchings told them it was "a piece of cake." Kitchings had traveled to Japan the previous summer for a series of games with the Southeastern Conference all-stars. He had endured a 16-hour flight, with several stops and plane changes en route from Birmingham to Atlanta to Portland to Tokyo.

The team attended a bullfight in Madrid, and most of the basketball players ended up cheering for the bulls.

"How can you go to Spain and not see a bullfight," said junior guard Aaron Lucas. "I won't do it again, but at least I can say I did it once."

On the bus ride from Madrid to Barcelona, the team stopped at Zaragoza for lunch. The Spanish usually have lunch around 2 p.m. or later, so none of the traditional Spanish restaurants were open. The day was saved, however, when a McDonald's was spotted.

As the team was leaving the Hotel Colon in Barcelona for a game, a woman snatched a bag that assistant coach Rick Callahan was carrying, and she fled. Fortunately, the Barcelona policia were nearby. They ran the would-be thief down and recovered the bag.

How'd You Get?

In my travels around the world, I have discovered that South Carolina Gamecocks are everywhere, but so are Clemson Tigers.

In 1998, my wife, Margaret, and I took a two-week cruise to the Baltic Sea. We had already visited Oslo, Copenhagen, Stockholm, and Helsinki, when we boarded a tour bus at the pier for a trip to downtown St. Petersburg, Russia.

A man seated across the aisle noticed my Gamecock jacket and asked, "Are you from Carolina?"

When I replied in the affirmative, he asked where I lived, and I said Columbia. He said, "We live in Charlotte."

He said he attended Carolina from 1946 to 1950. I graduated in 1951. I introduced myself and he jumped out of his seat and exclaimed, "How did you get to be Tom Price? I was in your wedding."

Margaret and I hadn't seen Carolyn or Jim Davidson in 48 years. He, Jim Bigger, and Frank Sherer—all three from York County—had lived next door to me in Preston Hall for two years. All three had served as ushers in our wedding at Charleston in June of 1950. Sherer once pitched a no-hit, no-run game for the Gamecock baseball team.

There were at least three groups with connections to Clemson aboard the cruise ship. I met a Clemson professor in Guatemala. While in Seattle, I visited a navy frigate. The sentry on duty at the gangway was from Clemson.

In 1989, while in Kingston, Jamaica, with the basketball team, trainer Jim Price and I were eating breakfast in the hotel when we noticed a familiar face at a nearby table. He looked at us and said, "You're Jim Price and you're Tom Price."

His name escapes me now, but he was one of Coach Weems Baskin's track athletes from the 1960s.

During a trip to Alaska in 1992, the young lady giving the National Park Service lecture at the glacier near Anchorage was asked by a tourist if she did that year round.

"This is a summer job," she replied. "I'm a student at the University of South Carolina." She was from New Jersey.